The Performance of Nations

The Performance of Nations

Edited by
Jacek Kugler
and
Ronald L. Tammen

ROWMAN & LITTLEFIELD PUBLISHERS, INC.
Lanham • Boulder • New York • Toronto • Plymouth, UK

Published by Rowman & Littlefield Publishers, Inc.
A wholly owned subsidiary of The Rowman & Littlefield Publishing Group, Inc.
4501 Forbes Boulevard, Suite 200, Lanham, Maryland 20706
www.rowman.com

10 Thornbury Road, Plymouth PL6 7PP, United Kingdom

British Library Cataloguing in Publication Information Available

Library of Congress Cataloging-in-Publication Data
The performance of nations / edited by Jacek Kugler and Ronald L. Tammen.
   p. cm.
  Includes bibliographical references and index.
  ISBN 978-1-4422-1704-1 (cloth : alk. paper)
  ISBN 978-1-4422-1706-5 (electronic)
  1. Political stability—Economic aspects—Cross-cultural studies. 2. World politics—Cross-cultural studies. 3. Political indicators—Cross-cultural studies.
4. Central-local government relations—Cross-cultural studies. I. Kugler, Jacek.
II. Tammen, Ronald L., 1943–
JC330.2.P47 2012
320.01′1—dc23

                   2012026585

Printed in the United States of America

Contents

Figures and Tables

FIGURES

Chapter 3

Chapter 4

Chapter 5

TABLES

Chapter 12

Chapter 13

Acronyms

BRIC	Brazil, Russia, India, and China
CINC	Composite Index of National Capability
DAD	Development Assistance Database
DOE	Department of Energy
EC	European Communities
ECSC	European Coal and Steel Community
EEA	European Economic Area
EEC	European Economic Community
EFTA	European Free Trade Area
EMU	Economic and Monetary Union
EU	European Union
FATA	Federally Administered Tribal Areas
FCR	Frontier Crimes Regulation
FDI	foreign direct investment
GDP	gross domestic product
GFS	Government Finance Statistics
GSDP	gross state domestic product
GSP	gross state product
GTD	Global Terrorism Database
HDI	Human Development Index
IAS	Integration Achievement Score
IECC	International Energy Conservation Code
IFS	International Finance Statistics
IMF	International Monetary Fund
OECD	Organisation for Economic Co-operation and Development
OLI	ownership, location, and internalization
OLS	ordinary least squares

PCGSDP	per capita gross state domestic product
RPA	relative political allocation
RPC	relative political capacity
RPE	relative political extraction
RPP	relative political performance
RPR	relative political reach
SATP	South Asia Terrorism Portal
UNESCO	United Nations Educational, Scientific and Cultural Organization
UNSD	United Nations Statistics Division
VIF	variance inflation factors
WGI	Worldwide Governance Indicator

Introduction

This book is the result of a five-year collective effort by more than a dozen scholars associated with the TransResearch Consortium (TRC). Founded by three public policy/business schools,[1] the TRC is designed as an incubator for emerging new ideas in world politics.

The research challenge of the TRC team was to develop and test specific measures of the performance of nations at the global level. Over time and with promising results, the scholars involved realized that the measures used to compare one nation with another globally would be even more powerful at the subnational level. And that then led to experimentation with issues at the local level within the United States. Thus the original objective of this research effort mutated, by reason of successful applications, from one to three levels of analysis: Global (national), Subnational (provincial and state), and Local (city).

This natural progression was encouraged by the end goal of developing a means to compare societies to each other and over time, vertically as well as horizontally. In a sense this book represents a sign along the road to developing a social science indicator similar to the ubiquitous applications of GDP and GDP per capita in economics. Political science has long valued the universality of these concepts and the powerful applications they allow for measuring and comparative purposes. It was the chase after the elixir of a political science counterpart that led to this volume.

Despite its universal appeal, as a concept GDP remains limited in some ways. It does not include the nonmonetized economy, the black market, the subsistence economy, or volunteer work, and it fails to address why the public sector is approximated by inputs, not outputs. Yet GDP remains the gold standard for cross-national economic comparisons. And GDP per capita is the measure of choice for assessing the average productivity of individuals across and within nations. Is there a GDP-like indicator that would

1

allow scholars to compare governmental functions across time and space and across types of governments? That was our challenge. Various attempts have been made to develop proxies for government performance, but none of them has allowed scholars to measure the effectiveness and efficiency of governments, the performance of governments, vertically and horizontally—from the international to local levels.

In order to find our GDP-like political indicator, the various scholars contributing to this effort developed, tested, and integrated three distinct measures of political performance. They are Extraction, Reach, and Allocation. Extraction approximates the ability of governments to appropriate portions of the national output to advance public goals. Reach gauges the capacity of governments to mobilize populations under their control. Allocation evaluates the share of public revenues provided to competing national priorities contrasted to the optimal allocation based on maximizing economic growth.

Each of these measures was tested empirically to determine if significant and substantive results followed from its application. These tests, as cataloged in this book, establish the universality of the political performance concept.

The first chapter defines and outlines our system of measuring the three variables that constitute political performance. The following chapters use that system to demonstrate its utility at the three levels of analysis. We begin with Abdollahian, Kang, and Thomas formally linking performance with growth. Then J. Kugler, Tammen, and Thomas show how political performance has an impact on conflict and growth with an eye on emerging powers. Genna, Yesilada, and Noordijk use these ideas to test the effects of political performance on European integration. T. Kugler, Boussalis, and Coan discuss how political performance influences migration. And Arbetman-Rabinowitz and Johnson evaluate the impact of political participation on societies whose development is affected by oil and energy resources.

Moving to the subnational level with a concentration on critical internal issues involving the key regions of East Asia and South Asia, Johnson, Arbetman-Rabinowitz, and Swaminathan assess the political roots of instability in China while Umar-Wahedi and Arbetman-Rabinowitz explore similar phenomena in the context of Pakistan. T. Kugler, Boussalis, and Coan address how political performance affects the distribution of direct investment in India and China while Feng and Paul analyze Indian government performance against the backdrop of religion and growth. Swaminathan and Thomas maintain the South Asian theme when they evaluate the implications of political decisions on birth and deaths in India.

Moving down a level of analysis and focusing on the United States and applications at local levels, Nelson considers the role of political performance in the creation of U.S. energy codes. Finally, in a cross-disciplinary move designed to engage the emerging field of civic capacity in public administration, Nishishiba, Arbetman-Rabinowitz, Kraner, and Jones examine the impact of local political performance on public service outcomes. A short final chapter brings the various themes into focus.

These demonstrations clearly do not exhaust the number of applications of the general measures of political performance we have developed. They serve, however, to illustrate, similar to GDP and GDP/per capita, how the measures of political performance proposed here can be used in cross-national analysis over time and how they can be disaggregated to the provincial and local levels. To our knowledge, this is the first time that aggregate cross-national political performance measures have been formalized and empirically tested. Our expectation is that other scholars will find new and novel ways to use the political performance measure.

To that end, the data set we offer in this volume has some unique virtues. It is general, consistent, and ideologically and culturally unbiased. It measures all types of governments uniformly, from democracies to dictatorships. We carefully define the elements required to estimate each of the three indicators of political performance. Based on these formulations, we provide detailed, standardized cross-national assessments for all societies from 1960 to 2007. A far more detailed state/provincial level assessment has also been compiled for the United States, China, India, and the EU (contact the TransResearch Consortium for details). Finally, individual TRC researchers have compiled political performance data in detail across specific countries of high personal interest including Brazil, Bolivia, Nigeria, Thailand, Indonesia, Pakistan, Mexico, and Japan. Readers can utilize and extend this information to additional nations and augment the time coverage.[2]

Finally, a word about language: In this volume, we use the terms *political capacity* and *political performance* interchangeably. The literature sometimes draws distinctions between the two but most frequently uses both words as synonyms. To add to the confusion, the terms *efficiency* and *effectiveness* also are thrown into the mix when discussing governmental capabilities. We are familiar with the debates over subtle differences in all of these words and specifically whether capacity is a component of performance. And we appreciate the input (capacity) and output (performance) distinctions drawn by some. But for our purposes, it would be confusing to draw narrow, even artificial, distinctions across the fourteen chapters in this book, particularly since we have defined Extraction, Reach, and Allocation as operationalizing the concept of Performance and two of these are inputs and one an output function. So, with apologies to the wordsmiths, herein Performance equals Capacity. Effectiveness and efficiency will stand on their own.

ACKNOWLEDGMENTS

The editors and authors wish to gratefully acknowledge the assistance of the TransResearch Consortium and the three founding organizations, the La Sierra School of Business, the School of Politics and Economics at Claremont Graduate University, and the Mark O. Hatfield School of Government at Portland State University. These three academic institutions provided the time and resources to bring this project to fruition. We also wish to thank all the faculty and student members of the TRC who have displayed an uncanny sense of dedication and mission over many years of effort and particularly in the difficult collection of subnational data in challenging regions of the world.

NOTES

1. The School of Politics and Economics at Claremont Graduate University, the Mark O. Hatfield School of Government at Portland State University, and the School of Business at La Sierra University.

2. To assist in this process, we provide a detailed summary of the formulations used in this volume. A more extensive technical presentation will appear in a subsequent publication.

I

DEFINING AND MEASURING EXTRACTION, REACH, AND ALLOCATION

1

Political Performance

Marina Arbetman-Rabinowitz, Jacek Kugler,
Mark Abdollahian, Kyungkook Kang, Hal T. Nelson,
and Ronald L. Tammen

CONTEXT: THE IMPORTANCE
OF POLITICAL PERFORMANCE

The world is in flux, but modern communications bring home that observation in increasingly dramatic fashion. The global recession, the rise of China and India, unstable states, terrorism, revolution in the Middle East, aging populations stressing governments . . . these world trends not only capture our attention but they bring focus to the role of governments at the global, national, and subnational levels. Although borders may be disappearing into the new communications ether, ground truth remains centered on the role of governments that influence and control both beneficial and adverse events in their spheres of operation.

We know so much about the role of governments and yet we have so few tools for analyzing their effectiveness, their performance in the near term and over time. No issue could be more important in the policy world. Understanding the linkages between government performance and violence, stability, economic growth, and demographic changes would not only help rationalize policy choices but assist governments and nongovernmental organizations in the search for the magic formula bridging development and stability.

In response to these world dynamics, the goal of our research team was to create measures of political performance that provide an objective assessment of government capacity across time and nations and within societies.

In order to be universal, this assessment must be independent of the type of government, the level of economic productivity, human rights, or the wealth of society. To accomplish these goals we needed to measure the ability of governments to implement policies chosen by governing elites, to determine if the population is mobilized in support of such goals, and to assess if allocations maximize the goals of that government.

We define political performance as the ability of governments to reach their population, to extract economic resources from that population, and to allocate those resources to secure the long-term survival of the political structure. Governments may choose to brutally impose policy (e.g., Stalin in the USSR) or to convince populations to support policy objectives (e.g., U.S. presidents). Most societies will use a mixture of strategies to advance policy. For example, laws can impose new tax obligations while persuasion may mobilize public support.

The key to our approach is efficient extraction from a mobilized population and effective implementation of public allocations. Governments that advocate policies that fail to meet goals will not meet the expectations generated. Failing governments may succeed in the short term through coercion, but will be challenged or replaced in the long run (e.g., Egypt or Libya 2011). Governments that perform effectively will be sustained over time (e.g., Brazil, China 2011).

Figure 1.1 illustrates the process of political performance inputs and outputs. A government receives inputs from society as it extracts revenues and mobilizes the population to support its goals. Government outputs take some portion of the resources extracted from its population and reallocate them for transportation, environment, infrastructure, national defense, police, and welfare programs, among other priorities. Following this path of inputs and outputs, we can evaluate the performance of governments—those that squander public resources are ineffective and will in the long run be replaced; those that utilize public revenues to advance national growth are retained and rewarded by internal stability.

This process is illustrated by the performance of authoritarian regimes in the USSR and China. The USSR's political regime collapsed when economic and political expectations were not fulfilled. Attempts to stabilize political control under perestroika failed largely because they did not revitalize the economy. The underperforming political system led to the collapse of the Soviet empire in 1991—an event that shook the foundations of world politics.

China faced similar challenges in 1989 but did not suffer the same fate. When the movement toward political openness culminated in the Tiananmen Square demonstrations, China's elites were able to retain full political controls and subsequently even continued to liberalize the economy. China's political performance was sufficiently high to ensure stability, through

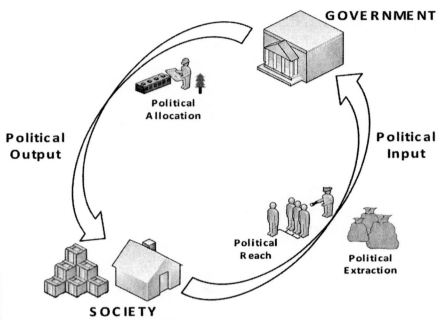

GOVERNMENT

Political
Allocation

Political
Output

Political
Input

Political
Reach

Political
Extraction

SOCIETY

Figure 1.1.   Components of Political Performance

force, and simultaneously encourage fast growth. Stripped of its moral component, this is a remarkable response.

Can this economic growth be maintained without political liberalization, or is political liberalization a requirement for long-term stability? We anticipate that our measures of political performance will provide answers to such questions.

Political performance does not reflect economic success, regime characteristics, or political values embraced by a government. Rather political performance is related to success in achieving government-defined policy outcomes. An effective government will achieve desired policy outcomes; a weak one will not. Political performance emulates in the political and institutional arena what GDP approximates in the economic field. Just as a rising GDP per capita indicates financial success, political performance reflects policy success. And like GDP, Political Performance numbers are void of political content, though not void of political uses.

Political performance measures should be parsimonious, robust, and simple. For maximum utility, these measures should be capable of aggregation from district to province/state to nation. These measures should be accessible across time. Again we take our cue from successful measures of economic productivity. Using 2010 GDP purchasing power, for example, the largest global economy is that of the United States followed by China, which recently passed Japan as the number two nation.

We know that the United States continues to dominate the global economy, that China is growing, and that Japan—seen as a contender in the 1980s—is rapidly declining. India is a likely contender expected to overtake Germany in the next decade. That no nation from Europe is among the top three shows a dramatic relative decline following World War II and perhaps accounts for the need of the EU to emerge as a coherent representative of the European conglomerate. Given these trends, our goal is to produce equivalent assessments with measures that incorporate political performance and reflect the relative power distributions in world politics.

Consideration of per capita purchasing power helps to clarify the political performance setting. Establishing the United States at 100 percent, we find that Japan is 74 percent as productive while China lags at about 20 percent and several European nations match or exceed the performance of the United States. This simple comparison provides a shortcut to understand why China, whose population is five times larger than that of the United States and about ten times that of Japan, still lags in political influence.

These assessments are crude and camouflage much. Yet no such comparisons are possible for political performance across the international system. Is the performance of China and India comparable? Can we effectively compare the political performance of China, Russia, and the United States? Can we gauge the political performance of Vietnam, Brazil, and Indonesia? Can we reflect accurately the political performance of Texas, California, and Oregon? All these can be assessed with economic measures. This book attempts to fill this vacuum in the political arena.

THE INTELLECTUAL ENVIRONMENT

Initial forays into the measurement of government have relied on the idea that capable governments are able to enact their social, political, and economic goals. Governments and their elites make different decisions about resource allocation. Some invest heavily in social programs while others act to facilitate economic growth or seek security objectives. Measurements of well-being or of freedom capture such choice indirectly, but they do not measure the innate ability of governments to make those choices.

The historic search for political performance measures is full of twists and turns. We lump previous efforts into two distinct camps. First, Deutsch (1966), Rokkan et al. (1970), and Gurr (1974) among others used a variety of indicators to reflect the well-being of a population. Their estimates were published initially in the *World Handbook of Social Indicators*. Consistent with this approach, the World Bank's Human Development Index tracks selected basic indicators of political performance motivated in part by assessments required by the Millennium Development Project.

The second camp has theoretical foundations in democracy research, with a focus on participation, representation, electoral choice, institutions, and performance of the bureaucracy (Campbell, Converse, Miller, and Stokes 1960; Verba and Nie 1972; and Fiorina 1981).[1] This focus reflects government and elite choice in resource allocation and places democratic systems of government over other forms of governance. The goal of this approach is not necessarily "performance" but how such performance is executed.

Both of these approaches pose problems. First, our objective is to develop an index independent of type of government or the well-being of populations. For example, how can we assess Argentina's political performance compared to that of Iran? How does either country compare to the Netherlands, the United States, or China? Current data sets shed little light on these questions. The Human Development Index captures mainly effects already included in GDP per capita by mixing variables such as economic development, regime structure, national resources, language, class, tribal structure, culture, and religion. But this obscures a rational assessment of political performance. Secondly, the democracy measures are applicable mainly to electoral systems and do not travel well across systems with numbers of competing political parties.

Measuring the performance of governments has been elusive because of the lack of a commonly held definition. What is political performance? The World Bank states that "governance is the manner in which power is exercised in the management of a country's economic and social resources for development" (World Bank 1992). We argue that the concept the World Bank is trying to capture is "good" governance, not "effective" governance. Indeed, the World Bank effort is confounded by the incorporation of norms that include, among others, justice, ethics, and institutional quality and that prevent an impartial assessment of political performance (World Bank 2007).[2]

Approaching GDP calculations from this perspective would require consideration of levels of corruption, the ethics of business, the values of society, and trust within society. These elements no doubt affect overall measures of productivity, but they are not reflected in objective assessments of productivity or wealth. How you get there is a different question from what you get. We are interested in the objective estimation of political performance.

A THREE-PRONGED APPROACH TO
POLITICAL PERFORMANCE: INPUT
AND OUTPUT FUNCTIONS

Governments in possession of vast material resources can pursue their objectives more easily since money is fungible. But money alone is not sufficient. Governments also require human resources. Elites need to convince their population to accept common goals. The existence of a black market labor sector shows that a segment of the population defies government rules and operates outside the legal realm. A correlation may well exist between low revenue extraction and low reach insinuated by a large black market labor sector, but conceptually these two concepts are different. For example, a country like Colombia that has a large drug sector will show relatively few people working outside the official labor sector, but conspicuous spending will disclose large amounts of untaxed money. Conversely, a subsistence economy will show many people who eat what they produce but are heavily taxed on the little money they produce from migrant labor.

We have developed two measures to capture such differences: one related to extraction and the other to reach. These two elements provide the input to political performance.

The output function is represented by allocation. Government goals must be reasonably public with expenditures and budgets following such goals. Otherwise support for the government will drop. Continued failure will lead, even when coercion is used, to a change in governments (e.g., USSR 1989; Egypt or Libya 2011).

This perspective is conceptually and pragmatically attractive because it permits measure disaggregation and allows testing at different levels of analysis. Political performance can be constructed at the national level, which results in cross-national comparisons, or at the subnational, provincial, and state level, which results in intranational comparisons. And finally political performance measures can also be used to capture local government performance at the state, district, or city level, if data is available. At any level of analysis, the policy questions addressed have similar structural constraints: governments that reach and extract resources from their populations will be able to successfully implement desired policies.

Knowing the political capacity of a province or city can help a central government trying to implement an education or health program, for example. Allocating more resources to a city, district, or state that is highly capable will increase the prospects for national success. Less capable provinces will provide fewer benefits to the central government (Rouyer 1987). Of course allocating to the most efficient will deprive the needy from resources they desperately require but cannot efficiently utilize. In Afghanistan, for example, the United States is expected to allocate about $65 billion dollars in economic aid in 2010 to a society whose overall product is less than $20 billion. We rate the Afghani political extraction level at an astonishingly low 20 percent of normal, and less than 10 percent compared to other societies at war. With such low political capacity, external resources are likely to be dissipated or lost even if participants have the best of intentions.

Politically capable state/provincial government officials also will be far more effective at lobbying their central government than comparable weak provincial governments. In the same vein, provinces with elevated political performance will use human and material resources more efficiently and will implement an allocation portfolio more effectively because elites wish to maximize their long-term political support. Thus our three-pronged approach of two inputs, Extraction and Reach, plus our one output of Allocation.

THE FIRST INPUT TO POLITICAL PERFORMANCE: POLITICAL EXTRACTION

Relative political extraction (RPE) measures the ability of a government to obtain resources from a population given their level of economic development. Efficient governments are able to meet or exceed their expected extractive capabilities while inefficient governments fail to reach expected extraction levels. Public revenues set the preconditions to implement a set of policy choices: governments that perform effectively will be able to implement policy and pursue their political and economic goals while preserving political stability. The opposite is true of inefficient governments.

Governments require public resources to enact policies. Conducting economic or political activity with government oversight requires sufficient government revenue and presence to ensure compliance. Unlike economic exchanges, policy implementation requires either persuasion or coercion. Like taxes, policy regulations are frequently opposed by the affected parties who would generally choose to pursue their activities without any constraints. Such transactions are seldom voluntary.

Contrast this with an economic transaction that is usually voluntary where the parties exchange a product for money. At the point of the transaction both parties voluntarily choose to accept the exchange. Of course over time one side may consider the price to be too high, particularly when the same item is offered at a lower price, while the seller is then satisfied—and vice versa. Political transactions on the other hand are not voluntary. While you may enjoy witnessing the imposition of a ticket on a speed violator that recently overtook you on the freeway, such cooperative feeling will not be present if you have been stopped for violating the speed limit.

Extracting taxes and imposition of restrictions on previously legal action are supported when they affect others, but seldom when they affect you directly. For this reason the extraction of tax revenues to be directed to public policy is supported in general but opposed when applied to the individual.

Political extraction conflates voluntary and coercive compliance. Organski and Kugler (1980) illustrate this shortcoming well: "It is evident to us that a highly capable political system need not be free, democratic, stable, orderly, representative, and participatory or endowed with any of the other desiderata." Government extraction assesses the extractive efficiency of government given levels of productivity, but does not indicate whether the government choices are optimal or if they are supported by the majority of the population.

In other words, political extraction is an agnostic measure of performance that does not reflect democratic principles, optimal allocations, or lack of coercion. We do postulate that regardless of the procedures used, a government that maintains high levels of extraction over a long time span (a decade or so) is capable because the population complies with the demands of that government and through its contributions allows the implementation of governmental goals.

The original insight for the use adjusted tax indicators emerged from a conversation with Richard Musgrave, then at the University of Michigan, who pointed out that the IMF was using "tax effort" indicators to measure government performance. Lotz and Morse (1967) and Bahl (1971) utilized adjusted tax ratios to measure the economic penetration of governments within their societies. Organski and Kugler (1980) were the first to realize that such ratios provided an indirect measure of political performance. Most developing societies raise insufficient revenues to meet their public policy goals. How much tax revenues a government can extract is a function of the level of economic development as well as the economic profile of the country. For example, an economy heavily dependent on oil revenues or other exports makes it far easier to raise tariffs at the point of exit than to tax individual income or their products.

Realizing that most governments extract less than they would optimally desire, and noting that countries with similar economic profiles achieve very different levels of fiscal income, it follows that governments that are political efficient are able to extract more under similar economic circumstances.

Differences in political extraction measure approximate differences in the political performance of governments. Early assessments of political extraction demonstrated the empirical validity of the relationship between resource extraction and political performance. A natural empirical test was provided by the outcome of severe international conflicts where both sides stood to lose core territory.

Based on this approach, Organski and Kugler (1980) demonstrate that the early success of Germany and Japan or the collapse of France in World War II can be better explained by high political capacity than by military expenditures. Likewise the different performance of Russia in World War I and the USSR in World War II follows directly from comparing the ability of the czar and Communist governments to extract resources from their populations. Such measures solved a major puzzle. Combining GDP and political extraction allowed comparisons of power that anticipated the outcome of conflicts between societies at very different levels of economic development.

Consider the Vietnam War. Comparisons of resource extraction in Vietnam, despite high levels of U.S. support and the much greater wealth of the South, show that the extraction capabilities of South Vietnam continued to be low while those of the much less-endowed North were extraordinarily high and increased as the conflict was waged. Consistent with the outcome of the conflict and contrary to alternate military or economic measures of capabilities, power measures anticipated the collapse of South Vietnam concurrent with the withdrawal of U.S. troops (Organski and Kugler 1980). Multiple applications to conflicts in the Middle East, Afghanistan vs. Russia, Iran vs. Iraq, and the internal conflict between North and South Sudan have confirmed that political extraction is an integral political component of capabilities (Kugler and Lemke 1996; Kugler, Benson, Hira, and Panasevitch 1997; Benson and Kugler 1998; Tammen et al. 2000).[3]

Political extraction, as a general concept, has applications in political demography and political economy. The extractive capacity of a government is essential to assess changes in fertility and mortality or to anticipate development trajectories. Arbetman, Organski, and Kugler (Organski and Kugler 1980; Organski et al. 1984; Arbetman, Kugler, and Organski 1997) initially examined the relationship between political capacity and demographic change.

That work shows a systematic relationship between declines in fertility and mortality in a population and the concurrent rise of political extraction. Following up on the early results, Rouyer (1987) assesses sources of political capacity at the province level in Indian states and shows that the effectiveness of regional population planning programs depends directly on the levels of political extraction in each state. Swaminathan and Thomas (2007) revisit the political capacity of states in India and show that levels of infant mortality and other physical survival measures are directly related to political extraction.

Applying these measures to economic development, Leblang (1997) found a similar strong relationship between political extraction and economic performance. Formalizing such insights and applying a general equilibrium dynamic model called POFED, Feng et al. (2000; 2008) demonstrate how political extraction directly affects population changes, fertility, and economic growth. Their model accounts for more than 60 percent of the variance in economic performance across societies compared to the 30-plus percent consistently found using economic factors alone. This approach avoids the dreaded "Africa exception" where growth models that work in other societies fail to account for Africa's economic development (Schultz 1999; Easterly 2008).

Subcomponents of development also respond to political extraction. Alcazar (1997) shows that inflation declines with political extraction. Feng and Chen (1997) and Feng (2003) indicate that increasing the extractive ability of the government raises private and foreign direct investment. Following up on this work, Coan and Kugler (2008) show that foreign direct investment is attracted to regions with high and low variance political extraction. Benson and Kugler (1998) conclude that political extraction is a very effective means to compare the domestic power of competing groups within a nation and link the severity of civil war to levels of political extraction. From a similar perspective, Johnson (2007) suggests a strong relationship between subnational capabilities and the severity of civil war. These are just a few of the many examples testing the role of extractive capacity in the implementation of governmental goals.

Measuring Political Extraction

Initial work on measurement of government capability either relied on the effects of policy outcomes—e.g., physical well-being—or levels of democracy within a country that reflect the governmental structure. Such efforts are based on the idea that capable governments share and enact social, political, and economic goals. We believe that governmental elites make different decisions about resource extraction and allocation.

Some invest heavily in social programs while others act to facilitate economic growth in the private sector. Some place security at the top of their agenda while others seek alliances or integration to assure stability. Some seek to subsidize education while others rely on the private market to provide these services. Some provide housing, utilities, transportation, sanitation, water, and electricity to their populations while others choose to provide these services through the private sector. Some provide heath and a deep welfare structure while others minimize or delegate such services to families and the private sector.

Measurements of well-being or of freedom capture these choices but in our view fail to measure the innate ability of governments to make or implement their own choices. Our approach is to measure the marginal ability of governments to implement new options—controlling for commitments they previously made. Thus a society that has chosen to educate its population through the public sector will expend far more than one that provides similar services largely through the private sector. Likewise a society with universal health coverage supported by general revenues will differ substantially from a society where these services are largely private or where support for these activities is paid from special funds not directly related to general taxation. The reason for the variation in controls applied at different levels of development and within societies is to capture systematically these differences—otherwise tax revenues alone would reflect political capacity and our work suggests that they do not.

The measure of relative political extraction takes into account the economic profile of an economy and compares the actual levels of extraction to its predicted value based on economic endowment:

$$Relative\ Political\ Extraction = \frac{Actual\ Extraction}{Predicted\ Extraction}$$

Several alternate economic models that have been tested to account for levels of extraction depend upon the level of development of a country as well as its particular mix of resources. Developed and developing countries differ quite sharply based on differences in the structure of their economies and the patterns of tax collection. For developed countries, controls for GDP and health and education expenditures are important to account for differences in levels of wealth and the distribution of wealth throughout a population.

Per capita income determines to a large degree the amount of resources a government can extract simply because as the survival level is approached, resistance to additional extraction will rise—or in extreme cases produce famine among the population. Governments of less-developed countries extract proportionally less resources from their populations not because their requirements are met (far from it), but because the economic base determined by the per capita productivity of individuals in that society is much smaller.

This restricted economic base limits policy choice for these regimes. Extracting fewer resources means that there is less to allocate. The policy demands of the population may not be as readily expressed in resource-constrained societies compared to those in wealthier countries (where governments can express their policy preferences by choosing to allocate public resources to health care, education, welfare, or other social programs).

Developed countries face fewer limitations on extraction based on a larger availability of fiscal resources, but at the same time they face far stiffer opposition to raising existing taxes (Arbetman 1990). Taxation in developed countries is not generally limited by available resources but by the political pressures to implement or dismantle choices to have public or private provision of services like health, education, welfare, and social services. Arbetman (1990) illustrates this process with contrasting examples of Sweden and Japan. Establishment of extensive public institutions that deliver educational and health services in Sweden requires a greater degree of tax collection. A lack of similar public institutions in Japan does not indicate a lesser ability to extract resources; instead it reflects a desire by the government to persuade the population to obtain these services by private means.

The extractive capabilities of countries are empirically calculated based on resources extracted from the population. Resources obtained from sources that require no popular decision are excluded because they do not indicate the ability of governments to extract revenues to advance their view of the public good. Mineral production or oil profits are an easy revenue target. A government lucky enough to have large deposits of oil or other minerals does not have to impose tax cost on the population but can simply levy tariffs on local or foreign producers subsidizing government. Taxation of imports and exports does not pressure the population.

Controls for these revenue sources are critical in determining a government's extractive capacities from the population. Likewise, subsistence agriculture is excluded because such production is usually produced and consumed by the household, making it difficult to identify or tax. The level of income across societies needs to be adjusted because a higher per capita productivity indicates a potential for increased taxation—of course controlling for the choice of allocations already made by societies. The general equation developed to capture these differences can be found in this endnote.[4]

The systematic controls included will vary across levels of development and differ for intrastate estimations. For this purpose we have developed two distinct models.[5] The use of these two models depends on the set of nations that are compared. For historical analysis or to contrast developing societies today, agriculture is the appropriate control variable that captures the effects of a subsistence economy. Model two applies as the impact of subsistence agriculture declines, populations become urban, economic productivity increases, and income rises. Per capita gross domestic product now effectively reflects the tax base.

The logic of political extraction is perfectly adapted to the subnational context. Efficient subnational governments are able to extract resources from their populations and administer services more equitably than competing less-efficient units. Inefficient or less-capable subnational governments extract fewer resources from their populations and allocate such resources less equitably.

Measuring the political capacity of state or provincial governments presents several challenges not encountered in the estimation of political capacity across countries. First, taxation efforts are not standard—diverse provinces may use a multitude of tax schemes and also gain transfers for taxes collected at the national level. For example, some states within the same nation may impose income taxes, while others rely on sales and property taxes. Moreover, large portions of state or province revenues are composed of transfers from the national government. Many such transfers are fixed by legislature-imposed formulas, but others depend on the political acumen of the provincial or state leaders.

Like the cross-national measure of political extraction, relative provincial political capacity must control for the economic endowment of provincial governments. The measure captures how state governments are performing based on their economic endowments, or in other words, whether provincial governments are performing in terms of resource extraction to anticipated levels based on their economic endowments.

Due to the differing taxation structures as well as the domestic accounting systems, adjustments in the estimation are required for each national tax structure. This does not impact intrastate comparisons as the scores are relative within a given country. Cross-national comparisons at the provincial level require far more care when fiscal systems differ fundamentally.

Adapting national-level models of political extraction to the subnational level requires familiarity and understanding of individual national tax structures. For example, Nigeria's tax structure is complicated by the wealth of oil resources in Niger Delta States. Historically, the tax structure in Nigeria was highly centralized, with the transfer of resources from the central to local governments constitutionally designated. The continued conflict and protest over the outflow of resources from oil-producing regions led to a constitutional reform in 1997 that established a revenue-sharing mechanism for oil states. Now, oil-producing states are able to retain up to 13 percent of the revenue generated from oil taxes before transferring money to the central government (Johnson 2007).

This creates serious problems for cross-temporal comparisons. Moreover, while the oil-producing regions are now relatively flush with public sector revenues, Nigerian states that do not have oil are dependent on transfers from the central government where funds can be significantly depleted by corruption. Industrial development of the poorer regions depends on developing a viable infrastructure, but such provinces are highly dependent on taxes from oil revenue (up to 90 percent of revenue is generated by oil production; IMF Country Report Annex 2005) that they do not directly control. Variations in the extractive capacity of provinces is frequently far larger than across nations.

Variables included in political extraction estimates at the subnational level rely on specific elements unique to a province.[6] Similar to the national-level estimation of political extraction, controlling for agriculture is appropriate for less-developed provinces while controlling for GDP per capita is appropriate for the estimation of provincial extraction in the more highly industrialized portions of the nation. Additional control variables such as manufacturing/GDP or service/GDP are appropriate based on the economic structure of the province.

Government transfers complicate estimates. Extraction should only reflect political elements. Politics occurs when central government transfers are allocated following negotiations on an annual basis. When a fixed constitutional formula for transfers of resources from the central to regional governments applies, only changes in that formula reflect politics (Arbetman and Johnson 2008). Additional attention needs to be paid to resources governments can tax without putting pressure on the population. In provinces where natural resources exist, it may be easier for governments to collect revenues generated from exploitation of mineral resources or to tax tourists anxious to visit unusual attractions. Where possible, it is important to control for these resources because they do not reflect the link between the population and government.

Data difficulties abound but are not insurmountable. Not only is this data far less standardized, but it is also far more difficult to compile and integrate. Some countries do not publish data on the productivity of the public sector (industrial or mining) because this information is believed to challenge national security. Subsidies from central governments are frequently augmented without reporting to cover unusual events. Such augmentations are particularly difficult in centralized systems that provide much of the resources but also affect decentralized systems, particularly if the event is a hurricane or earthquake that causes severe damage and requires massive reconstruction efforts. The estimates for subnational-level extraction are often driven by the country accounting system and data availability.

THE SECOND INPUT TO POLITICAL PERFORMANCE: POLITICAL REACH

The second input component to governance and governmental capabilities is Relative Political Reach. Reach combined with Extraction represent the inputs available to government to make policy choices. Reach establishes the degree to which the government influences and penetrates into the daily lives of individuals. Different conceptualizations of the relationship between the state and society range from discussions of social capital (Putnam 2000) to broader definitions and examinations of governance, which generally focus on the responsiveness of regimes to measurements of demands by the population for governmental action.

The interaction between state control and social demands often concentrates on domestic distributions of influence, which, in any system, provide insight into how the political system works. These approaches focus on the presence of the government in normal individual interactions, reflecting the degree that a government is able to mobilize the human resources of its population. The proposed measure of relative political reach (RPR) is based on the logic that interactions of the population and government provide a distinct view of the ability of governments to operate efficiently.

Measuring Political Reach

In order to perform effectively, governments must have an ability to mobilize both human and economic resources. Political reach measures the ability of a government to mobilize the human resources of a population. Governments that are able to mobilize human resources can implement their desired policy agenda; governments that are limited in their mobilization of human resources are less able to enact or enforce policies. Political reach also reflects the degree to which the population accepts the presence of government in their lives.

Societies characterized by little trust in government elites are more likely to actively avoid the government, reducing involvement in economic and other interactions. This can also reflect a lack of trust. Human resources in a population are important not only because individuals will produce more but also because they can be mobilized to support the agendas of policy makers, including the choice to go to war or significant economic reforms (Arbetman 1990).

Relative political reach estimates the degree the government is involved in economic activities of the population relative to the expected degree given the education and employment of the population. The groundwork for this measure can be found in Organski (1958) and was initially modeled and expanded by Arbetman (1990). Below, we address existing methods for identifying the size of the informal economy, also defined as the degree to which economic activity occurs outside the purview of the government. While recognizing that a direct measure of informal activity poses challenges, particularly in cross-country analysis, we believe that we can measure the informal sector through evaluation of the size and expected size of the economically active population of a society.

The informal sector, also called the black economy, shadow economy, parallel economy, informal economy, irregular economy, or cash economy, essentially describes transactions that are "untaxed, unmeasured, or unregulated" (Smith 1986). Several approaches to measuring the informal sector have been proposed.[7] At the national level, informal interviews are used to assess the extent to which economic interactions take place in the formal and informal markets. Such interviews aim to establish a benchmark for total economic interactions. Pettinati (1979) used this approach successfully in Italy. He shows that this is an accurate and useful method to approximate the informal sector, but generality is difficult to maintain and inconsistent aggregation procedures severely affect cross-temporal and cross-national comparisons.

A second method to approach the informal sector is to estimate tax fraud and tax evasion based on differences in GNP and in income and expenditure based on household and individual surveys (Tanzi 1983). The main problem generalizing this approach cross-nationally is that measuring tax evasion does not reflect economic activity that occurs beyond tax evasion.

A third method relies on monetary indicators that identify the demands on currency because the ratio of currency to demand deposits can provide information about the velocity of currency circulation. Thus, the ratio of currency demand divided by the size of economic output (total GNP) can be used to approximate the size of the informal sector. This approach yields consistent results in developed countries but runs into a number of problems when dealing with less-developed economies (Arbetman 1990).

Formal theorists have taken a different route to dealing with reach, establishing a labor market where an informal sector does not exist and making comparisons across market types. Scholars use labor participation to estimate the size of the informal market, looking in the change in size of the economically active population, or who and how many earn money in the labor market over time. The advantage of this approach is that cross-national and cross-temporal comparisons can be made. The shortcoming is that only those who earn money are counted. Our reach measure employs activity rate—economically active population discounting for part-time workers and employment—as the dependent variable.

The measure of relative political reach models labor participation taking into account the demographic profile of the country:

$$Relative\ Political\ Reach = \frac{Actual\ Activity\ Rate}{Predicted\ Activity\ Rate}$$

Political reach is intended to reflect the ability of elites to mobilize human resources—countries that have little involvement with entire segments of the population are not able to mobilize these resources effectively. Also note that a significant difference exists between countries at similar levels of development.

For example, Tanzania and Botswana can arguably be compared as African nations that have some degree of similarity in economic development, although most would identify Botswana as the more economically successful. However, the Tanzanian government has a much greater reach, or active involvement in the lives of the population, and a much smaller informal sector. Tanzania is more readily able to mobilize support for policies and implement them effectively.

An additional relevant example is Nigeria. Nigeria possesses a great deal of material resources in its wealth of oil and mineral reserves; however, it has very low levels of political reach. The Nigerian government will likely experience difficulties in mobilizing the population behind policy changes or in national efforts. Arbetman (1990, 1994) and Arbetman and Ghosh (1997) demonstrate the relationship between government inefficiency and the level and rate of change of black market activities.

Developed and developing countries differ quite sharply in the structure of their economies and the patterns and allocation of expenditures as well as the level of barter and subsistence production. Governments in developed countries have built the infrastructure to be involved in economic interactions of the population, but developing societies, particularly the least developed ones, rely on subsistence and make government interaction prohibitive. The general equation developed to capture differences for reach is outlined in this endnote.[8]

While recognizing that a direct measure of informal activity poses challenges, particularly in cross-country analysis, we believe that we can see "the shadow" of the informal sector through evaluation of the size and expected size of the economically active population of a society. Governments in possession of material resources can pursue their objectives more easily since money is fungible.

Governments also need human resources; to obtain those resources they need to convince their population to abide by their goals. The existence of a black market labor sector shows that there is a segment of the population that defies the government rules and operates outside their realm. Our measure of relative political reach looks at a model of labor participation taking into account the demographic profile of the country. The specific formula for calculating reach is in this endnote.[9]

The reach indicator is calculated following the same methodology as the political extraction indicator. Reach proposes that at every level of economic development a certain activity rate is required to meet the output. If that output is met with a lower than average activity rate, that gap represents undeclared labor.

Consistent once more with the extraction measure, the lower the ratio, the less the government can reach the population because more people dare to defy the "rules of the game" and work outside government scrutiny. On the other hand, a high ability of the government to mobilize human resources increases the probability the government will gain support to implement their desired policies.

Reach can be measured at the cross-national and the subnational level. As before, relative political reach measures the degree to which the population accepts the presence of government in their lives. Populations in provinces or states characterized by low government reach are more likely to actively avoid the local government, cutting out involvement in economic and other interactions. Government-building in such environments is unlikely.

At the state level reach needs to be adjusted slightly. Instead of considering social security expenditures that are not local, the province or state percent of population over sixty-five years old is used as a control. The other adjustment applies to the education variable. In developing provinces where schooling is not prevalent, we use enrollment or completion of primary school. For the countries where literacy is still an issue (e.g., Sudan or Afghanistan), we use that variable.

THE THIRD VARIABLE OF POLITICAL PERFORMANCE: POLITICAL ALLOCATION

While both Reach and Extraction define the inputs available to government from society, we also need to understand what value government provides to society. As such, political performance reflects the interplay between inputs and outputs.

Focusing on outputs, we provide a theoretical and measurable framework that answers the fundamental question: how do fiscal allocation policies affect the prospects for economic development? We posit that all governments wish to advance economic prosperity for political support, but some are distracted by national security considerations or the need to secure personal gains through corruption. Thus how government allocates public expenditures, seen directly by budget spending, reflects the constrained political choices governments pursue to advance economic growth.

The intuition is as follows. In the long term, political survival depends on policies that ensure economic development. Had the USSR successfully solved the growth problem, we postulate, its collapse could have been avoided. The United States owes its stability as much to the long record of sustained growth as it does to its democratic institutions. And China has avoided collapse largely because their public expenditures focused on creating a competitive economic system with accompanying economic growth that now sustains the stability of that one-party regime. Similar arguments can be made about the Middle East nations that now face serious instability following long-term economic ineffectiveness despite in most cases a very large natural wealth base.

Measuring Political Allocation

First, Relative Political Allocation measures how public expenditures are prioritized in the government budget. Second, Allocation identifies the gaps between actual expenditures and the "best" expenditures that maximize economic growth on any portion of the development path. By mapping each government's political allocation choices to its economic achievements, we identify the political levers governments use to achieve growth. This novel conception of political allocation reflects public sector expenditures on security, infrastructure, education, health, housing, or welfare compared to the optimal expenditure levels that maximize economic growth. Such allocations echo the explicit choices governments make in distributing public goods and relate them to economic performance. We argue that at each level of development, either over- or underallocating sectoral resources will hinder societies' path to prosperity.

How governments achieve optimal growth by implementing different fiscal policies remains one of the most fundamental questions in endogenous economic growth theory. Barro (1990) suggested a simple general equilibrium model to show how tax-financed government services affect production and utility level. Easterly and Rebelo (1993) effectively investigated the empirical association between the development level and fiscal structure. Abdollahian, Arbetman, and Kang (2009) empirically show that fiscal policies are linked to political capacity. We believe these contributions put forward an important foundation.

While previous work focused on the relationship between the aggregated fiscal policies and economic growth, we shift our attention to the optimality of public sector expenditure allocations. All government allocations are politically motivated, and the emerging budget portfolio indicates priorities advanced by leading elites. The motivation for our Allocation index is to provide an observable measure of the effect of policy choices on growth.

Our approach helps determine the best combination of fiscal policies for growth because we seek to know what happens over time and across countries at given levels of development. As the importance of issues facing a government varies, more or less money will be allocated to different public sector expenditures to affect economic outcomes. In addition, by mapping how budgetary expenditures are allocated differently across governments, we can reveal the political preferences of government.

To construct RPA, we start with Solow's (1957) growth accounting approach that looks at growth as a function of technology, capital, and labor. Specifically, to capture that economies tend to converge on balanced growth we follow Hall and Jones (1999) by using income intensive capital instead of total capital. However, we extend this work by including public sector expenditures as an added input to technology and income intensive capital.

For the first step, we estimate each country's distinct social production function that specifies the output of an entire economy for all combinations of technology, capital, and government budget allocation. This social production function denotes the political economic process of converting private capital inputs and public spending into total income of the society.

Government budgets or public spending is further decomposed into a portfolio of eight different dimensions: General Public Spending, Defense, Public Ordering, Economic Affairs, Housing, Health, Education, and Social Protection.[10] How much a government spends in each budget category reflects their political choices and priorities to provide output value to society. The government budget that maximizes growth is estimated based on different combinations of these expenditure categories that vary with the level of development achieved by each society.[11] Figure 1.2 shows conceptually the first step of our approach.

Once we have the expenditures across these eight budget categories, we can then move to our second step for creating Allocation. Here the approach is similar to focusing on a government's actual budgetary allocations compared to what seems to be the best allocation given all other governments' performance. By summing up the absolute distance values for every component, we obtain the allocative "inefficiency" score for each country for a given year.[12] Relative Political Allocation is then consistent over time and across countries. Figure 1.2 visually illustrates the calculation procedure (for details see the general appendix).

Our Relative Political Allocation measure reflects the difference between economically optimal allocations and political reality. This difference elegantly captures the outputs governments provide to society. Governments choose an allocation strategy that maximizes their own preferences, which of course may differ from economic optimality. These decision makers are constrained by security, self-interest, staying in power, and many other political considerations.

We do not judge the morality of these allocations, just that they directly show political choices. Notice we do not advocate maximizing economic growth at the expense of political reality or any other priorities. The goal is to provide an impartial index of allocation performance that measures the degree of each country's political public spending choices. This is why we

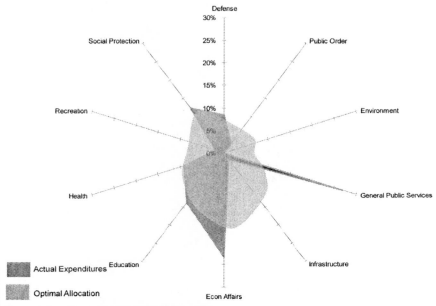

Figure 1.2. Measuring Political Allocation

perform our second step that benchmarks a government's performance relative to other governments.

One implication for Allocation is that over time, budget differences from more optimal allocation expenditures will reduce societal economic growth. This in turn impacts society and the amount of available inputs, via Reach and Extraction, accessible to government to provide future goods and services back to society. Thus we come full circle, understanding how government and society interact and the role politics play in our input/output cycle.

CONTRASTING POLITICAL
PERFORMANCE MEASURES

A major objective of our work is to show that the measures of political performance do not simply reflect the wealth or productivity of societies. We must look at both the economic and political effects of government and society to understand the evolution of societies—and these dimensions are distinct. The economic side of the equation is already captured by economic variables (GDP or GDP/per capita and related variants) and indicators that reflect the economic openness in terms of monetary, investment, financial freedom, or property rights. We show that political performance measures are distinct from economic indicators and are poorly approximated by measures based on the type of governments—authoritarian; democratic—or preferences for freedom of the press, human rights, or equality. These may or may not reflect the performance of governments.

We are interested in objective measures of political performance. We will show that highly coercive regimes like Nazi Germany, Stalin's Russia, pre–World War II Japan, or North Vietnam performed very well under war conditions. These regimes did not have a democratic system and did not support freedom of the press or human rights. By our definition these governments reached very high performance standards. This is not to say that democracies that advance the freedom of the press and support human rights and civil equality are ineffective.

Britain in World War II or France in World War I performed magnificently. Regime does not ensure performance. We know that regardless of structure, societies may perform well or poorly. Russia collapsed in World War I and the USSR in 1991 because their governments performed poorly. France failed to stop Nazi Germany because of major deficiencies in their political performance. Performance varies and it is not directly related to the attributes commonly associated with "good" and "bad" governments. Our objective is to show that such measures are not equivalent and can be biased depending on political beliefs.

To assess the value of proposed measures of political performance, we compare and contrast elements of political capacity against existing indicators of economic and alternate political performance assessments. We show that our measures of political performance are independent of economic measures and differ from alternative political assessments. To do so we present a series of comparisons that captures these components.

As a first cut we evaluate the cross-national and cross-temporal relation between the per capita income, the continuous Freedom House measures of economic openness, and the political performance measures. Most important, it is clear that GDP per capita and Relative Political Extraction, Relative Political Reach, and Relative Political Allocation are not correlated. Participation measures do not reflect the productivity of populations.

On the other hand Freedom House measures are all related to GDP per capita, and in some cases like Freedom from Corruption this association is at a very high level.[13] This suggests that Freedom House indicators capture in large part the effects of wealth and do not necessarily reflect political organization. Further, different Freedom House indicators are quite strongly related to each other,[14] suggesting that an aggregation of such mea-

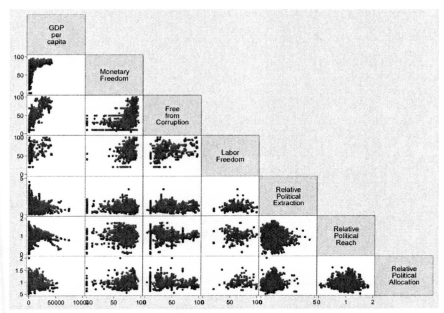

Figure 1.3. Relationships between GDP per Capita, Freedom House Measures, and Political Capacity

sures using factor analysis or related techniques will reflect the same patterns as those already disclosed by individual subcomponents.[15]

A similar picture emerges from internal relationships at the World Bank Worldwide Governance Indicator (WGI).

The relationship among Relative Political Extraction, Relative Political Reach, Relative Political Allocation, and GDP per capita support the findings in the previous figure but in a much larger sample. The World Bank Worldwide Governance Indicators are strongly related to GDP per capita[16] and also even more than before among themselves.[17] Such strong relationships suggest that World Bank Indicators, like the Freedom House indicators, are directly influenced by the wealth of populations. Again, the high interactions among them make it unlikely that any aggregation into an overall index will produce a picture different from that provided by these subcomponents.[18]

We noted before and show in detail in chapter 3 that the form of government does not relate directly to political performance in war. Democratic France mobilized effectively and extracted successfully during World War I but failed to do so in World War II. Likewise, Russia's monarchy mobilized and extracted resources poorly for World War I but the Soviet government

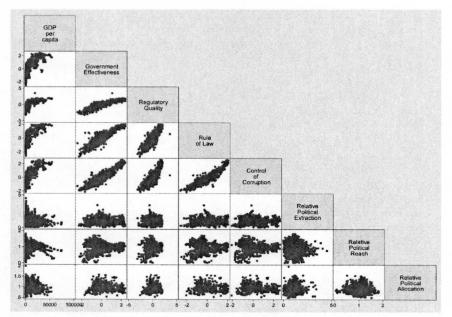

Figure 1.4.   Relationships between GDP per Capita, Worldwide Governance Indicator (WGI), and Political Performance

did so very effectively under a more totalitarian regime of Stalin during World War II. Authoritarian Japan extracted the most and mobilized fully during World War II while democratic Britain did likewise only until the United States entered the conflict. Democracy may provide the population with a higher quality of political life, but it does not guarantee high government political performance.

Now we turn to tests of governmental effectiveness at the subnational level. Considerable variation exists across countries in the type and level of authority granted to subnational jurisdictions. Decentralization is driven by constitutional structure, demands by hinterland regions for local autonomy that increase with national income growth, greater relative hinterland population, and increasing national population (Arzaghi and Henderson 2005).

Germany and the United States are commonly held examples of highly federalized systems. American state governments have revenue-raising authority, directly regulate large sectors of their economies (finance, insurance, real estate, etc.), and implement and enforce relevant federal legislation. Even in unitary countries, subnational governments play an important role in government service delivery and typically have authority for local planning and land use at a minimum. In sum, due to the substantial authority invested in subnational governments, measures of governmental effectiveness for these units are critical to explain and predict important socioeconomic outcomes.

We expect that measures of governmental effectiveness at the subnational level are more valid for cross-sectional analysis than their international counterparts comparing federal to unitary systems. Subnational jurisdictions operate under the same constitutional system and therefore have similar revenue-raising authority and constitutional structure (unitary vs. federal), as well as service delivery mandates. In spite of these theoretical advantages, much less quantitative measurement work has been performed on governmental effectiveness at the subnational level. Because of a lack of relevant international indicators, we focus our robustness tests on existing U.S. measures of governmental effectiveness.

Indicators used to measure government capacity in the American states can be divided into three categories:

1) Indicators based on tax or expenditures data versus expert survey indicators. State expenditures data have also been used to proxy the relative size of the state governmental intervention in policy areas (Lester and Lombard 1990; Grossback et al. 2004). State short-term state fiscal health has also been employed as a measure of government capacity. (Among others see Berry and Berry 1990; Bacot and Dawes 1997.)

2) The size or professionalism of state legislatures and bureaucratic resources has also been used as a measure of administrative capacity. (For a review see Gerber and Teske 2000; also Squire 2007; Potoski 2001; Shipan and Volden 2006.)

3) The final category of government effectiveness indicators is elite survey measures. The most notable of these is the Pew Center on the States' Government Performance Project, which assesses state government performance along four different dimensions: Money, People/Human Resources, Infrastructure, and Information Technology. Each dimension has scoring criteria and measures to assess state performance codified by Pew Center staff and outside experts.[19] Although not specified in the methodology, Pew also calculates an overall score for each state, apparently a summation, or an index of, the four survey dimensions. The stated goal of the Pew surveys are to "assess the capacity of state governments as a whole to produce results—including the cumulative skills and leadership of elected and appointed officials, career civil servants and not-for-profit and private-sector partners."[20] The surveys were performed in 1999, 2001, 2005, and 2008.

Each of the above measures of governmental capacity suffers from significant construct validity issues as an aggregate measure of government performance. Regarding expenditures indicators Huang et al. (2007) found state environmental expenditures negatively predicted the adoption of state renewable energy quotas. However, the measure doesn't capture state administrative costs associated with energy, but rather costs of administering the natural resources.

Western states with large public land holdings therefore rank higher in expenditures, which is not necessarily an indicator of commitment to environmental protection or progressive energy policy. This admonition also applies to the heavily cited work by Lester and Lombard (1990) whose highest expenditure states all have large public land holdings. Furthermore, absolute measures of revenues or expenditures do not capture the large fixed costs associated with service delivery, and thus overstate the relative spending of states with small populations compared to large states. While expenditures might be an appealing indicator of governmental performance, they typically cannot control for relevant structural socioeconomic variables.

Fiscal health measures are also commonly used measures of governmental capacity, although it's not theoretically clear what the relationship between state borrowing and government performance is. A state like California with large deficits due to initiative mandated spending on education and "get-tough-on-crime" could have better educational attainment and public safety outcomes due to its high spending levels than other states that don't borrow money to pay for service delivery. We consider state fiscal health belonging in the category of expenditures indicators, but oriented toward the short term.

An important contribution to governmental capacity literature is legislative professionalism. One legislative performance indicator operationalizes professionalism as an equally weighted index of legislator compensation, time demands, and staff resources benchmarked against U.S. Congress (Squire 2007). However, legislative professionalism measures are intended to capture the capacity of one branch of government and say nothing about the state's willingness and ability to implement policies. Nor is the theoretical justification for the equal weighting of the index made explicit.

Finally, the Pew Government Performance Project is undoubtedly the most data intensive indicator of governmental effectiveness. Yet, the causal logic for the measures is underspecified in two aspects: why the chosen dimensions are important and why they are evaluated the way they are.

1) While certainly important, the selection criteria for the four dimensions of People, Money, Infrastructure, and Information Technology

are not explicated. Furthermore, these four dimensions correlate with each other at .75–.80.

2) The second open question is why the Pew evaluative criteria for each dimension equate to government performance. The criteria emphasize performance budgeting and strategic planning functions in its evaluation dimensions. The high correlations between dimensions indicate that perhaps what is being measured is the degree of performance budgeting and strategic planning across the four areas.

In sum, by focusing on planning functions and not sociopolitical outcomes such as education, public health, economic competitiveness, and environmental protection, the evaluation dimensions seem to measure *potential* governmental performance, or perhaps potential management performance. In spite of the lofty goal quoted above to "assess the capacity of state governments as a whole to produce results" the Pew indicator's scope is actually more modest: to "assess the quality of management in state government."[21]

Given these issues with the internal validity of the survey and expenditures indicators, let us now compare them to one another. Figure 1.5 shows the scatterplot of various indicators of government performance along with gross state product (GSP) per capita. The correlations are for 1999–2008 as the Pew survey was administered in 1999, 2001, 2005, and 2008. The Pew data is linearly interpolated in missing years. Relative political extraction and reach data for 2006 are also used for 2007–2008.

The correlation coefficients presented here are not large (substantive), but are significant at the 95 percent confidence level. Unlike international indicators of governmental effectiveness, none of the U.S. indicators is strongly correlated with productivity measured as GSP per capita. Legislative professionalism has the strongest positive correlation with GSP/capita (.25) while RPE is negative associated (-.33). The effectiveness indicators also show interesting relationships with each other. The Pew indicator is positively correlated with RPR (.22), but negatively correlated with RPE (-.20) and uncorrelated with legislative professionalism.

This analysis shows that a wide range of subnational government performance indicators have been employed, at least for the United States. Each one has its strengths and limitations. Fiscal and expenditures data are easy to acquire, but not theoretically robust. Legislative professionalism correlates positively, but weakly, with relative political extraction but is primarily a useful measure of legislative capacity. The Pew Center's Government Performance indicator is designed to measure state administrative innovation, but is unsurprisingly uncorrelated with legislative professionalism. A larger formal economy (relative political reach) correlates with legislative professionalism.

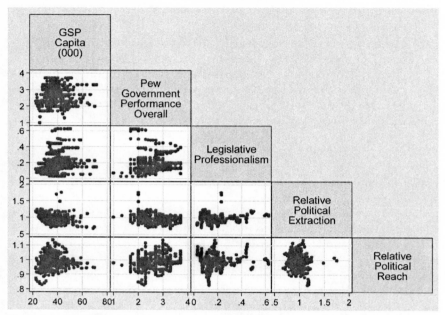

Figure 1.5.   Relationships between GSP per Capita and Government Performance Indicators

Finally, relative political extraction is negatively correlated with GSP per capita and legislative professionalism. This is unsurprising as revenue-based measures (tax revenue/GSP) of political capacity are higher for small population states that tend to be more agrarian (and thus lower income). The regression model of RPE for the United States controls for state population. This specification helps to ameliorate, but cannot eliminate, a positive bias in political capacity predictions due to the higher fixed costs of service delivery and infrastructure provision in states with small populations.

To summarize, at the international level we have established with these tests that the proposed measures of governmental effectiveness are independent of each other, and are also independent of wealth, democracy, economic freedom, and measures of governance. At the national level for the United States, we have also demonstrated that political extraction and reach are analytically distinct from wealth and from other measures of government performance. Political reach and extraction are also the broadest measure of government performance and the only indicators that control for the structural characteristics present in each state. They are also objective. We theoretically assumed when constructing these indicators that politics and economics are independent, and that they interactively account for the working of the social fabric. The tests provided in this book strongly suggest that these insights are correct.

POLITICAL PERFORMANCE APPLICATIONS

The following provides a visual assessment of the three components of political performance. We chose data for 2003–2005 to illustrate the level of and variation in the three measures of political performance.

Political extraction has the following characteristics. The least developed societies have massive variance in their ability to extract resources from the population. At the very bottom of the least developed societies are "failed" states—Sudan, Iraq, and Myanmar—that extract minimally and perform very poorly. As development proceeds, less-developed societies increase their political extraction. Among the most developed societies few fall below the norm. When populations earn on the average $30,000 or more, variation in levels of extraction diminishes. Outliers such as Norway and Iceland had welfare packages much larger than those of other societies but were unable to sustain them.

Consistent with expectations, development produces stable political environments, but political opportunities reside with the less-developed societies that have a large potential to accelerate growth with effective political intervention. Indeed, developing societies that mobilize their resources effectively have the largest potential to expand—as is the case of Brazil and China in 2005–2011. They also have great potential to fail if political extraction and reach weakens; instability can overwhelm societies like Mexico.

The assessment of political reach reflects patterns detected in the political extraction assessment indicating these two measures are not related.[22] Again the variance in reach among the least developed societies is very large, while that among the most developed societies is very low.

Finally an inspection of allocation shows consistency. Among the least developed societies, allocations again vary substantially and variance declines as the level of development rises. From a growth perspective, Pakistan and Indonesia allocate very poorly, while the Bahamas does an exceptional job given resources. Finally Luxembourg is an outlier among the most developed societies—but this may well be due to the banking secrecy laws that fail to reflect overall productivity.

The results confirm that political performance is not related to personal wealth. Some less-developed societies extract, reach, and allocate resources far more effectively than the more-developed set. On the other hand there is much more variance in the performance of the least developed societies—generating much higher levels of risk over time among

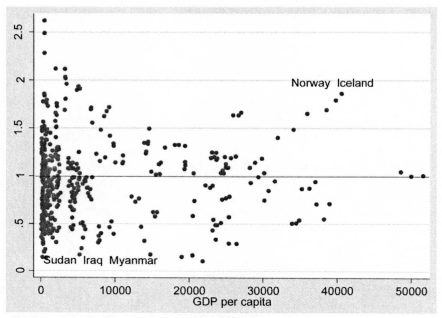

Figure 1.6.   Extraction by Level of Development, 2003–2005

these populations—than among the most developed societies. These results are consistent with our intuitive expectations.

CONCLUSIONS

Most previous assessments of political performance have been determined by movement toward democracy and the provision of freedoms (Bueno de Mesquita et al. 2003). Our perspective on politics is very different from this view. While wealthier societies are more stable and more consistent, they do not necessarily extract, reach, and allocate resources more efficiently than their authoritarian counterparts. One may well ask, given such results, if the competitive democratic system in the United States that allows substantial freedom to its population is more capable of resolving political disputes than the noncompetitive single-party system of China that imposes numerous restrictions on the freedoms of its population. Our measures suggest that this question may well need to be revisited.

In addition to seeing how our measures Reach, Extraction, and Allocation look across countries, we also can compare the political performance of the United States, Russia, and China over time. The performance of the United

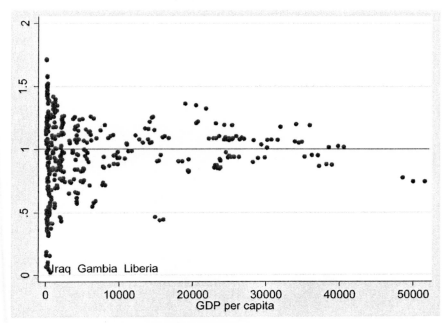

Figure 1.7.   Reach by Level of Development, 2003–2005

States is consistent over time, hovering around the norm (mean performance = 1.0) from 1970 to 2006. Extraction is above average for most of the period.[23] Extraction varies the most, probably reflecting the effects of wars and business cycles, but these are minor compared to those registered in less-developed societies. Relative Political Reach consistently hits the mean. From the growth perspective, allocations improve steadily, most likely reflecting the demise of the Cold War. They drop markedly after 9/11 with the shifting U.S. policy focus on security and the associated increase in the defense budget. Overall, however, this picture is consistent with our expectations for a developed, stable society.

The assessment of Russia is based only on data following the collapse of the USSR as data prior are both scarce and of suspect quality. The reorganization of government is captured by the dramatic decline in extraction and a moderate decline in reach. Growth allocations are not available during the most intense crisis when we expect a dramatic decline, but Russia's performance since 2000 suggests that the current slow recovery should continue. Reach has stabilized, so hopefully better Allocation policies or stronger Extraction performance can stabilize Russia's future.

Let's turn to China's performance. We see a steady decline in the capacity

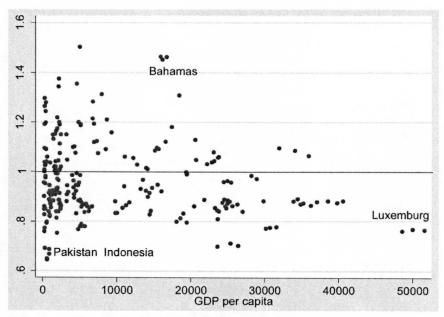

Figure 1.8. Allocation by Level of Development, 2003–2005

of the government to extract resources as the party's hold on the economy declines. Reach remains constant, indicating that political mobilization is not affected. Somewhat surprisingly, the allocation measure suggests sluggish performance given optimal growth, but a constant improvement over time indicates the government is maintaining an effective hold over the economy.

These pictures indicate that structural changes in political performance do take place, but they are rare. Variability in these indicators is associated with lower economic performance, and they indicate instability. Stable societies are those where variations in political performance are minimized.

Many international political economy colleagues recognize the link between politics and political economy but have labored under the impression that while most economic phenomena could be effectively measured, politics was far more elusive. The empirical chapters of this book are designed to show that the contrary is true. Political and economic behavior can be approximated with equivalent levels of reliability.

We contend that political performance represents a major factor when evaluating issues associated with political economy and conflict. Until now, we have been constrained by the absence of consistent indicators to mea-

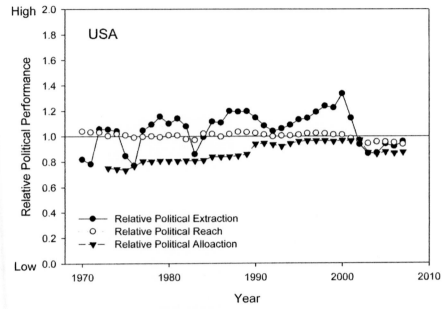

Figure 1.9.   United States Political Performance, 1970–2007

sure levels of political performance. This book provides the evidence necessary to redress that gap in our knowledge.

NOTES

1. This scale of democracy has continued to be an important measure in political research, with extensive measures of the degree of democracy found in the Freedom House Index and democracy/autocracy measures available in Polity IV.

2. The World Bank study covers 212 countries and territories for 1996, 1998, 2000, and annually for 2002–2006. The indicators (voice and accountability, political stability and absence of violence, government effectiveness, regulatory quality, rule of law and control of corruption) are based on several hundred individual variables measuring perceptions of governance, drawn from 33 separate data sources constructed by 30 different organizations.

3. Assessments of Relative Political Capacity as a useful indicator in identifying national capabilities can be found in Kugler and Domke (1986) and more recently in Kadera and Sorokin (2004).

4. $y_{it} = \alpha + x_{it}\beta + \epsilon_{it}$

where y_{it} is adjusted tax revenue for country i at time t, x_{it} is a vector of variables that determine potential tax collection, and ϵ_{it} is the white noise disturbance.

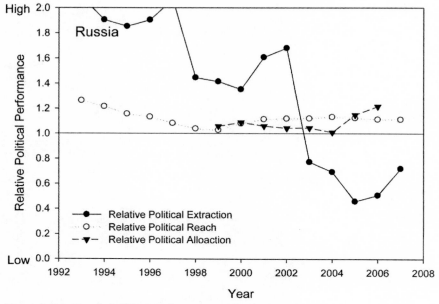

Figure 1.10.   Russia Political Performance, 1993–2007

5. Two equations are used to estimate RPE.
Developing societies (Model 1):

$$\frac{\text{Tax}}{\text{GDP}} = \alpha + \beta_1(\text{time}) + \beta_2 \left(\frac{\text{Mining}}{\text{GDP}}\right) + \beta_3 \left(\frac{\text{Agriculture}}{\text{GDP}}\right) + \beta_4 \left(\frac{\text{Exports}}{\text{GDP}}\right)$$
$$+ \beta_5(\text{Crude Oil Production per year}) + \beta_6(\text{OECD}) + \epsilon$$

Developed societies (Model 2):

$$\frac{\text{Tax}}{\text{GDP}} = \alpha + \beta_1(\text{time}) + \beta_2 \left(\frac{\text{Mining}}{\text{GDP}}\right) + \beta_3 \left(\frac{\text{Exports}}{\text{GDP}}\right) + \beta_4(\text{Crude Oil Production})$$
$$+ \beta_5(\text{GDP per capita}) + \beta_6(\text{OECD}) + \epsilon$$

The RPE estimation for our sample is as follows:

VARIABLES	(Model 1) Tax/GDP	(Model 2) Tax-GDP
Time	0.0000416	0.000366***
	(0.0000661)	(0.00 00672)
Mining/ GDP	0.0560***	0.102***
	(0.00801)	(0.00835)

VARIABLES	(Model 1) Tax/GDP	(Model 2) Tax-GDP
Agriculture/GDP	− 0.145*** (0. 00697)	
Exports/GDP	0.0340*** (0.00424)	0.0746*** (0.00422)
Oil Production	− 0.00001*** (0.00000081)	− 0.0000067*** (0.00000084)
OECD	0.0220*** (0.00260)	0.0624*** (0.00333)
GDP per Capita		− 0.00000103*** (0.00000016)
Constant	0.162*** (0.00331)	0.105*** (0.00214)
Observations	6,544	6,528
R-squared	0.188	0.139

Standard errors in parentheses
*** p<0.01, ** p<0.05, * p<0.1

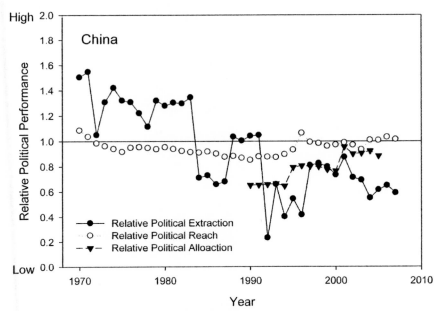

Figure 1.11. China Political Performance, 1970–2007

6. The basic model of political extraction at the sub-national level is as follows:

$$\frac{State\ Revenue}{GDP} = \alpha + \beta_1(time) + \beta_2\left(\frac{State\ Mining}{GDP}\right) + \beta_3(State\ GDPpercap)$$

$$+ \beta_4\left(\frac{transfers}{GDP}\right) + + \beta_4\left(\frac{State\ Oil\ Production}{GDP}\right) + \epsilon$$

7. For an exhaustive overview, see Frey and Weck (1983).

8. $y_{it} = \alpha + x_{it}\beta + \epsilon_{it}$

where y_{it} is active population ratio to total population for country i at time t, x_{it} is a vector of variables that determine potential reach capacity, and ϵ_{it} is the white noise disturbance.

9. $\dfrac{Activity\ Rate}{Population} = \alpha + \beta_1(time) + \beta_2(Education) + \beta_3(Population\ Age) + \beta_4$

$(Social\ Security) + \beta_5(Urbanization) + \beta_6(Population) + \beta_7$
$(GDP\ per\ Capita) + \beta_8(Bureaucracy) + \epsilon$

where
Activity Rate / Population = (Active Population- Unemployment*) / Population
Bureaucracy = Government Wages / Total Expenditures
Education = Secondary Education Attainment
Pop Age = % Population less than 16 years old
Population = Total Population
Social Security = Social Security Taxes / GDP
Urbanization = % Urban
GDP per Capita = GDP per capita in 2000 constant US dollars
* Part time workers should be excluded are unavailable. Alternatively economically active population adjusted by unemployment can be used.
The RPR estimation for our sample is as follows:

VARIABLES	Activity Rate
Time	0.000870***
	(0.000142)
Education	11.04***
	(2.200)
Population Age	−0.00237***
	(0.000379)
Social Security	0.135*
	(0.0697)
Urbanization	−0.00197***
	(0.000107)
Population	8.90e-11***
	(0)

GDP per Capita	0.00000551***
	(0.000000313)
Bureaucracy	− 0.244***
	(0.0299)
Constant	− 1.028***
	(0.286)
Observations	6,380
R-squared	0.150

Standard errors in parentheses
*** $p<0.01$, ** $p<0.05$, * $p<0.1$

10. There are many other government categories of budgetary expenditures, but these are the main expenditures that are consistent across almost all governments. For example, environment and recreational budgets exist, but are mainly for highly developed societies only.

11. For the first step, we estimate the frontier production function with optimal spending ratios reflected in beta coefficients:

$$GDP\ per\ capita = TotalFactorProductivity \times \left(\frac{Capital}{GDP}\right)^{\alpha_1} \times (GeneralPublic/cap)^{\beta_1}$$
$$\times (Defense/cap)^{\beta_2} \times (PublicOrder/cap)^{\beta_3} \times (EconAffair/cap)^{\beta_4}$$
$$\times (Housing/cap)^{\beta_5} \times (Health/cap)^{\beta_6} \times (Education/cap)^{\beta_7}$$
$$\times (SocialSecurity/cap)^{\beta_8}$$

For estimation purpose, taking logs,

$$\ln GDP\ per\ capita = \alpha_0 + \alpha_1 \ln\left(\frac{Capital}{GDP}\right) + \beta_1 \ln (GeneralPublic/cap) + \beta_2 \ln$$

$(Defense/cap) + \beta_3 \ln (PublicOrder/cap) + \beta_4 \ln (EconAffair/cap) + \beta_5 \ln (Housing/cap) + \beta_6 \ln (Health/cap) + \beta_7 \ln (Education/cap) + \beta_8 \ln (SocialSecurity/cap) + \epsilon$

The RPA estimation for our sample is as follows:

VARIABLES	ln GDP per capita
ln Capital/GDP	0.130***
	(0.014)
ln General_Public_spending	0.043***
	(0.004)
ln Defense_spending	− 0.006***
	(0.002)
ln Public_Order_spending	0.03***
	(0.001)
ln Econ_spending	0.016***
	(0.005)
ln Housing_spending	0.008***
	(0.003)

ln Health_spending	0.022*** (0.006)
ln Education_spending	0.024*** (0.007)
ln Social_spending	0.009*** (0.003)
Constant	10.05*** (0.088)
Observations	3,088
Wald chi2(9) = 1564.72	

Standard errors in parentheses***
p<0.01, ** p<0.05, * p<0.10

12. For our second step, we then calculate the allocation inefficiency scores for the Relative Political Allocation (RPA) index as follows:

$$RPA = 2 \times \left(1 - \frac{|Country\ i's\ Ineff. - Lowest\ Ineff.\ in\ the\ sample|}{Country\ i's\ Ineff. + Lowest\ Ineff.\ in\ the\ sample} \right)$$

RPA is bound between 0 and 2. The upper bound (2) indicates super-optimality, the mean (1) indicates normal performance, while the lower bound (0) indicates sub-optimal allocation.

13. R^2 .16 − .73

14. R^2 .12 − .80

15. Recent extensive evaluations show that these relationships remain constant. Extracting the strongest relationships, we find that trade freedom and freedom from corruption are most strongly related to GDP per capita. Monetary, investment, and property rights lag behind. Freedom from corruption in particular has a substantive impact on per capita GDP as do monetary and investment freedom. Property rights lag behind.

16. R^2 .38 − .65

17. R^2 .58 − .92

18. More detailed regression analysis indicates the independence of performance indicators and GDP per capita. Relational coefficients are never significant. The $R^2 = 0.004$ for RPE with agriculture adjustments; and $R^2 = 0.0001$ for RPR and RPE with productivity adjustments. Further analysis confirms the independence of performance variables at different levels of economic development. Additional analysis confirms our theoretical suspicions. Government size is not associated with RPR or the RPE's but it is related to GDP per capita, suggesting the effects of economies of scale. RPR and the RPE's have a very weak relation other indicators (Strongest is $R^2 = .08$ for RPE with productivity controls) but such relations are not significant in regressions.

19. http://www.pewcenteronthestates.org/template_page.aspx?id = 353 60

20. http://www.pewcenteronthestates.org/template_page.aspx?id = 35362

21. The first quote comes from the website describing the Government Performance Project's methodology: http://www.pewcenteronthestates.org/template_page.

aspx?id = 35362. The second quote is the header for the 2008 individual state reports. For example, see: http://www.pewcenteronthestates.org/uploadedFiles/PEW_WebGuides_AZ.pdf

22. $R^2 = .01$

23. Extraction drops substantially after 2000—reflecting the significant tax cuts enacted during the George Bush administration.

REFERENCES

Abdollahian, Mark, Marina Arbetman, and Kyungkook Kang. 2009. "Exploring Optimal Public Expenditure Frontier: Stochastic Social Production Frontier Approach." Paper presented at the annual meeting of the International Studies Association, New York City, NY.

Alcazar, Lorena. 1997. "Political Capacity and the Use of Seigniorage." Marina Arbetman and Jacek Kugler, eds., *Political Capacity and Economic Behavior*. Boulder, CO: Westview Press.

Arbetman, Marina. 1990. "The Political Economy of Exchange Rate Fluctuations." PhD diss., Vanderbilt University.

———. 1994. "The Concept of Political Penetration." The Center for Politics and Economics, ed., *Proceedings of the Conference on Political Capacity and Economic Behavior*. Claremont, CA: Claremont Graduate School.

Arbetman, Marina, and Dipak Ghosh. 1997. "Political Capacity and Black Market Premiums." Marina Arbetman and Jacek Kugler, eds., *Political Capacity and Economic Behavior*. Boulder, CO: Westview Press.

Arbetman, Marina, and Kristin Johnson. 2008. "Power Distribution and Oil in the Sudan: Will the Comprehensive Peace Agreement Turn the Oil Curse into a Blessing?" *International Interactions* 34 (4): 382–401.

Arbetman, Marina, Jacek Kugler, and A. F. K. Organski. 1997. "Political Capacity and Demographic Change." Marina Arbetman and Jacek Kugler, eds., *Political Capacity and Economic Behavior*. Boulder, CO: Westview Press.

Arzaghi, M., and J. V. Henderson. 2005. "Why Countries Are Fiscally Decentralizing." *Journal of Public Economics* 89: 1157–89.

Bacot, A. H., and R. A. Dawes. 1997. "State Expenditures and Policy Outcomes in Environmental Program Management." *Policy Studies Journal* 25 (Fall): 355–70.

Bahl, Roy W. 1971. "A Regression Approach to Tax Effort and Tax Ratio Analysis." *IMF Staff Papers* 18 (November).

Barro, Robert. 1990. "Government Spending in a Simple Model of Endogenous Growth." *Journal of Political Economy* 98 (5): 103–26.

Benson, Michelle, and Jacek Kugler. 1998. "Power Parity, Democracy, and the Severity of Internal Violence." *Journal of Conflict Resolution* 42 (2): 196–209.

Berry, F. S.. and W. D. Berry. 1990. "State Lottery Adoptions as Policy Innovations: An Event History Analysis." *American Political Science Review* 84 (2): 395–415.

Bueno de Mesquita, Bruce, Alastair Smith, Randolph Siverson. and James Morrow. 2003. *The Logic of Political Survival*. Cambridge, MA: The MIT Press.

Campbell, C., P. E. Converse, W. E. Miller, and D. E. Stokes. 1960. *The American Voter*. New York: John Wiley and Sons.

Coan, Travis, and Tadeusz Kugler. 2008. "The Politics of Foreign Direct Investment: An Interactive Framework." *International Interactions* 34 (4): 402–22.

Deutsch, Karl. 1966. "Social Mobilization and Political Development." Jason Finkle and Richard Gable, eds., *Political Development and Social Change*. New York: John Wiley and Sons.

Easterly, William. 2008. "Can the West Save Africa?" *NBER Working Paper* no. 14363.

Easterly, William, and Sergio Rebelo. 1993. "Fiscal Policy and Economic Growth: An Empirical Investigation." *Journal of Monetary Economics* 32 (3): 417–58.

Feng, Yi. 2003. *Democracy, Governance, and Economic Performance: Theory and Evidence*. Cambridge, MA: The MIT Press

Feng, Yi, and Baizhu Chen. 1997. "Political Capacity and Private Investment." Marina Arbetman and Jacek Kugler, eds., *Political Capacity and Economic Behavior*. Boulder, CO: Westview Press.

Feng, Yi, Jacek Kugler, Siddharth Swaminathan, and Paul Zak. 2008. "Path to Prosperity: The Dynamics of Freedom and Economic Development." *International Interactions* 34 (4): 423–41

Feng, Yi, Jacek Kugler, and Paul Zak. 2000. "The Politics of Fertility and Economic Development." *International Studies Quarterly* 44 (4): 667–93.

Fiorina, M. P. 1981. *Retrospective Voting in American National Elections*. New Haven, CT: Yale University Press.

Frey, Bruno, and Hannelore Weck. 1983. "Estimating the Shadow Economy: A Native Approach." *Oxford Economic Papers* 35 (1): 23–44.

Gerber, B. J., and P. Teske. 2000. "Regulatory Policymaking in the American States: A Review of Theories and Evidence." *Political Research Quarterly* 53 (4): 849–86.

Grossback, L. J., S. Nicholson-Crotty, and D. Peterson. 2004. "Ideology and Learning in Policy Diffusion." *American Politics Research* 32 (5): 521–45.

Gurr, T. R. 1974. "Persistence and Change in Political Systems, 1800–1971." *American Political Science Review* 68 (4): 1482–1504.

Hall, Robert, and Charles Jones. 1999. "Why Do Some Countries Produce So Much More Output per Worker than Others?" *Quarterly Journal of Economics* 114 (1): 83–116.

Huang, Ming-Yuan, et al. 2007. "Is the Choice of Renewable Portfolio Standards Random?" *Energy Policy* 35: 5571–75.

Johnson, Kristin. 2007. "Sub National Capabilities and Internal Conflict." PhD diss., Claremont Graduate University.

Kadera, Kelly, and Gerald Sorokin. 2004. "Measuring National Power." *International Interactions* 30: 211–30.

Kugler, Jacek, Michelle Benson, Andy Hira, and Dimitry Panasevitch. 1997. "Political Capacity and Violence." Marina Arbetman and Jacek Kugler, eds., *Political Capacity and Economic Behavior*. Boulder, CO: Westview Press.

Kugler, Jacek, and William Domke. 1986. "Comparing the Strength of Nations." *Comparative Political Studies* 19 (1): 39–69.

Kugler, Jacek, and Douglas Lemke. 1996. *Parity and War*. Ann Arbor, MI: The University of Michigan Press.

Leblang, David. 1997. "Political Capacity and Economic Growth." Marina Arbetman and Jacek Kugler, eds., *Political Capacity and Economic Behavior*. Boulder, CO: Westview Press.

Lester, J. P., and E. N. Lombard. 1990. "The Comparative Analysis of State Environmental Policy." *Natural Resources Journal* 30: 301–20.

Lotz, Jorgen R., and Elliott Morse. 1967. "Measuring 'Tax Effort' in Developing Countries." *IMF Staff Papers* 14.

Organski, A. F. K. 1958. *World Politics*. New York: Alfred A. Knopf.

Organski, A. F. K., and Jacek Kugler. 1980. *The War Ledger*. Chicago: University of Chicago Press.

Organski, A. F. K., Jacek Kugler, Timothy Johnson, and Youssef Cohen. 1984. *Births, Deaths and Taxes*. Chicago: University of Chicago Press.

Pettinati, Paolo. 1979. "Illegal and Unrecorded Employment in Italy." *Economic Notes* 8: 13–30.

Potoski,. M. 2001. "Clear Air Federalism: Do States Race to the Bottom?" *Public Administration Review* 61 (3): 335–42.

Putnam, Robert D. 2000. *Bowling Alone: The Collapse and Revival of America Community*. New York: Simon & Schuster.

Rokkan, S., A. Campbell, P. Torsvile, and H. Valen. 1970. *Citizen's Election Parties, Part II*. New York: David McCay.

Rouyer, Alwyn. 1987. "Political Capacity and the Decline of Fertility in India." *American Political Science Review* 81 (2): 453–70.

Schultz, T. Paul. 1999. "Health and Schooling Investments in Africa." *Journal of Economic Perspectives* 13 (3): 67–88.

Shipan, C. R., and C. Volden. 2006. "Bottom-Up Federalism: The Diffusion of Anti-smoking Policies from U.S. Cities to States." *American Journal of Political Science* 50 (4): 825–43.

Smith, Stephen. 1986. *Britain's Shadow Economy*. Oxford: Clarendon Press.

Solow, Robert. 1957. "Technical Change and the Aggregate Production Function." *Review of Economics and Statistics* 39 (3): 312–20.

Squire, P. 2007. "Measuring State Legislative Professionalism: The Squire Index Revisited." *State Politics and Policy Quarterly* 7 (2): 211–27.

Swaminathan, Siddharth, and John Thomas. 2007. "Saving the Next Generation: Political Capacity and Infant Mortality Decline in India's States." *International Interactions* 33 (3): 217–42.

Tammen, Ronald L., Mark Abdollahian, Carole Alsharabati, Brian Efird, Jacek Kugler, Douglas Lemke, Allan C. Stam III, and A. F. K Organski. 2000. *Power Transitions: Strategies for the 21st Century*. New York: Chatham House.

Tanzi, Vito. 1983. "The Underground Economy in the United States: Annual Estimates, 1930–80." *IMF Staff Papers* 30 (2): 283–305.

Verba, S., and N. Nie. 1972. *Participation in America: Political Democracy and Social Equality*. New York: Harper and Row.

World Bank. 1992. *Governance and Development*. Washington, DC: The World Bank.

———. 2007. *Strengthening World Bank Group Engagement on Governance and Anticorruption*. Washington, DC: The World Bank.

II

CROSS-NATIONAL
PERFORMANCE

2

Setting the Stage

The Politics of Economic Growth

Mark Abdollahian, Kyungkook Kang, and John Thomas

CONTEXT AND INTELLECTUAL ENVIRONMENT

History is rife with revolution and reform. From the widespread European social revolts of 1848 to Middle East unrest in 2011, government economic performance matters. In this chapter, we investigate the political determinants of economic performance. For almost all governments, maintaining an environment that fosters economic prosperity is a top priority to enhance their own political survival. Where are the political opportunities for success or the constraints for failure? What are the politics of economic performance or the economic cost of politics?

Here we begin to unravel these questions by looking at our three political indicators—extraction, reach, and allocation—and how they relate to economic performance over time. Although seemingly simple questions, it is only recently that we have a long enough track record of economic performance to compare to political promises. This chapter first identifies the short-term effect of political capacity on economic growth using econometric analysis. Then we investigate five countries from the long-run economic growth perspective, to detect the role of political capacity. The ultimate objective is to provide a workable approximation of the effect of policy choices on economic growth at the national level.

In order to understand the political determinants of economics, we must first start with the traditional foundations explaining economic growth.

Vast differences in standards of living over time and across countries are a recurrent puzzle for economists. Almost two centuries after Adam Smith released *An Inquiry into the Nature and Causes of the Wealth of Nations* in 1776, this question was posed again by Robert Solow (1956) and T. W. Swan (1956). The Solow-Swan growth model mathematically modernizes the process of wealth or capital accumulation depending on inputs in the economy and their efficiency. This simple but powerful framework has been widely accepted by economists as the basis for most explanations of economic growth.

Two principal findings of the Solow-Swan model were empirically validated by Mankiw, Romer, and Weil (1992) and Barro and Sala-i-Martin (1992). First, every economy is expected to converge onto its own "potential" output level. This potential output is defined by productivity change, capital, and labor. Economists call this the steady-state income. Thus a nation's population size defines the pool of available labor potentials, with larger more populous nations having a distinct advantage, if the proper financial markets and investments are made productively. Second, the farther a country is from its economic potential, the faster the economy should grow to reach that potential and thus the opportunity for high economic growth.

Following Solow-Swan, a new growth economics emerged, called endogenous growth theory, that addresses how technology or knowledge represents a key component in economic changing the productivity of potentials (Romer 1990; Grossman and Helpman 1991; Aghion and Howitt 1997). Here economic growth rates equal the accumulation rate of new ideas that allows a given quantity of input to produce more output. This view emphasizes the importance of individual motivation to implement private research and development activities to reward productive efforts.

Progress of pushing the economic potential envelope is an inherent outcome of profit-maximizing behaviors. As in popular rags-to-riches stories in Horatio Alger's novels, the main engine of growth is reduced to the result of individual achievements driven by economic competition. The stages of economic development are a testament to the impact of technological progress, where primary economic activities are in the agrarian sector, secondary activities in the manufacturing sector, tertiary activities in the services sector, and quaternary activities in the knowledge or information technology sector.

This explanation is still unsatisfying in many ways. The neoclassical analysis including the new growth theory rests on the assumption of a perfect market economy: let the market do the work and the outcome will be optimal. There is no need for government intervention as any competitive equilibrium leads to a Pareto efficient allocation of resources where everyone is better off without affecting the resources of third parties. Thus individual efforts and achievement for private gains will be transformed to the whole social welfare without losses. We know, however, the real world is a bit more complicated than the outcomes produced by profit-maximizing individuals.

Social structures that determine an individual's socioeconomic incentives are largely not under his or her control. Chronic social problems such as prolonged political violence, black market activity, crime, or capital flight cannot be remedied by private effort alone. With real macro-level constraints, one cannot expect every individual to pursue private interests that are compatible to public interests. Indeed Baumol (1990) maintains that in societies without strong legal enforcement, seeking economically productive achievements is less attractive to the most gifted individuals than participating in lucrative criminal activities such as rent seeking.

This line of reasoning is further advanced by Murphy, Shleifer, and Vishny (1991), who show how politically strong governments can provide productive economic incentives that encourage individuals to pursue private activities that are socially beneficial. In a similar vein, Hall and Jones (1999) emphasize the positive role of political institutions and policy makers that encourage investment and production rather than consumption or rent seeking.

Thus the challenge for politicians and policy makers to induce economic growth appears to be rather simple and straightforward: identifying the determinants of economic potentials and implementing political reforms that increase or realize public benefits. The rapid growth of Asian Tigers from the 1960s to the 1980s, with their financial commitments and focus on manufacturing using new technology, is a good example of realized economic potentials. The realization of these economic potentials was made reality by government policy.

Despite low economic performance, the Asian Tigers grew more rapidly than Latin American counterparts because they utilized the economic potentials of having an abundance of land, labor, and capital that just needed to be tapped into. The neoclassical model anticipates that once a nation is closer to its potential output level, its economy grows slower as there is less room to increase production beyond potential levels. The United States and Europe are advanced economies with sophisticated capital and financial markets with developed technology. Their levels of economic growth are smaller in spite of sophisticated political machinations.

This implies that the same dynamics that have propelled the United States and EU to economic preeminence will also drive the growth of the developing world toward economic parity, under the right structural conditions of economic inputs and political initiatives. It also implies that both rich and poor countries can experience sluggish economic growth when structural conditions are not politically exploited.

While most developed countries successfully realize their greater potential output levels and enjoy higher standards of living, average growth rates of their countries are relatively low with small fluctuations. Many sub-Saharan African countries also experience low growth as they are caught in chronic "poverty traps" since their economic potentials fall far short of the world average. Despite having an abundance of potential labor, undeveloped financial and capital markets coupled with little benefits from technology limit economic growth. Government's role cannot be overlooked as a facilitator to either empower or constrain economic growth potential as markets do not operate by themselves. Only when government can secure an economic environment where productive individual decisions can be made can it achieve the primary goals of long-term economic growth.

THE SHORT-TERM IMPACT OF POLITICAL PERFORMANCE ON ECONOMIC GROWTH

Unfortunately or fortunately, there is no pure market economy in the world. Political systems assume the role of coordinator to facilitate the nation's economic goals such as economic growth, full employment, low inflation, efficient income distribution, and so on. To advance goals, governments project their political capacity on economic realms mainly through fiscal policy. Policy makers create a detailed list of goods and services that are assumed to make the best use of the nation's resources. Governments design individual incentive structures to encourage certain types of production or consumption that alter the path of economic growth. By levying taxes and providing public goods, fiscal policy limits resources left in people's hand to spend as they like. This can distort or empower economic growth.

While conventional economic approaches to fiscal adjustment emphasized the macroeconomic stabilization perspective, some political economists view fiscal policy as an active political channel to better support economic growth. Barro (1990), Barro and Sala-i-Martin (1992), and Turnovsky and Fisher (1995) suggested general equilibrium models to show how tax-financed government services affect production and utility level. Aschauer (1989), Easterly and Rebelo (1993), and Alesina, Perotti, Giavazzi, and Kollintzas (1995) investigated the empirical association between the development level and the fiscal structure.

Even though there are questions remaining on the importance of fiscal policy as the main instrument of economic policy in any country, we still need to investigate how that policy really works in practice. Since previous work focuses on the relationship between the aggregation of fiscal policies and economic growth, policy makers often fail to realize what specific aspects of detailed budgetary expenditures are critical in economic development. The concept of political performance or political capacity enables us to examine the performance of government's fiscal policy implementation to enhance the productivity of an economy from multidirectional aspects.

Specifically, the effectiveness of government performance should be evaluated in terms of first, its ability to raise revenues as budget adjustment (Relative Political Extraction: RPE); second, the prudence to purchase goods and provide services as government spending (Relative Political Allocation: RPA); and third, the quality of political infrastructure that reduces the transaction costs between society and government (Relative Political Reach: RPR). The more revenues a government has, the more policy choices are provided. The more policy choices given, the more its population can enjoy being productive. However, too much or too little extraction and injudicious spending coupled with large segments of the population unaffected by government policy is a recipe for economic disaster. We believe that "sufficiently" extracted resources spent in "optimal proportions" given budget constraints thorough "effective" channels is the political balancing act that turns potential economic promise into real growth reality.

Before proceeding with detailed explorations, we pay special attention to two theoretical concerns commonly highlighted in the fiscal policy assessment: the temporal dynamics and the interaction effect with income. First, we need to keep in mind that the realization of political capacity via fiscal policy can emerge either immediately or several years later. Some sectors of an economic system may respond sluggishly to policy changes. To varying extents it often takes a certain amount of time for firms to shift from one product to another, for workers to shift from one job to another, and for resources to be mobilized from one use to another. This is one of the practical shortcomings of fiscal control over markets since some economic actors should endure temporal losses until normal operations.

Second, the impact of relative political extraction (RPE) may not be generalized when levels of socioeconomic development differ across countries. Contrary to relative political reach (RPR) and allocation (RPA), taxation directly affects purchasing powers of individuals. If fiscal policies are poorly administered as distortionary tax, it may discourage economically desirable activities such as consumption or work. This is relevant to the reason why the need for a fiscal stimulus has been widely accepted in developed countries. If a well-established economy already enjoys an appropriate level of the provision of public goods, excessive extraction can worsen business cyclical swings, especially in a recession. One cannot conclude, however, that the appropriate approach to stimulating advanced economies is also helpful in the design of an optimal tax system for developing countries that suffer from a lack of an adequate level of public revenues. In sum, the search for a generalized impact of political extraction applicable for all kinds of economies may be misguided.

Accordingly, we estimate the degrees of temporal contribution of political capacity changes to the growth of individual income over one- to five-year durations. To consider the income effect of taxation, we investigate the impact of political extraction on economic growth based on the presence of interaction with the level of income per capita. From empirical investigations with 116 countries from 1970 to 2007, figures 2.1 to 2.3 illustrate how 0.1 unit changes of three elements of political capacity affect the percentage growth rate of GDP per capita over one- to five-year lags.[1]

RELATIVE POLITICAL EXTRACTION (RPE) AND SHORT-TERM ECONOMIC GROWTH

In figure 2.1, Relative Political Extraction is found to have salient impacts on economic growth, but the directions of change vary with levels of per capita income. In the case of least developed societies (when individual income level conditioned on $800, which is considered the low-income criterion by UNESCO), raising 0.1 unit of RPE at the previous year is expected

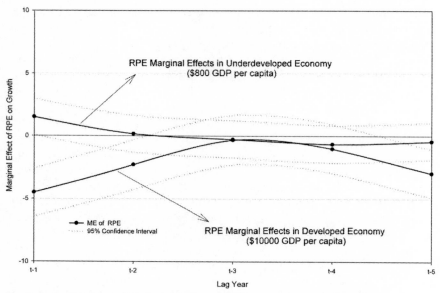

Figure 2.1.   Relative Political Extraction and the Growth of GDP per Capita (Underdeveloped Case and Developed Case)

to increase 0.15 percent of growth rate at the current year.[2] However, in the case of most developed societies (when individual income level conditioned on $10,000, which is considered the high-income level by UNSD), as 0.1 unit of RPE rises at the previous year, 0.45 percent of growth rate is expected to be reduced at the current year.[3] Either of those impacts is instantaneous and vanishes after the second year. To put it another way, increasing RPE is an attractive option to immediately boost economic productivity of countries that suffer chronic poverty while excessive RPE can dampen economic growth in relatively wealthy societies.

This result is closely related to the famous "Samuelson rule" that has been the prevailing guide to public good provision (Samuelson 1954). Obviously, as governments provide more public goods, the aggregate welfare of the population increases. To finance pubic good provision, however, individuals should forgo certain amounts of their disposable incomes to pay taxes. According to the rule, the ideal fiscal condition that maximizes the welfare of the population is that people pay marginal taxes for public goods that are just equal to the marginal benefits they receive.[4]

This simple principle determines the optimal level of political extraction for the whole economy. Recall the marginal benefits of individuals from public goods are decreasing while marginal costs of government for public goods are decreasing. Then we can postulate that the marginal benefits of public goods are more likely to prevail over the marginal taxes in developing societies where the initial levels of public goods provisions are relatively low. Conversely, in developed societies, individual burdens are more likely to outweigh the public benefits since diminishing marginal returns occurs in the provision of extra public goods.

Thus it appears that we must look further to understand the nonmonotonic impact of political extraction on economic growth. For developed societies that already reached the balanced growth path with a fair amount of public good provision, extra burdens from adding marginal taxes appears to dampen economic activities of the population. Consistent with the standard macroeconomics explanations, excessive levels of RPE may work as a contractionary fiscal policy to reduce aggregate demand.

This short-term pain is usually used to correct the inflationary problems of business cycle expansion, but is always unpleasant to policy makers who are concerned about their popularity. By the same token, lowering RPE can work as expansionary fiscal policy to close a recessionary gap since a fiscal deficit can be financed from the well-established capital market with lesser political effort. On the contrary, the Keynesian saturated stimulus packages such as Bush and Obama administrations' tax cuts may be costly in underdeveloped societies. First, in fragile societies such as Afghanistan or Sudan, the prerequisite of state building is maintaining the monopoly of legitimate violence that can reduce political resistances stemming from regional or local elites. From this perspective, extracting essential revenue for military force is never easy, but is a crucial task at the initial stage of state building (Organski 1997; Benson and Kugler 1998). Once the government can successfully finance such administration, however, it can achieve a stable investment environment that fosters private investment (Johnson 2007).

Second, in view of the underdeveloped state of capital markets, effective resource extraction should be implemented to expand internal investments by discouraging consumption of nonnecessity goods relative to saving. Thus, governments with strong RPE are able to increase the pool of resources from which investment to generate future revenues is made. Establishing such growth-facilitating tax systems must be the central concern in developing countries (Bird 1992). In sum, the effect of RPE on economic growth is conditional on the level of development. This issue should be further analyzed from multifaceted perspectives.

RELATIVE POLITICAL REACH (RPR) AND SHORT-TERM ECONOMIC GROWTH

Figure 2.2 illustrates the general impact of relative political reach (RPR) on economic growth. Effective political reach is shown to exert positive effects

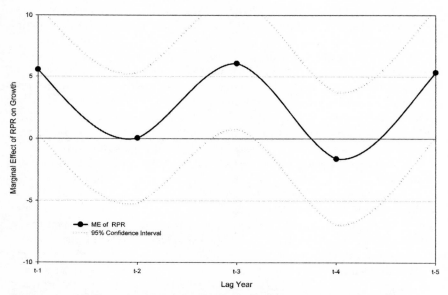

Figure 2.2.   Relative Political Reach and the Growth of GDP per Capita

on income growth immediately and persistently while short-run fluctuations appear. As 0.1 unit of RPR at previous year increases, 0.55 percent of growth rate is expected to rise at current year. Then the positive effects of RPR on growth reappear at the third and the fifth year. Contrary to RPE, this impact can be generalized for either developed or developing societies since RPR is not directly related to individual purchasing power.

Conceptually, RPR measures the performance of political process that converts intrinsic values of social assets into economically productive capitals. De Soto (2000) adeptly explains that the principal problem of less-developed countries is a lack of established "hidden conversion" processes that transform assets from "dead" into "liquid" capital rather than an insufficiency of physical assets. Many individually owned assets inherently have latent potentials, but they need to be converted into tradable forms for further economic transactions. After going through multiple transactions, each dispersed individual endowment is transferred into additional production process.

For example, consider a simple case of an individual who sells to a car dealer her unnecessary used car that is worth $3,000 to finance her new business to generate extra revenue greater than $3,000. The dealer then sells the used car to another customer who is willing to pay more than the dealer's buying cost. This series of deals is economically productive since dead capital (unnecessary used car) is converted to liquid capital (transferred ownership) by hidden conversion process (trading) to enhance all participants' welfare. Note the key of this conversion process is to secure legal contract enforcement by the political authorities to reduce individual vulnerability to prevailing opportunistic behaviors. If the government does not have a legal means such as a "pink slip" to reach individual trades with political power, agents should bear vulnerability and risk involved with unsecured economic transactions to impede efficient trades.

To put it specifically, a government with strong political performance can facilitate the economic process that transfers economic potential of dispersed individual endowments into additional production to generate greater values.

Additionally, from the government side, the strong political capacity to reach the private sector is essential to controlling its economy because it helps to structure the environment within which exchange is repeated, information is collected, and incentives are presented. Without efficient political institutions that monitor economic transactions, most economic behaviors would be carried out in extralegal realms.

The underground economy expands because government cannot access the information on extralegal transactions that are commercially and financially invisible. In the countries in which the underground economy prevails, governments suffer weak political capacity due to the failure to extract resources and cannot generate revenue that provides productivity-enhancing public goods. In circumstances like this, a vicious cycle of under-development repeats itself.

In sum, RPR directly reflects the quality of institutionalized governance that reduces social transaction costs in the whole economy. In fact, this idea is theoretically compatible with the New Institutional Economics theories that emphasize the role of socially devised constraints on individual action to facilitate economic exchanges (classic references include Demsetz 1964 and Alchian 1965). RPR also measures the visibility of social resources to be mobilized for pubic administrations. A government equipped with the well-established institutional environment can implement legal enforcement more effectively. The benefit of increasing RPR is obvious in terms of economic growth.

RELATIVE POLITICAL ALLOCATION (RPA) AND SHORT-TERM ECONOMIC GROWTH

Figure 2.3 explains the relationship between relative political allocation (RPA) and economic growth. Effective fiscal spending seems to boost economic growth immediately; 0.1 unit increase of RPA at the previous year is

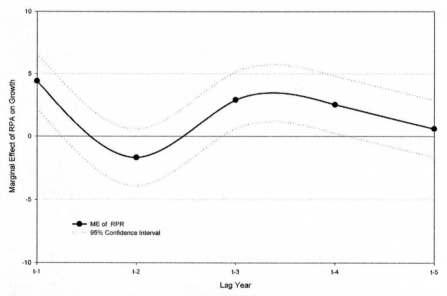

Figure 2.3. Relative Political Allocation and the Growth of GDP per Capita

expected to induce about 0.44 percent of economic growth. While the second-year impact is less clear, possibly due to social adjustment costs, we can expect persistent positive impact from three to five years.

While previous studies focused on the relationship between the aggregation of public policies and economic growth (Aschauer 1989; Easterly and Rebelo 1993; Alesina, Perotti, Giavazzi, and Kollintzas 1995), we shift our attention to the optimality of public sector expenditure allocation that is politically motivated. As already discussed in the previous chapter, RPA provides an objective measure of the government efficiency to optimize its development potential using fiscal spending.

Considering both economic optimization and political feasibility, government makes a decision to purchase goods and services either for current uses (such as military spending or public order) or for future benefits (such as infrastructure investment or research spending). As a result, each expenditure item can be either overallocated or underallocated. This approach sharply contrasts with the standard macroeconomic literatures on fiscal policy that generally deal with only the scale of fiscal policy with expansions or cuts.

Wealth alone is not the key to development. Political performance and wealth levels combine to generate growth. The subset of budgetary allocations represents the larger choices governments have to make. If government adopts fiscal policy strategies to increase spending of public sectors with strong positive impact on domestic production (such as education or economic affairs) and to decrease low productivity public expenditures (such as military defense), then we can consider that government has strong political capacity to improve economic growth.

From a pure economic perspective, fiscal allocations must be paid for by taxes. Unless these are optimized, both have harmful impacts on economic output. Governments, however, make policy choices to attain a variety of frequently incompatible goals. In part, they attempt to attain economic prosperity, and in part they seek to preserve political stability. Indeed, fiscal considerations are constrained by internal political situations. If so, economic growth is entirely dependent on whether the regime is capable or not, rather than whether the regime type is democratic or autocratic.

As will be shown later, this should lead well-entrenched autocracies (e.g., China in 1990s or South Korea in 1980) and strong democracies (e.g., United States) to make reasonably efficient allocations in public expenditures enhancing growth. Weak societies (e.g., Pakistan and Sudan), on the other hand, make consistently poor allocations regardless of political turnovers. Given these political constraints the policy choices made by the elites determine the growth trajectory. The relationship between RPA and economic growth explains why some autocracies grow rapidly and why some democracies are growth laggards. We agree with Olson (1996, p. 22) that "the sums lost because the poor countries obtain only a fraction of—and because even the richest countries do not reach—their economic potentials are measured in the trillions of dollars."

This wide disparity between government policy and economic optimality is frequently attributed to the notion that there is no free lunch. The complex pattern of fiscal allocations, indeed, reveals their preferences and the structural constraints facing policy makers that vary with socioeconomic conditions.

COMPARATIVE CASE STUDIES: THE ROLE OF POLITICAL PERFORMANCE IN LONG-TERM ECONOMIC PROSPERITY

One of the major shortcomings in neoclassical growth theories is that they overlook the intrinsic characteristic of government policy that causes economies to grow over extended periods of time. The literature instead focuses on the general process through which the growth of capital converges on long-run equilibrium levels—eventually zero growth rates. Therefore, this body of theories does not provide a satisfactory explanation for various historical records of economic performances around the world.

Economic growth is frequently impeded by inadequate institutional structure, a lack of commitment and political will of policy makers, imperfect capital and labor markets, and so on. Especially for preindustrialized societies, it is critical to have an independent consolidated political authority with an effective performance to formulate and pursue development strategies. Since neoclassical growth theories neglect these crucial political factors, their applicability for economic development is incomplete, especially when we design country-specific reform processes.

This section illustrates country-to-country comparisons of several stylized facts to show the relationship between political capacity and long-term economic prosperity. In particular, we will examine in detail the trends of economic prosperity and political performance from 1970 to 2007.

The United States

Figure 2.4 shows that the United States has shown a characteristic trajectory commonly found in most advanced industrialized countries. It performs averagely in terms of every component of relative political capacity (RPC). Since the United States has already reached the balanced growth path, policy change is usually driven by the adjustment purpose of short-term macro fluctuation such as recession or presidential leaderships.

Note the levels of RPR and RPA do not have drastic variation while RPA

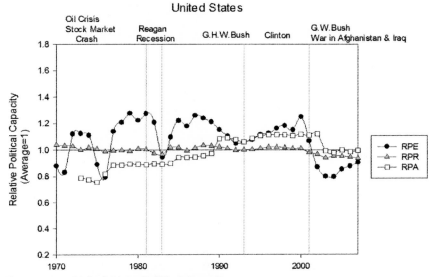

Figure 2.4a.   United States Political Capacity

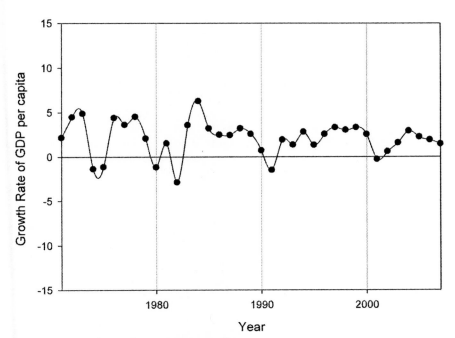

Figure 2.4b.   United States Economic Performance

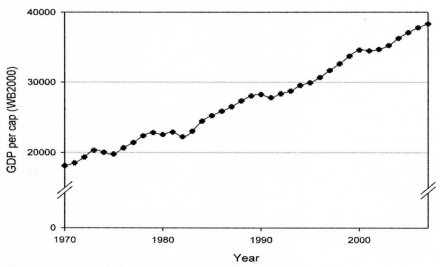

Figure 2.4c.   United States GDP per Capita and Income

shows moderate and gradual improvement along the time series. By contrast, the levels of RPE show a wider range from below 0.7 to above 1.2.
This data explains how the U.S. federal government has managed macro-
economy by manipulating tax rates while the allocating patterns of fiscal
spending have been improved. For example, during Volker's stagflation
control in the late 1970s, the United States implemented high extractive
policy, but Reagan readily abandoned it temporarily to recover from serious
recession from 1981 to 1983. After undergoing a relatively stable period in
the 1990s, the new structural break occurs after the 9/11 attack. The G. W.
Bush administration suffered a serious decline in optimal allocation due to
war spending, associated with low reach policy as economic stimulus. We
know the consequence of the policy. After 2000, the United States has
shown sluggish growth as shown in the figure 2.4.

China

In figure 2.5, the data shows how China's macroeconomic performance
has been affected by different Chinese leaders pushing various strategies.
China exemplifies some patterns of structural change that affect economic
development. The Cultural Revolution (1966–1976) and its aftermath
ruined the economy with excessively high political extraction. After the
Fifth National People's Congress that introduced a mixed planned-market
economy in 1980, the level of political extraction drastically dropped while

political reach still remained relatively low and political allocation was unidentified. Since the early 1990s, the Chinese government has been consistently emphasizing a low RPE and high RPA strategy. The level of RPR is also moderately boosted during the period. Such economic transformation is shown to be directly related to high economic growth. This result is consistent with Feng (2010)'s recent examination of Chinese economic growth from the perspective of the political business cycle.

In particular, the severe fluctuations in political capacity are closely related to the leaderships. Before Li Xiannian's leadership in the early 1980s, China suffered chronic poverty associated with the high level of extraction. This is a typical example of the active but predatory government that extracts resources beyond sustainable levels. Interestingly, after the Tiananmen protest of 1989, the level of RPE drastically dropped. Then, after Jiang Zemin's inauguration as president in 1993, Chinese government boosted the RPA level while maintaining a relatively low RPE level. This drastic shift of political capacity affects the economic trajectory of China, showing a steeply growing pattern after the early 1990s. Indeed, the leaderships of Jiang Zemin and Hu Jintao showed their ability to recover from the economic disaster of the Cultural Revolution with effective fiscal and administrative measures.

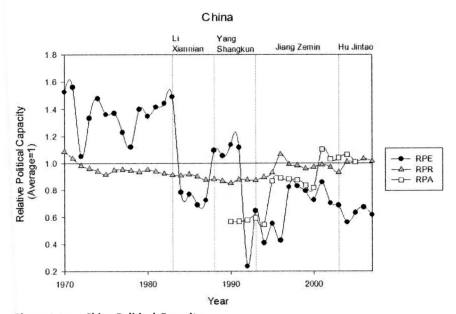

Figure 2.5a. China Political Capacity

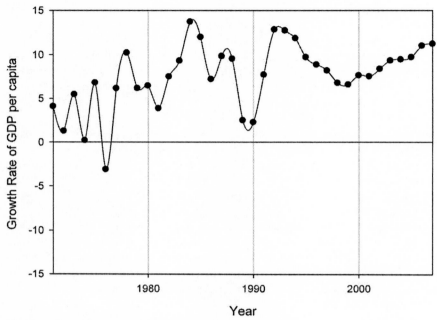

Figure 2.5b.   China Growth Rate of GDP per Capita

Pakistan

In figure 2.6, Pakistan's summary shows the devastating consequence of poor political capacity failing to convert potential natural resources into economic value. Especially Pakistan has a chronic problem of low RPA that has hindered economic development. According to Todaro's (2000) report, for example, the Pakistani government paid military spending more than twice as high as spending on health and education combined in 1994. As a result, Pakistan has suffered high infant mortality and illiteracy rates that are common to many underdeveloped nations.

Pakistan also demonstrates poor political extraction performance. A highly stratified and traditional societal structure of Pakistan has raised an obstacle to sufficient self-financing. This problem worsened after the Bhutto and Sharif regime collapsed. Although unprecedented inflows of foreign assistance have been implemented by the United States in compensation for Pakistan's commitment to fighting terror since 2002, the leaderships of Pakistan have not been willing to escape from the brink of collapse on their own initiative. The sharp declines of political extraction and persistently inefficient political allocation reflect how seriously Pakistan's political institutions have lost their competence. As a result of poor governance, Pakistan

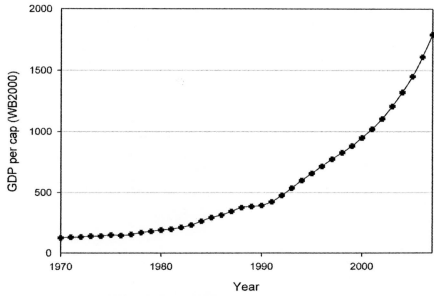

Figure 2.5c. China GDP per Capita and Income

ranks tenth below several African countries, Afghanistan, and Iraq in terms of *Foreign Policy*'s annual Failed State Index.

Pakistan is important evidence to show that regime type cannot be a good guide to political performance. Regardless of regime types, Pakistan's economic situation has been consistently bleak due to the combination of insufficient extraction and poor spending. Despite generous foreign aid and extensive natural gas reserves, Pakistan's economic development has been hampered by continuing concerns about political uncertainties and questions about the quality of its institutions.

South Korea

In figure 2.7, the case of South Korea shows that consistently high levels of RPR and RPA have been the main drivers to achieve economic prosperity. Firm commitment and political will of governmental leadership saw a remarkable development of the economy based on efficient policy implementation. The peculiar combination of strengthened financial institutions, flexible economic planning to encourage private savings, and external capital infusion from the United States and Japan enabled South Korea to successfully carry out export-oriented industrialization without excessive internal extraction.

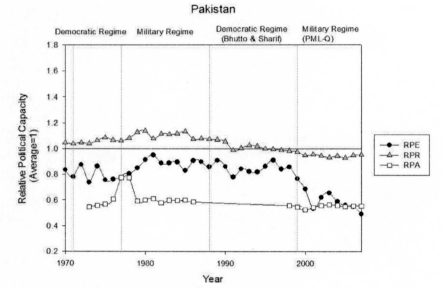

Figure 2.6a.   Pakistan Political Capacity

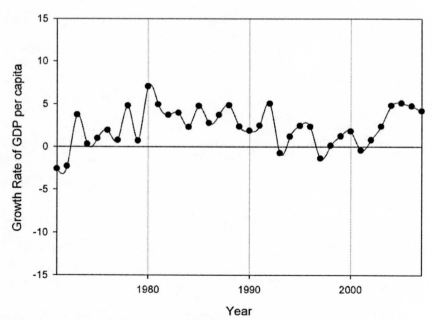

Figure 2.6b.   Pakistan GDP per Capita Growth Rate

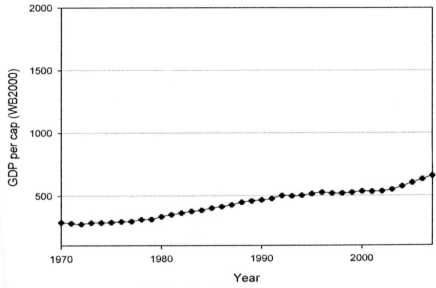

Figure 2.6c.   Pakistan GDP per Capita and Income

Note that there has been little significant shift of political capacity although South Korea underwent several political and social upheavals. The overall trend of each RPC component shows no significant distortion after the 1979 assassination of President Park and the 1987 June Democratic transition. Rather, RPR and RPA drop and RPE increases during the period of the Asian financial crisis and under the leftist President Roh's government rule. Political performance in South Korea has been more affected by socioeconomic shocks or partisan politics rather than political turmoil as seen in the case of Pakistan.

Sudan

Finally, figure 2.8 illustrates the case of Sudan. Sudan is one of the worst cases in lost opportunities for the poor. Undergoing prolonged civil war, the government has totally lost its political capacity. The administrations without effective authority to make collective political decisions have not been able to provide reasonable public resources for sustained development. Political reach and allocation have been chronically stagnated along the whole period. Since the leaderships have been highly vulnerable to major structural changes in the society through several decades, economic markets are always uncertain and consumers and producers suffer limited information.

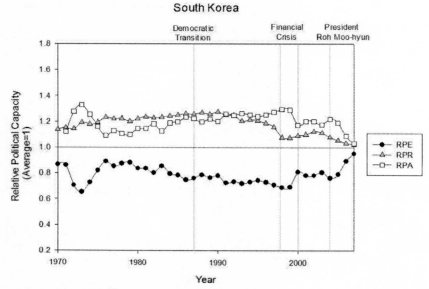

Figure 2.7a.   South Korea Political Capacity

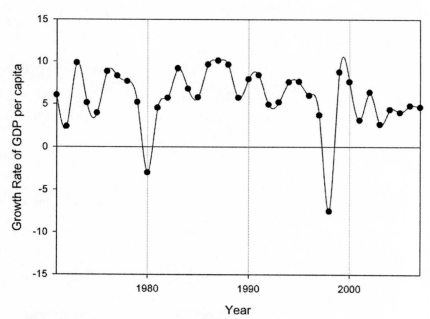

Figure 2.7b.   South Korea GDP per Capita Growth Rate

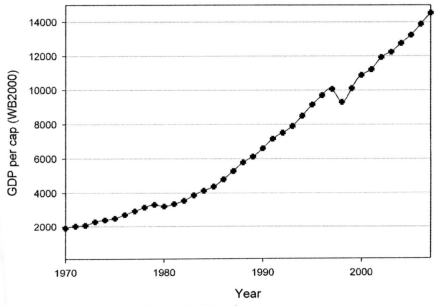

Figure 2.7c.   South Korea GDP per Capita and Income

Worst of all, after the overthrow of Sadiq al-Madhi's coalition government that mobilized enormous internal resources for ending the southern civil war, Sudan literally became a "failed" state in terms of every component of political capacity. Consistent with Myrdal's (1968) theory of circular and cumulative causation in underdeveloped societies, Sudan's low level of political capacity and low productivity are mutually reinforcing socioeconomic phenomena. Therefore if Sudan is to turn the tide of its economic misfortune, the government should endeavor to function "normally." Besides the matter of foreign aid, Sudanese leaderships should take their own political responsibility for the future well-being of their people.

CONCLUSIONS

In neoclassical growth theories, any increases in GDP that cannot be explained by either growth of labor or growth of capital are credited to an independent process such as technological improvement. This term has been referred to as the Solow residual. Despite its symbolic name, the "residual" accounts for approximately half of the historical growth in most industrialized economies from 1874 to 1986 (Blanchard and Fischer

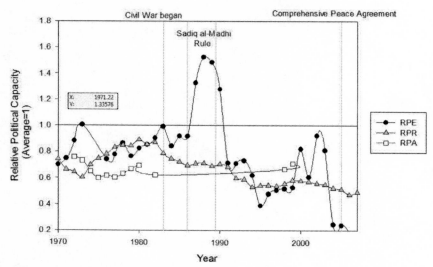

Figure 2.8a.   **Sudan Political Capacity**

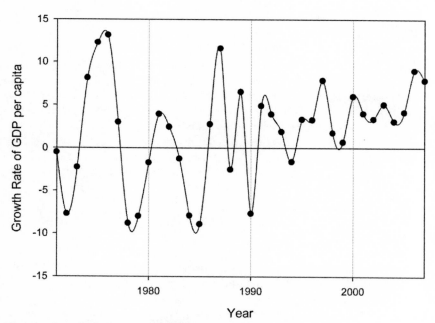

Figure 2.8b.   **Sudan GDP per Capita Growth Rate**

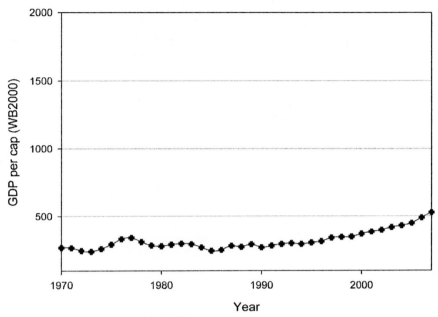

Figure 2.8c.   Sudan GDP per Capita and Income

1989). Unsurprisingly, this ad hoc treatment fails to provide a satisfactory explanation on how to improve intrinsic potential of economies that causes them to achieve prosperity over extended periods of time. Advances in growth theory try to overcome shortcomings of the neoclassical theories by emphasizing the determinants of long-term growth rates, such as savings and human capital investments; an active role for political performance in promoting short-term and medium-term growth has been neglected. Existing theories are insufficient to provide a practical policy guide for achieving rapid growth.

Our main argument is that given the political and economic constraints, the proper policy choices enhance the likelihood of economic success. We emphasize the importance of the political ways in which policy decisions made by leaderships can affect the welfare of millions of people. While we are "bringing back in" the politics that is disregarded as residual by neoclassical economists, our approach is also distinguished from comparative political studies since we concentrate on the efficiency side of political performance rather than the normative side such as democracy or freedom.

Our empirical results and several historical cases show the role of extraction in economic growth of less-developed countries is different from the case of developed countries. In developing countries, the most critical task for economic growth is to raise resources to finance government expenditure. Without an efficient mechanism for generating public revenues, government cannot achieve its political and economic goals with self-sufficiency.

With sufficient resources, government should implement growth-generating reallocation of public expenditure. Given its budget constraints, the government should utilize its inputs in optimal proportions. Clearly, the historic records of successful economic growth can be attributed to the political will of leadership to extract public revenue and to carry out development plans. Despite the "good" will of leadership, however, economic growth in developing countries can be impeded by political inefficiencies arising from inadequate institutional structure that hinders the population from working in legal realms.

Improved political capacity, improved political performance, is necessary to increase economic efficiency. And economic efficiency is the building block for development and growth.

NOTES

1. We implement estimations with the dynamic panel technique suggested by Arellano and Bond (1991). The entire model contains GDP per capita of 1970, Polity IV, and Year as control variables within AR (1) structure. Arellano-Bond GMM estimator helps to correct potential problems of endogeneity and autocorrelation that are often detected in macroeconomics models.

2. For forty countries with 469 observations, GDP per capita in World Bank 2000 is lower than $800.

3. For twenty-nine countries with 657 observations, GDP per capita in World Bank 2000 is higher than $10000.

4. Technically, the Samuelson Rule states that the sum of marginal rates of substitutions—between the public good and the private—should equal the marginal rate of transformation between the two goods.

REFERENCES

Aghion, Philippe, and Peter W. Howitt. 1997. *Endogenous Growth Theory*. Cambridge: MIT Press.

Alchian, A. A. 1965. "Some Economics of Property Rights." *Il Politico* 30: 816–29.

Alesina, Alberto, Roberto Perotti, Francesco Giavazzi, and Tryphon Kollintzas. 1995. "Fiscal Expansions and Adjustments in OECD Countries." *Economic Policy* 10 (21): 205–48.

Arellano, M., and S. R. Bond. 1991. "Some Tests of Specification for Panel Data:

Monte Carlo Evidence and an Application to Employment Equations." *Review of Economic Studies* 58: 277–97.

Aschauer, David. 1989. "Public Investment and Productivity Growth in the Group of Seven." *Economic Perspectives* (Sep.): 17–25.

Barro, Robert. 1990. "Government Spending in a Simple Model of Endogenous Growth." *Journal of Political Economy* 98 (5): S103–S125.

Barro, Robert, and Xavier Sala-i-Martin. 1992. "Convergence." *Journal of Political Economy* 100 (2) 223–51.

———. 1995. *Economic Growth*. New York: McGraw-Hill.

Baumol, William. 1990. "Entrepreneurship: Productive, Unproductive, and Destructive." *Journal of Political Economy* 98 (5): 893–921.

Benson, Michelle A., and Jacek Kugler. 1998. "Power Parity, Democracy, and the Severity of Internal Violence." *Journal of Conflict Resolution* 42 (2): 196–209.

Bird, R. 1992. *Tax Policy and Economic Development*. Baltimore: Johns Hopkins University Press.

Blanchard, Olivier, and Stanley Fischer. 1989. *Lectures on Macroeconomics*. Cambridge: MIT Press.

Demsetz, Harold. 1964. "The Exchange and Enforcement of Property Rights." *Journal of Law and Economics* 7: 11–26.

De Soto, Hernando. 2000. *The Mystery of Capital: Why Capitalism Triumphs in the West and Fails Everywhere Else*. New York: Basic Books.

Easterly, William, and Sergio Rebelo. 1993. "Marginal Income Tax Rates and Economic Growth in Developing Countries." *European Economic Review* 37 (2–3): 409–17.

Feng, Yi. 2010. "National Agenda, Politics, and Macroeconomic Performance: An Empirical Study of Growth, Inflation, and Employment in China." *Journal of Chinese Economic and Foreign Trade Studies* 3 (2): 97–109.

Grossman, Gene, and Elhanan Helpman. 1991. "Quality Ladders in the Theory of Growth." *Review of Economic Studies* 58 (1): 43–61.

Hall, Robert E., and Charles Jones. 1999. "Why Do Some Countries Produce So Much More Output per Worker than Others?" *Quarterly Journal of Economics* 114 (1): 83–116.

Johnson, Kristin. 2007. "Sub National Capabilities and Internal Conflict." PhD diss., Claremont Graduate University.

Mankiw, N., D. Romer, and D. Weil. 1992. "A Contribution to the Empirics of Economic Growth." *Quarterly Journal of Economics* 107 (2): 407–37.

Murphy, Kevin M., Andrei Shleifer, and Robert W. Vishny. 1991. "The Allocation of Talent: Implications for Growth." *Quarterly Journal of Economics* 106 (2): 503–30.

Myrdal, Gunnar. 1968. *Asian Drama: An Inquiry into the Poverty of Nations*. New York: Twentieth Century Fund.

Olson, Mancur, Jr. 1996. "Big Bills Left on the Sidewalk: Why Some Nations Are Rich, and Others Poor." *Journal of Economic Perspectives* 10 (2): 3–24.

Organski, A. F. K. 1997. "Theoretical Link of Political Capacity to Development." Marina Arbetman and Jacek Kugler, eds., *Political Capacity and Economic Behavior*. Boulder, CO: Westview.

Romer, Paul M. 1990. "Endogenous Technological Change." *Journal of Political Economy* 98 (5): S71–S102.

Samuelson, P. A. 1954. "The Pure Theory of Public Expenditure." *Review of Economics and Statistics* 36: 387–89.

Solow, Robert M. 1956. "A Contribution to the Theory of Economic Growth." *Quarterly Journal of Economics* 70 (1): 65–94.

Swan, Trevor. 1956. "Economic Growth and Capital Accumulation." *Economic Record* 32: 334– 61.

Todaro, M. 2000. *Economic Development.* New York: Longman.

Turnovsky, Stephen, and W. H. Fisher. 1995. "The Composition of Government Expenditure and Its Consequence for Macroeconomic Performance." *Journal of Economic Dynamics and Control* 19: 747–86.

3

How Political Performance Impacts Conflict and Growth

Jacek Kugler, Ronald L. Tammen,
and John Thomas

CONTEXT

The Political Performance of nations is based on the ability of governments to achieve desired goals. Governments achieve desired goals by optimizing resource extraction, by reaching populations, and by allocating revenues to advance public goals. When threatened by domestic challenges or foreign opponents, more-capable governments are expected to outperform less-capable opponents.

The same is true for long-term economic performance. Capable governments in societies that adopt viable economic strategies are expected to perform far better than those that cannot bring their political house to order. From this perspective, capable governments can recover from disasters because they have the organizational capacity and they are able to mobilize their populations.

Most indicators of political performance conflate economic and political performance. Indeed, as we show in chapter 1, World Bank measures of political performance consistently overestimate the political capacity of the relatively affluent. Such measures imply that economic success is directly related to political performance. Our main contention is that economic capacity is not equivalent to political performance. We further argue that political performance is not related to the type of government.

75

While it is correct to assume that a relatively affluent society has institutionalized means to capture resources from its population, we believe that well-organized and relatively poor societies can raise political performance far above that of their more-affluent counterparts. Moreover there is a tendency to associate democratic performance with economic success and political efficiency. Again we believe that this is not necessarily so. And we offer figure 3.1 as evidence.

Affluent nations, concentrated among democratic regimes, clearly benefit from their fiscal resource base, which can be tapped by the government. Indeed, among the most developed societies, extraction approaches 60 percent of total output. Yet this high level sets limits to the government's ability to *increase* revenues. Developed societies function effectively but have little room to maneuver under the stress of war or an economic downturn.

By contrast, developing societies extract lower levels of revenues but are capable of mobilizing far more because there is much slack in their revenue extraction. Under stress, successful developing societies, such as Japan in World War II or North Vietnam in the 1960s, were able to multiply their "normal" capabilities by tapping new sources of revenue.

This is not a general pattern. Many developing societies are not effective revenue collectors and are only capable of grabbing public resources from among the low-lying fruit—particularly oil revenues or tariffs from exports. These sources of public revenue are difficult to hide and require limited

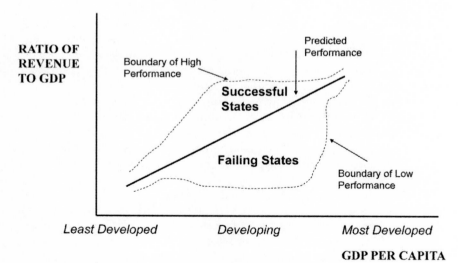

Figure 3.1.   Political Extraction and Economic Performance

government capacity to obtain. Saudi Arabia is a case in point. Controlling for oil revenues, this society approaches the capabilities of Yemen. The least developed societies are constrained. The very poor cannot extract resources without directly reducing the health and lifespan of populations that already exist at the margin of survival.

An important pattern emerges. The most developed societies are constrained because they have already captured much of the resources available and further extraction would face well-organized resistance. The least developed societies extract little and are constrained by the lack of productivity in society. The developing societies have the most to gain or lose. Raising extraction is possible because production is not universally taxed, but at the same time lack of institutionalization and resistance to government presence inhibit revenue collection, resulting in government deficits and underinvestment in the public sector. We contend that the key to development can be traced to political performance. Governments that perform well politically succeed; those that do not fail and must live with low incomes and poverty.

The variance in RPE is a telling indicator. Developed societies are relatively stable because the variance in political performance around the mean (1.0) is very small (0.9 to 1.2). This predictability generates stability, but also limits the ability of governments to fundamentally alter already existing structures. Developed societies already have precommitted much of their large budgets. The ability of the governing elite to alter the economic path is constrained because they cannot dramatically alter their revenue flows.

Developing societies have great opportunity and equally great peril. The variance around normal performance (1) in political extraction is extreme (0.2–4.0) in peacetime. Major improvements can be followed by catastrophic declines in productivity. Budgets are limited and insufficient to provide for required public goods. There are frequent suboptimal allocations and major distortions. The government is able to alter extraction in a major way if sufficient motivation and reach are achieved.

The least developed societies are constrained by the lack of resources. It is very difficult to extract revenues for public goods from a marginalized and impoverished population. Societies that break away from such constraints and increase life spans, education, and nutrition can catapult from the poverty trap to rapid growth. In these societies political performance is the key to growth and prosperity.

The key to understanding these phenomena rests with establishing the validity of political performance. The following historical examples point the way.

VALIDATION OF POLITICAL
PERFORMANCE MEASURES

Total Conflict

A basic way to validate the measures of political extraction proposed in this volume is to evaluate how governments performed when their nations were at war. The reason is reasonably obvious. When the very existence of the government and the nation itself is at stake, governing elites maximize their extractive capacity (Kugler and Arbetman 1989; Benson and Kugler 1998; Bueno de Mesquita, Smith, Siverson, and Morrow 2003). A nation threatened by foreign invasion is expected to maximize resource extraction to avert defeat. We postulate that political performance—regardless of the type of government in power—is a key indicator of success in such a situation.

One challenge is to distinguish between "total" war, when the core territory is directly in peril, and "limited" war, when a nation can withdraw from conflict with territorial impunity. Few total wars have been waged, but a sufficient sample in the last century is available to validate the extractive capacity of nations. Therefore we will examine the performance of the great powers involved in World War I and II. Following Kugler and Domke (1986) each conflict is separated into "fronts." But instead of just using GDP to measure the capabilities on both sides in each front, we will add in RPE to the equation. Then we will take a look at the two resulting snapshots of history—one using just GDP and the other GDP and RPE. The general equation and definitions are found in this endnote below.[1]

World War I

First, we provide the snapshot of World War I based on power measurement using GDP. A similar exercise done with the CINC Index produces equivalent results but is less useful because CINC is also affected by variation in the number of nations included in each collation, thus distorting results.

Figure 3.2 shows the relative capabilities of Allied and Central Powers, obtained by adding the GDP output of these contenders:

The GDP-based power calculation for the Central Powers was about 70 percent that of the Allies. This suggests that the Central Powers should have been at a substantial disadvantage from the onset of World War I. Of course this is not consistent with the record. Not only did the Central Powers take the initiative but they defeated Russia in 1917 and then turned to the Western Front anticipating victory that was only thwarted by the entry of the United States.

A different pattern emerges when controls for political performance are introduced:

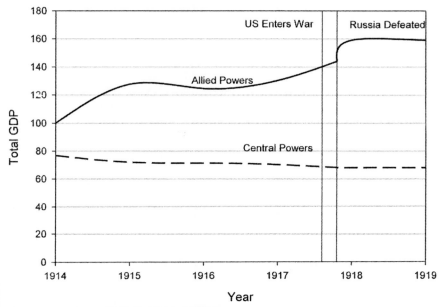

Figure 3.2.   GDP of Allied and Central Powers

Now we see that the Central Powers have a slight advantage over the Allies at the onset of the conflict, but that advantage evaporates into parity only to reappear as a modest gain when Russia collapses. The entry of the United States more than compensates for the loss of Russia and proves to be decisive in the defeat of the Central Powers. This assessment mirrors reality quite closely.

One of the attributes of this combined power measure is that calculations can be disaggregated into realistic component parts. We can, for example, look at the war based on the Eastern and Western Fronts. In 1914 based on GDP allocations to the Western Front, the Central Powers and Allies enter the conflict at parity (Allies/Central = 1.1). Yet, in 1915 through 1917, the Allied Powers become preponderant (Allies/Central = 1.8 for 1915–1917). Based on GDP assessments the Allied Powers should have defeated the Central Powers in the West. Of course this was not the case.

A similar story holds for the Eastern Front. The Central Powers allocate less than 70 percent of Russian GDP to the Eastern Front from 1914 to 1917. Yet it is Russia, not the Central Powers, that collapses. Finally, as the United States enters the conflict, the Allied Powers hold a 2/1 ratio in 1918.

Controlling for allocations by war fronts, GDP fails to account for the defeat of Russia and does not reflect the battlefield reality in the Western

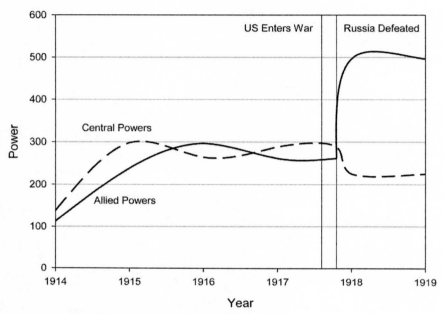

Figure 3.3. Power of Allied and Central Powers

Front from 1914 to 1917. It is only after the entry of the United States that GDP ratios predict the ultimate Allied success in the Western Front.

Political extraction is the key for rectifying the disconnect between GDP predictions and reality. In the Western Front, the Central Powers hold an initial advantage over the Allied Powers. This is reversed in 1916 and early 1917 to a ratio of approximately 80 percent. In the Eastern Front, the Central Powers match Russian capabilities in 1914 and 1915, and then gain ground so in 1917 Russia has less than 40 percent of Central Power resources.

Unlike GDP, the combined power index accurately anticipates the defeat of Russia. At the end of 1917, the withdrawal of Russia weakens the Allies but the infusion of resources from the United Sates decisively overwhelms the Central Powers in the Western Front (2/1 ratio). As most historians recognize, the intervention by the United States tipped the balance decisively.

World War II

Based on GDP (figure 3.4), or the CINC Index, the Axis Powers should have defeated the Allies in 1939 and 1940. And there is some evidence to

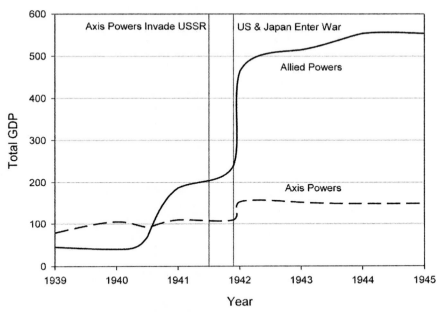

Figure 3.4. GDP of Allies and Axis Powers

support this assessment. France fell after offering only token resistance and Britain held by a thin thread during the Battle of Britain. But the GDP tide turns in mid-1940, and by 1941 and Operation Barbarossa, the GDP data mirrors reality by forecasting the Russian defeat of Germany in the long winter war. Chalk one up for GDP as a predictor of battlefield power. But don't rule out political extraction. The power measure that adjusts GDP with political extraction shows a very similar picture as demonstrated in figure 3.5.

The GDP and the adjusted power measure produce equivalent results and both reflect the ground truth of the war. The Axis Powers dominate in 1939 and early 1940, but the Allies close the gap during the Battle of Britain. The entry of the United States produces a 2 to 1 ratio in favor of the Allies (rather than the 4 to 1 ratio suggested by GDP).

The story by front is similar. Both calculation systems provide an accurate picture of the war in each front, but the political performance option appears more refined.

Incorporating political performance into a power equation provides more accurate and refined results than the far more frequently used military capabilities data, GDP, or the CINC Index.

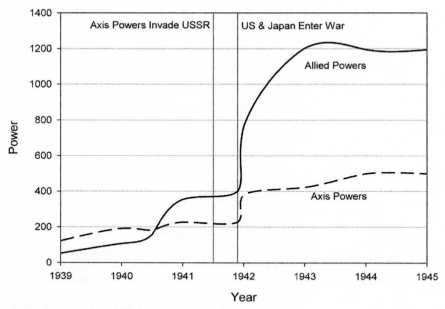

Figure 3.5.   Power of Allies and Axis Powers

Regime Types

Political extraction is independent of regime type. Consider first authoritarian regimes. Russia, a developing nation during World War I, was defeated because the czar's authoritarian regime was unable to mobilize its resources. Russia only managed to double its "normal" extraction capacity during WW I while Germany extracted four times as much from its population.

In World War II Japan was an authoritarian regime that mobilized resources far more effectively than any other contender. The USSR maintained a steady performance but did not match the exceptional effort by Japan. Germany actually increased its political performance during both World Wars despite losses on the battlefield. In sum, authoritarian regimes are capable of extracting effectively under stress.

The story is no different for democracies. France mobilized effectively during World War I but did a poor job during World War II. The United Kingdom performed very effectively both in World War I and II. Its highest performance was achieved during the Battle of Britain in 1940 and tailed off after the United States joined the war. The United States increased and maintained relatively high performance during both World War I and World War II but did not mobilize as much as Germany or Japan.

Given differences in levels of development it is difficult to make direct comparisons between authoritarian and democratic nations. But authoritarian Russia in World War I and democratic France in World War II failed to extract resources even in the face of imminent danger. France extracted effectively in World War I and the USSR did likewise in World War II. Associating regime type with political capacity clearly is inappropriate.

The modest evidence on hand suggests that the type of regime fails to predict the performance of governments. But it is worth some modest amount of speculation. Democratic regimes seem more capable of a sustained effort while authoritarian regimes seem to achieve short but high bursts of extractive capability.[2]

We have noted at the outset that political extraction can vary most among the less and least developed societies. For that reason the effects of politics should be far more pronounced in conflicts that involve the developing rather than the developed world. We now turn to that analysis.

The Developing World

Comparisons thus far concentrated on great powers or relatively developed societies. We now turn to conflicts where the less and least developed societies confront the most developed societies.

Again it is important to identify "total" wars. The intervention of third parties directly affects the outcome of conflicts involving the least developed societies. It is impossible to understand the outcome of the Korean War, for example, without taking into account the intervention of the United States and China. The direct intervention of these actors determined the eventual settlement. For the United States, Korea was far from a total war—the effort was limited, the resolve constrained. A negotiated outcome ended the war. There was no call for "unconditional" surrender. The vanquished were not occupied.

The Korean War was a "total" war from the perspective of both Koreas, but it was a "limited" conflict from the perspective of major powers. To make any valid comparisons we need to incorporate the effects of foreign intervention and aid into conflicts among the least developed and developing societies.

For this purpose we have selected major conflicts following World War II where relatively reliable political performance measures are available for the competing parties and the conflict approximated the characteristics of a "total war." The measure of power is augmented to incorporate the effects of foreign intervention and foreign aid. Power is calculated in this endnote.[3]

As a first cut we will evaluate wars in designated categories: for develop-

ing countries: Iran-Iraq; for wars of internal unification: North and South
Vietnam; for civil wars: Afghanistan.

Wars among Developing Nations: Iran-Iraq

The Iran-Iraq war of 1980–1988 is of interest because both contenders
are less-developed societies. Here again the relative economic capabilities,
GDP or CINC Index, of the contenders provide little information about the
ultimate outcome. Consider the results in figure 3.6.

Prior to the conflict, Iran is approximately three times larger than Iraq in
terms of GDP. Conditions for a war emerged as the Shah left Iran for exile
in mid-January 1979 and in the resulting power vacuum Saddam Hussein
saw an opportunity to reclaim full control of Shatt el Arab waterway.
Despite the decline in the Iranian economy since 1977, the disparity in
GDP strongly suggested that Iran was in a superior position. Again this does
not match reality.

Figure 3.7 represents GDP adjusted by political performance. Iraq compensates for a smaller base GDP by extracting more from the Iraqi population throughout the period. The 1977–1980 decline in Iranian capabilities
now does not appear so significant. Initial successes by Iraq during the conflict in 1980–1982 led to the occupation of over one thousand square kilo-

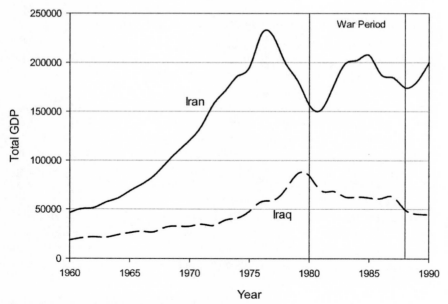

Figure 3.6.   Iran and Iraq GDP (Millions of US$)

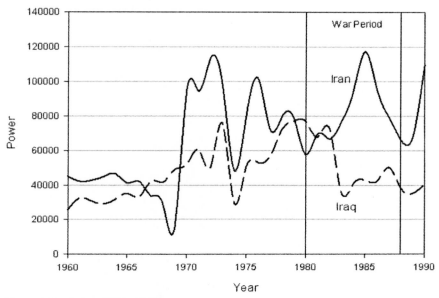

Figure 3.7. Iran and Iraq Power

meters of Iran. However the effort is stopped after both sides suffer massive losses in Khorramshahr. From 1982 to 1984 on Iraq adopts a defensive position with Iran gaining some ground. There is a war of attrition between 1984 through 1986. Note that Iraq recovers some ground in 1987–1988 largely because of the continued decline of an overextended Iran. Eventually a cease-fire was negotiated, followed by a peace agreement.

The story of figure 3.7 closely tracks the events of the war. Iraq fights and advances at parity reflecting its superior military capabilities. But it cannot overtake the larger but less mobilized Iran. This sets up the conditions for a long bitter war concluding in a draw and reimposition of the status quo ante.

Wars of Internal Unification: North and South Vietnam

The Vietnam conflict shows how political performance can alter anticipated outcomes of wars of internal unification. U.S. involvement started with a few advisors in 1950 and then increased sharply in the early 1960s. Combat troop deployment began in 1965 after the Tonkin Bay incident and accelerated in 1968 concurrent with the Tet Offensive. The U.S. military effort declined afterward and combat troops were withdrawn following the Paris Peace Accords of 1973. The civil war within Vietnam ended with the fall of Saigon in April 1975.

Measured by total output, South Vietnam towered over North Vietnam throughout the conflict. At no point did North Vietnam outproduce the South (figure 3.8). Political mobilization adds a different twist. North Vietnam extracted far more from far less. Their ability to extract and mobilize far exceeded that of the South, which was never able to reach even "normal" levels of performance under stress. One reason may be that the war was largely waged in the South, but intense bombing of the North should have limited the ability of that government to extract resources three and four times higher than normal performance. Moreover, the enormous foreign aid provided to the South needs to be considered.

The GDP comparisons, like CINC Index evaluations, indicate that South Vietnam should have dominated this conflict. At no time in this period did North Vietnam approach 70 percent of the output of South Vietnam. Counting the financial and military contribution provided by the United States, the result should have strongly favored South Vietnam. We know of course that the reverse was true.

Political performance explains this difference. With the inclusion of political performance in the power equation, North Vietnam dominates the South from the onset in 1950. Because of vastly larger RPC scores, North Vietnam has the strength to overthrow the government of South Vietnam

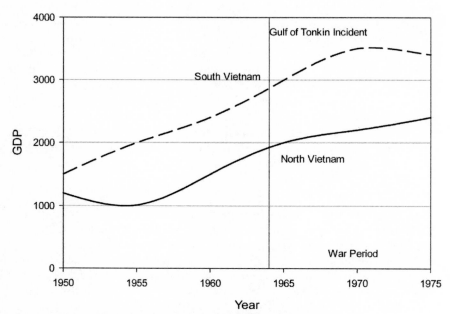

Figure 3.8.   North and South Vietnam GDP (Millions of US$)

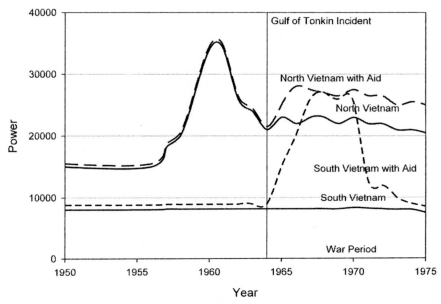

Figure 3.9.   North and South Vietnam Power

prior to U.S. intervention. Only the provision of massive amounts of resources and military forces stabilizes the war theater between 1965 and 1969. And U.S. withdrawal returns the picture to overwhelming Northern dominance.

The United States did not "lose" the war in Vietnam because of questionable generalship, weak political leadership, the draft, the American press, or a fickle American public. The United States lost the war in Vietnam because of a nation capable of generating very high levels of political performance—the ability to extract resources from a supportive population united in its commitment.

Intrastate Conflicts: Afghanistan

In wars of internal conflict, such as North and South Korea, Palestine-Israel, and South and North Vietnam, the two sides hold relatively clearly defined territory. The outcome is clear—either one unified nation emerges (Vietnam), the division into two states is reaffirmed (South and North Korea), or the issue is unresolved, resulting in a protracted conflict.

It is much more difficult to identify the competing contenders in intrastate wars where the parties are not as well established. The majority of intrastate conflicts are waged by parties that have no defined boundaries.

Rebels and the government commingle populations and resources. Internal conflicts in Afghanistan, the Congo, or Peru pose challenges because the warring parties cannot be easily identified.

It is difficult to estimate political performance with only government performance data and little information about insurgent forces. To partly overcome this serious analytical problem we turn to provincial level data. Generally, but not in all cases, each side in a domestic conflict controls certain, perhaps ill defined, geographic regions.

Such is the case with Afghanistan. Two phases are considered. The initial phase began in December 1979 following the Soviet troop deployment and ended in February 1989 when the last Soviet troops withdrew. The second phase started on 9/11 of 2011 following Al-Qaeda's strike on the twin towers in New York and continues to be waged as we write.

Phase I: USSR in Afghanistan 1979–1989   Phase I represents the period from 1987 to 1992 when the USSR and its Afghani allies faced off against the Afghan Mujahidin guerillas supported by the United States. Difficulties of obtaining information about the strength of the Mujahidin prevent systematic cross-temporal comparisons, but a telling picture emerges from a global assessment of the capabilities of the Afghanistan government prior to the war.

In 1960 the political capacity of the Afghanistan government hovered about 70 percent of normal, but just prior to the conflict this capability declined dramatically to about 40 percent of normal and continued to fall during the conflict to levels of less than 20 percent. Of course with only this indication one cannot say much about the outcome of conflicts without taking into consideration the relative capabilities of the opposing parties, but we can deduce that the Afghanistan government was a very poor partner.

Governments threatened by domestic challenges mobilize resources. But in this case, they demobilized. Where do slack resources go? We believe that very weak governments leave resources for the taking by the opposition. Not only was the Afghan Communist government incapable of absorbing the help provided by the USSR but it was losing control over the very population that was required to win the conflict. We surmise that the opposing Mujahidin guerillas were able to extract resources that the government left behind and to obtain new resources, such as from the United States and Pakistan. Therefore, with very crude data on capabilities and incorporating the far less generous external aid provided by the United States, we estimated in 1981 that the Mujahidin guerillas were poised to defeat the resident Russian troops.

This assessment was not found credible by the experts. The U.S. State Department argued that the authoritarian USSR government was not subject to the popular pressures that forced the U.S. government to reduce its involvement in Vietnam. The government was expected to impose no restrictions on the behavior of its troops in combat. It could impose swift and devastating punishment on local populations that supported guerrilla activities. In sum, the difference in the type of government was seen as the main reason for success or failure against a structurally weaker enemy.

We dissented. In a losing effort the United States endured higher casualties in Vietnam (50,000), spent more treasure ($530 billion in 1965 dollars), and fought longer (fourteen years) than did the USSR, which lost less soldiers (15,000), invested less heavily ($50 billion),[4] and withdrew earlier (nine years).

Phase II: United States in Afghanistan 2001–present   This conflict involves the United States–led coalition and its Afghani allies against the Taliban and Al-Qaeda. We have been able to construct provincial-level data for this period of analysis. For this domestic intrastate conflict, the provincial level is the appropriate level of analysis.

The two figures below show how political performance tracks violence as measured by political deaths. Figure 3.10a graphically displays the changes in political performance over time while figure 3.10b matches those changes in lockstep with violent deaths. Increases in political performance signal a decline in violent deaths while the converse also holds true. The steady decline in performance from 2001 to 2008 forecasts the resulting

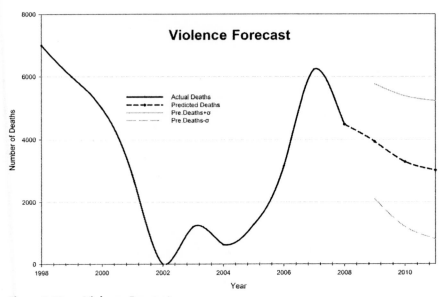

Figure 3.10a.   Violence Forecast

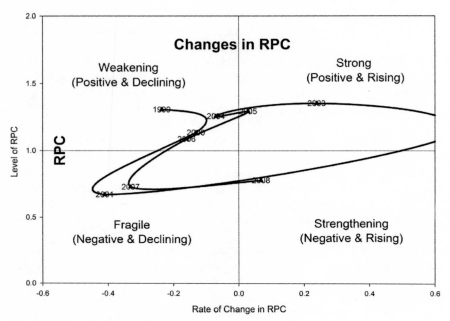

Figure 3.10b.   Changes in RPC

increase in violent deaths and the loss of government control in certain provinces. In fact, the entire U.S. strategy in Afghanistan, although not represented in this fashion, is based on increasing the political capacity of government at all levels of society. Higher rates of political capacity result in greater stability and trust in governmental actions.

External aid can mitigate insurgency but only if political performance is relatively high. The challenge for the U.S. position is to ensure that investments are absorbed efficiently be they on the civilian or military side. If corruption accounts for 20 percent at a minimum and low capacity stifles the remaining investment, then no amount of aid will resolve the current insurgency problems in Afghanistan. But a strengthened Afghan government, with higher political capacity, would lead to far more effective transfers of resources, which in turn would reduce the amount of violence and perhaps disinvest the insurgency.

POLITICAL EXTRACTION AND
THE GROWTH OF NATIONS

Global growth rates are strongly influenced by political performance. In previous sections of this chapter we have evidence that GDP alone is an inadequate predictor of power. But what about growth? We conclude that political performance may be the unseen hand that converts economic potential into assets, wealth, and stable prosperity.

The potential for growth is far larger among developing societies than developed. China and India may be growing at 8 to 10 percent annually while the mature economies of the United States and Europe lag far behind although with larger bases. Some nations do not grow at all, falling prey to the poverty trap. How then can we tell which nations will succeed while others fail? Clearly it is not the type of government since democracies have no monopoly on fast growth rates. Nor is it geography or natural resources. Political extraction gives us a strong clue as to the answer.

Political capacity can help us understand a wide variety of important development issues. It can suggest to us which nations will recover from conflict or disaster and which may suffer long-term negative effects. It tells us why only one of two countries, side by side, with similar populations and geographic placement has a successful growth pattern. It gives us useful information about long-term growth trends, which in turn helps shape the world of the future.

Consider the relationship among the United States, China, and India, the forecasted superpowers of the next half century. Economic estimates now widely circulated suggest the following relationships (see figure 3.11):

In this assessment China overtakes the United States in GDP, a proxy for power, before midcentury. India is not far behind, overtaking the United States by 2075 and catching up to China by 3000. If and when this comes about, for the first time in more than four centuries less-developed societies will control the majority of resources in the international system. This could well create tensions that may lead to conflict (Tammen et al. 2000).

The focus here is on the speed of this transition. Common assessments run the gamut. Some indicate that China may remain a regional power; others are concerned that China may seek to match U.S. military power and challenge its global influence; others are focused on stability within Asia and the potential for territorial conflict with India. We believe that all such assessments miss a fundamental structural point. Relations will depend in large part on the conditions that emerge and the level of satisfaction or trust among these powers.

What can we state about the potential structures in the future? Consider the anticipated relative capabilities of the United States and China using the measure of power developed above.

The very wide growth potential for China is driven by the large differences in attainable RPE over the period. If China takes the high road, it could double U.S. GDP output by midcentury; if the political system weakens it may well fail to catch up to the United States. High political capacity is of course associated with a more effective government that may make

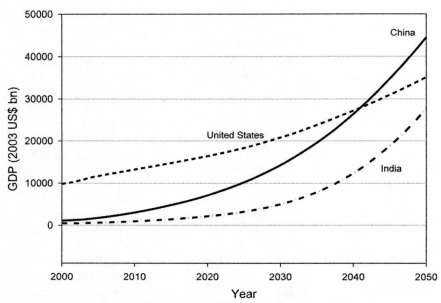

Figure 3.11.   Projected GDP of United States, China, and India

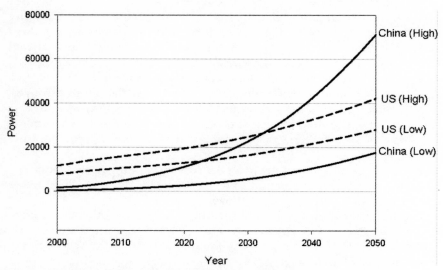

Figure 3.12.   Projected Power of United States and China

efficient demands, while a weak government is likely to be concerned with internal instability and react to the outside world rather than lead it.

From a transition perspective, the structural conditions in Asia are even more challenging. If India turns on its full potential, it may well challenge not only China but also the United States. Under such circumstances it is possible to anticipate that growing regional tensions may well become global issues. Here again, political performance will play a key role. If political capacity spreads prosperity and stability and contributes to the socialization of the world community into a common set of preferences, then even these wrenching economic and power transitions may be accepted peacefully by all parties.

CONCLUSIONS

The key conclusion is that an assessment of the political capacity or performance of governments is essential to understand the overall ability to influence others in the international arena. Our analysis of previous conflicts indicates that including political capacity elements in global, regional, and intrastate wars allows one to anticipate the potential outcome of conflicts far more accurately than with any other measure. Not only can this be done across states, but precision can be achieved if provincial-level data is used to assess local variances.

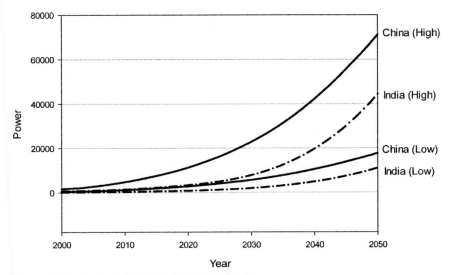

Figure 3.13.   Projected Power of China and India

The assessment of overall capabilities is important because developing societies have a far larger potential to grow. This is not only driven by economic factors, but it is also to a large degree determined by the ability of governments to advance their goals effectively. Strong societies succeed in achieving their potential while weak societies are far less likely to reach their potential. The potential overall size is still determined by the size of populations. Technological dispersion can make one set more effective than another, but it cannot overcome the limitations of human capital.

Small, effective societies like Switzerland or Israel cannot compete for control of the international system. Population size determines that limitation. On the other hand societies already endowed with large populations may improve their ability to extract and mobilize political resources and in so doing challenge for influence in the global arena. India, China, the EU, and the United States are known global players today but tomorrow Indonesia, Pakistan, and Brazil may ride the horse of political performance onto the global scene. Smaller nations may have to unite together to obtain similar scales of efficiency.

Political Performance is the beacon that will light the way for new nations, new developing giants living among us.

NOTES

1. $Power_{ik} = GDP_{Ik} * RPE_I$
    GDP_I = Gross Domestic Product Allocated to front k
    RPE = Relative Political Extraction
    i = Country
    k = Proportional allocation to front k
2. Democracies are thought to be likely to fight less but once engaged be more determined and patient in order to succeed (Bueno de Mesquita et al. 2003). We propose that success, endurance, and commitment during conflict depend on the level of political capacity of the government. Capable governments will wage war more successfully, will allocate more resources, and will fight longer than their less-capable counterparts. The regime type does not determine such capabilities.
3. $Power_{ik} = GDP_I * RPE_I + Foreign Aid_j * RPE_I$
    GDP_I = Gross Domestic Product Allocated
    RPE = Relative Political Extraction
    i = Recipient Country
    j = Donor Country
4. CIA (1987, p.1).

REFERENCES

Benson, Michelle, and Jacek Kugler. 1998. "Power Parity, Democracy, and the Severity of Internal Violence." *Journal of Conflict Resolution* 42 (2): 196–209.

Bueno de Mesquita, Bruce, Alastair Smith, Randolph Siverson, and James Morrow. 2003. *The Logic of Political Survival*. Cambridge, MA: The MIT Press.

Central Intelligence Agency. Directorate of Intelligence. February 1987. "The Cost of Soviet Involvement in Afghanistan." *CIA Declassification Release*. Washington, DC: Central Intelligence Agency.

Kugler, Jacek, and Marina Arbetman. 1989. "Choosing Among Measures of Power." Richard Stoll and Michael D. Ward, eds., *Power in World Politics*. Boulder, CO: Lynne Rienner.

Kugler, Jacek, and William Domke. 1986. "Comparing the Strength of Nations." *Comparative Political Studies* 19 (1): 39–69.

Tammen, Ronald L., Mark Abdollahian, Carole Alsharabati, Brian Efird, Jacek Kugler, Douglas Lemke, Allan C. Stam III, and A. F. K Organski. 2000. *Power Transitions: Strategies for the 21st Century*. New York: Chatham House.

4

Political Performance, Leadership, and Regional Integration in Europe

Gaspare M. Genna, Birol Yesilada,
and Peter Noordijk

Context

The European Union (EU) represents the largest area of economic and monetary union in the world, comprising twenty-seven sovereign nation-states and nearly 500 million people (European Commission 2008). There are numerous other regional integration efforts around the world but none on this scale of success. The scholarly community has only begun to pinpoint exact factors behind the deepening of regional integration even if we have an understanding of how and why states chose to enter into regional integration agreements initially.

Often, we are confronted with the question: why is regional integration in Europe such a success story while other regions have failed? By using the concept of Political Performance, we provide an explanation of regional integration that goes beyond current models in the literature.

We adopt a systemic approach to explaining regional integration that focuses on the capabilities of regional leaders and member-states and the level of similar preferences among all members of a regional integration project. The role of regional leaders in developing integration is not new.[1] Prior research has often assumed that these leaders would be capable of aiding integration based on their economic size. It is assumed that if the economic size asymmetry of the leader, vis-à-vis other members, is large and similarity of preferences is high, then the probability of integration increases.

Economic size asymmetry alone is not a satisfactory measure of capability. It is possible for a larger member-state to lack the ability to draw from its society the means to lead an integration effort. Therefore we include not the economic size but the regional leader's capability to mobilize resources in support of its policy preferences. This is represented by the Political Performance of the regional leader. This chapter will also include the role of the member-states other than the regional leader. A focus on regional leaders' capabilities can mask the work of member-states and lead to overestimating the leading state's role. Therefore it is important to also examine capabilities relative to other member-states in explaining regional integration.

The chapter begins by reviewing regional integration theories. It then examines the need to include the capabilities of member-states with special attention to the capabilities of regional leaders. This is followed by a design to test our hypotheses, followed by conclusions.

INTELLECTUAL ENVIRONMENT:
THEORIES OF REGIONAL INTEGRATION

Theories of international integration, like all political theories, are produced in order to better understand ongoing political events and solve distressing problems that preoccupy political leaders. Thus, they follow the times, and they compete with one another to set the trend. Those theories that get the most attention are "fashionable"; they are not necessarily the ones that will continue to provide inspiration for political thinkers a half-century, or even a decade, later.

In this chapter, several theories with varying degrees of staying power will be reviewed. None of them is sufficient to fully understand where the European Union (EU) is today, how it got that way, and where it will end up. But we will draw on those that are general enough and strong enough to give us part of the explanation. Political theorists also attempt to do three things: explain, predict, and prescribe. In this regard, theories of regional integration have done a better job of explaining what has happened than predicting what will happen. As such their utility for policy prescription has been rather limited.

Early theories of regional integration include federalism, functionalism, and Monnetism. *Federalists* believed that the vulnerable post–WW II states of Western Europe should join together in a political union in which they could exercise mutual self-help in the face of threats to their common security. By forming a federation under a common central authority, once-sovereign states could pool their individual capacities to organize their defenses, mobilize their resources and industrial strengths, and guide their economies in the direction of modernization and economic growth. The states would retain control over those aspects of their domestic affairs that were not seen to be vital for the common effort (Pentland 1973, chapter 5).

Unlike the federalists, the *functionalists* did not outline plans for an elaborate division of political responsibilities among member-states. Instead they concentrated on the immediate economic needs of post–WW II states (George 1990, 16–22). The leading functionalist theorist was David Mitrany (1966), who was interested not in the functional integration of European nations but in the creation of international organizations to fulfill certain specific needs. These included organizing relief efforts for war refugees, regulating air traffic, formulating and enforcing international health and safety standards, or promoting more efficient agricultural methods.

According to Mitrany's vision, several such organizations might come into being for different purposes and comprise different sets of member-states, sometimes including members from different continents and subregions around the globe. They would not all involve a given set of members found in a particular region. That is, they would not gradually become a collective state-like territorial entity in their own right.

Mitrany (1966, 64–65) rejected federalism on the grounds that it would replace the old states with a new, larger one without necessarily reducing human misery. Yet, he is generally regarded as a forerunner of a movement for *European* functional integration, which actually did achieve the first real success in that direction: the European Coal and Steel Community (ECSC). The ECSC was the brainchild of Jean Monnet. Monnet had served in the League of Nations as a liaison among France, Britain, and the United States during WW II, and after the war, as the head of the French economic planning commission.

Like Mitrany, Monnet believed that, when faced with their own inability to solve problems that could be solved only by international cooperation, states would, even though reluctantly, relinquish limited elements of their sovereignty and pool their efforts in international organizations. Government leaders of the Monnetist persuasion formulated a new agenda for the European six in the mid-1950s. The result was the creation, in 1958, of the European Atomic Energy Community (Euratom) and the European Economic Community (EEC).

Euratom achieved only modest results, largely because of the unwillingness of governments, especially that of France, to give up their sovereign control of what was considered a vital element of national strength. In contrast, the EEC achieved remarkable success as a customs union during the first decade of its life.² Yet by the end of that decade, its chances of achieving a full-fledged *political* union still appeared to be visionary. Monnet's ideas not only led to the creation of ECSC but influenced scholars like Ernst Haas to develop his theory of *neofunctionalism*.

Haas (1958 and 1964) was impressed enough by Monnet's strategy and tactics to put them into a theoretical framework that was more elaborate and academic in nature. He argued that functional integration would most likely occur if influential and powerful elites were motivated to take decisive steps toward it. He introduced a number of *neofunctionalist* concepts to help explain the steps toward regional integration that had already occurred, as well as elucidating any further steps that might occur. Two central concepts are *spillover* and *supranationalism*.

Spillover means that if the tasks of a regional organization were to expand, it would occur as a result of experiences with the tasks the organization was already performing. In other words, cooperation and success in one issue area would spill over into a similar cooperation in a related issue area among states. But Haas emphasized that there was nothing automatic in spillover. Task expansion by the regional organization would require political initiative. "Cross-national networks" were becoming more frequent and broader. This process of communication made it possible for elites to address common problems in concrete terms and to discover an "upgraded common interest."

According to Robert Keohane and Stanley Hoffmann (1991) this communications net corresponded to neither a federal nor a confederal framework; instead, it would be supranational as opposed to being intergovernmental. In the EU experience, this form of decision making became part of the governance structure with institutions like the European Commission, the European Parliament, the European Central Bank, and the European Court of Justice. Although the principal actors were nationally based, they came together predisposed to find common solutions to their mutual problems, and their method of arriving at decisions was by unanimous consent, avoiding votes, vetoes, and subsequent expressions of antagonism.

More contemporary variations on these theories came about as scholars tried to explain the complex nature of European Communities' (EC) transition to an Economic and Monetary Union (EMU) that characterizes the current nature of the EU with some exceptions (not all member-states are in the monetary union). One of these theories is a variation on intergovernmentalism that Andrew Moravcsik has developed as the "liberal intergovernmental" view of regional integration (1993 and 1998). According to this theory, the member-states are motivated primarily by economic interests when they decide to propose, accept, or reject compromises on EU policy issues. Moravcsik argues that these interests, as well as the institutional constraints, must be examined in order to understand policy outcomes.

Governments, according to Moravcsik, are not the billiard balls of international relations theory; they act "on the basis of goals that are defined domestically," with foreign policies "varying in response to shifting pressure from domestic social groups, whose preferences are aggregated through political institutions" (Moravcsik 1998, 481). Both neofunctionalism and Moravcsik's liberal intergovernmentalism emphasize economic issues central to their analyses of EU decision making. For Haas, initial integration of economic decision making gives supranational agencies the leverage to induce governments to support further integration.

According to Moravcsik, governments can be persuaded to pursue cooperation within the EU framework for economic objectives, but this is because they cannot attain their objectives unilaterally, not because they have been maneuvered into giving up their best interests by supranational policy entrepreneurs. There is no automatic spillover from fulfilling one policy commitment to reaching agreement on another. The process is controlled by the member governments coordinating their own agendas, with very limited help from the Commission.

Moravcsik's view of how EU decisions are made could, without too much trouble, be converted into a version of what is called rational-choice institutionalism proposed by Simon Hix (1994). It posits that national governments act rationally on behalf of their preferences, but Moravcsik downplays the significance of the EU's supranational institutions, whether the Commission, the European Parliament, or the European Court of Justice.

According to Hix (1994, 13) "if preferences change, outcomes will change, even if institutions remain constant, and if institutions change, outcomes will change, even if preferences remain constant." Thus, both preferences and institutions are important for analysis of what happens in any decision-making process for understanding deepening of regional integration and enlargement of membership. The example of the unanimity rule suggests that outcomes would change if the preferences of the last holdout changed to become more compatible with those of the rest of the members. But if the institutional rule were to change so that a qualified majority on the issue would suffice to adopt a proposed action, then the holdout can be ignored and concessions would not have to be made.

A more recent response to the rationalist and institutionalist approach to regional integration comes from the constructivist reinterpretation of neofunctionalism (Sandholtz and Sweet 1998; Risse 2004). Constructivists' explanation of EU integration argues that the deepening of integration is a consequence of an interaction of members' interests and social norms, in which actors are embedded, regulate their behavior, and constitute their identities, interests, and preferences. This is consistent with the constructivist argument that structures of world politics are social rather than material in character (Checkel 1999, 83–115).

When applied to EU integration, constructivists view EU policy making as "grounded in the accumulation of positive experiences of cooperation, which seep into the preference pattern of participating states and open the way to future integration. Cooperation among members develops into trust and a habit of coordination, which other actors are able to exploit and turn into specific instances of policy making" (Bicchi 2007). That is, constructivists focus on how European identities, with common norms, emerge and how such norms, in turn, affect the behavior of the players. These writers argue that this perspective captures intergovernmental bargaining much better than its realist or liberal intergovernmentalist alternatives.

Despite their relative explanatory powers of regional integration, none of these theories provides a satisfactory answer to the questions we propose in this study. Each of these theories of integration leaves out two important variables that are central to understanding regional integration. The first is the role of a regional leader in integration. The second is the capacity of each member-state to carry out proposed plans that would lead to the deepening of integration. The theories discussed above implicitly assume that all member-states have similar abilities and therefore treat capacity as a constant. But this is not the case and therefore a theory of integration must examine the role of capacity and how relative capacity among the member-states would influence the level of integration.

THE RELATIVE POLITICAL CAPACITY OF STATES AND REGIONAL LEADERS

As Arbetman and Kugler (1997) correctly observed, all countries face challenges of economic development with mixed results. Their answer to the challenge of uneven development is the role of government capabilities. Capable governments are able to resolve these challenges while those that lack capability cannot. Globalization produces yet another set of challenges with which all states must come to terms. Coming up with solutions is often easier than putting policies into action.

This is where state capacity becomes important because solutions that require a shift from closed to open markets can have detrimental effects to specific industries and groups. It would be up to the governments, both individually and in partnership, to smooth out the adverse effects of economic policy changes.

Regional integration is one method to deal with the challenges of globalization. By focusing on regional partnerships, states offer firms access to markets that have close proximity and consumers with similar tastes and preferences. Also within any region there can be enough of a variation in factor endowments that would allow the logic behind comparative advantage and economies of scale to be persuasive.

But the idealism of open markets may run counter to the desires of protected and entrenched economic sectors. Bargaining with groups that oppose regional integration is one way that state leaders can broker deals in order to garner vital support. However, offering incentives is not enough. The offers must be credible. Threatened groups require that the state have the ability to produce these incentives. Of course not all states can do this, but their regional partners may be able to fill in the capability gap, which would help assuage any doubts.

What incentives do states need to provide? Basically they are the same ones that all states at one time or another provide in order to foster development. These include stimulating economic growth without the debilitating effect of inflation, producing high levels of employment, and promoting technological advancement. A shift in policy orientation from relatively closed to open economies will harm the ability of some sectors, in the short term, to have these outcomes.

It will be the capable government that can change policies while maintaining these promises of development for the needed supporters. Therefore the idea of regional integration is tied to the capability of the state to smooth out the problems of the transition through incentives like sidepayments, worker retraining, improved social insurance, and so forth.

The Political Performance of governments is defined in chapter 1 as the "ability of governments to reach their population, to extract economic resources from a population, and to allocate those resources to secure the long-term survival of the political structure." Political performance is derived from governmental ability to reach, extract, and allocate efficiently inside their countries, provinces, or states. Given the advanced state of development of EU nations, it was anticipated that the reach variable would not be as relevant and that proved correct. Allocation data is very difficult if not impossible to acquire given the complexities of the EU and member-nations. But the extraction variable has proved most powerful.

We define political extraction throughout this volume as the capacity to tap resources in order to carry out the policies adopted by a country's government. In similar words, it is the ability of the government to extract material resources in the society and mobilize these to advance goals. Extraction is a key component of understanding the deepening of integration. It helps to clarify why states partner with each other and seek to deepen integration. While all member-states could have sufficient capability to deal with the policy transition independently, it would be highly unlikely for this to occur given the uneven distribution of capabilities.

Partnerships of only equally capable states are also unlikely for the following reasons. Since regional integration, by definition, is a partnership among neighboring countries, this reasoning would limit cooperation to only those that happen, by geographic luck, to border countries with sufficient capacity to carry out the necessary reforms. Also there is the problem of enforceability of agreements. The partners would need to have the capacity to not only carry out the internal policies changes but also be independent enforcers to prevent free-riding by partner states. This would stretch the capacity of any one state if they have equivalent capabilities.

The final and related issue is the occurrence of economic shocks. Such a shock in any one member's market can lead it to defect from regional agreement because of the current political leadership's need for survival. Similarly capable states may not be able to aid the troubled partner given limited capacity especially if the economic shock spills over the political boundaries.

Therefore it is unlikely for similarly capable states to deepen their integration. First, the idealism of integration can evaporate when agreed-upon goals fail to materialize. Second, the farsighted pragmatism of credible execution may override any idealistic tendency among leaders. If the scenarios of free-ridership and defections produced by economic shocks are in the minds of negotiators, then they would seek out some sort of assurance that the capacity resources used in creating and deepening integration would not be wasted. It is unlikely to see leaders enter into long-term partnerships that use resources unwisely. If the scenario of similarly capable states leads to a theoretical dead end, then an alternative scenario of asymmetry of capability can prove to be the answer.

Some researchers have examined the role of asymmetric power distribution in explaining the level of regional integration (Efird and Genna 2002; Efird, Kugler, and Genna 2003; Genna and Hiroi 2004). All other things being equal, this research assumes that greater economic power translates to greater capability. However, does this assumption really hold? Do higher levels of national output correlate with higher levels of performance of governments?

The theory of integration proposed in this chapter hypothesizes that states that lack or have low levels of political performance necessary to open markets will require the partnership of a regional leader due to its high level of political performance. It is also theorized that the likelihood for a regional partnership formed by the regional leader and other member-states will improve with higher levels of mutual status quo satisfaction.

The role of a leader is first brought to attention in the works of Charles Kindleberger (1973, 1981, 1984, and 1986), who drew attention to subtle differences between *hegemony* and *leadership*. According to Kindleberger, the United States' role in restructuring of post–WW II international regimes was best described by *leadership* and not by *hegemonic stability* as argued by Robert Keohane (1984). For Kindleberger (1986, 841–842), hegemony has uncomfortable overtones of force, threat, and pressure whereas a leader can lead without "arm-twisting, to act responsibly without pushing and shoving other countries." In this regard a crucial issue that arises in economics is what has been called "the agency problem" (Jensen and Meckling 1976, 305–60).

The dilemma revolves around interests of the agent who is hired to carry out a task for the principal and those of the principal itself. When the two interests clash, the agent might be tempted to pursue his own interests at the expense of his principal! Typical solution involves the principal's decision to "add to the wage bill the expense of monitoring the agent's actions and of bonding him to cover the possible loss from malfeasance" (Kindleberger 1986, 845).

In the world of politics a similar relationship exists between majority and minority in democratic governance. Majority exercises restraint toward minority not only because roles might change in the future but also due to common ethical concern for the larger polity. In international relations, a similar relationship can exist as a contract between the leader and followers—that effective leadership will be met with effective followership. Our view on this relationship is that effectiveness of this leadership-followership relationship largely depends on the relative political performance of the stakeholders.

If a state possesses sufficient capacity to unilaterally open markets, integrate into the global economy, and deal with any negative shocks, then regional partnerships would not be necessary. States that lack sufficient levels of performance would venture into partnerships with others that could subsidize their political performance. The political performance of the regional leader would carry the policy transition costs of the less capable partner(s) and perhaps help partners in time of economic downturns (Genna and Hiroi 2007). This leads to our first set of hypotheses:

H_1: A state's Political Performance is associated with the level of regional integration with other states.

A state's political performance is theorized to include extraction of material resources. The extraction of material resources would aid in developing regional integration efforts because the wealth accumulated by the state can be redistributed to those that are harmed by greater market competition. Also, joining a regional integration that has undergone a series of stages of "deepening of integration," like the EU, could require the state to commit to fiscal responsibility, among other things.

The state's capability to extract taxes would therefore contribute to a successful implementation of regional integration. Using the capabilities asymmetry arguments just discussed above, as a state's level of this capability decreases, the new member-state might then need aid from a regional leader. In fact we do see some evidence of this by examining how the more economically powerful countries are net contributors to the EU's social cohesion and common agriculture policy funds, while the less economically affluent are net recipients. Therefore, it is crucial to see the independent effect of extraction on integration as well.

Based on these observations we propose the following second set of hypotheses:

H_2: The higher a state's relative political extraction, the higher the level of regional integration with other states.

H_3: The higher a regional leader's relative political extraction, the higher the level of regional integration of one state with other states.

We do not assume purely benevolent behavior of the regional leader. The regional leader would use this carrying capacity in order to shape agreements toward its preferences. The final bargain would be an exchange of capacity for regional economic policies (such as fiscal responsibility or conditions of labor mobility) that the leader prefers. Knowing that its policy preferences would be constrained, the smaller partner would integrate with a regional leader whose preferences are not distant from its own. This would reduce its "cost of integration" while improving benefits of the desired openness. Therefore there is an interaction between a regional leader's capacity and level of satisfaction among partners. The regional leader's relative political performance (RPP) conditions the effect the level of satisfaction has on the level of regional integration.

H_4: The higher the level of satisfaction among partners, the higher the level of regional integration as a regional leader's political extraction increases.

To move from closed to open markets and to further integrate require transition costs. These costs must be borne by someone, with the state being the assumed entity given its role in promoting economic stability. A state's level of capacity can promote or harm the likelihood of regional integration. However, states will seek out others to aid them in these transitions given the lack of political performance. Regional leaders are likely candidates since they possess ample performance. Since trading carrying capacity for preferences is a reality, smaller states would partner with larger states that share similar policy preferences. Finally, a regional leader is not immune to the costs of regional integration. It too will help or hinder regional integration depending on the type and level of performance it has in supply. The next step is to test these ideas using available data.

MODELING

We test our hypotheses using a directed dyadic relationship between European countries with a time series span from 1981 to 2007. As we further explain in this section, our timeframe begins in 1981 due to data limitations. Our formula is provided in this endnote.[3]

For the dependent variable, the level of regional integration, we use updated data compiled by Efird and Genna (2002) (also see Efird, Kugler, and Genna 2003; Feng and Genna 2003; and Genna and Hiroi 2004). The measure is referred to as the Integration Achievement Score (IAS), which is based on the work pioneered by Hufbauer and Schott (1994). IAS codes regional integration projects around the world by using implemented treaty text.

The score is an index of the following six categories: degrees of trade in goods and services, capital mobility, labor mobility, supranational institutional importance, monetary policy coordination, and fiscal policy coordination. Each category is given a value from 0 to 5, using a Guttman scale, with higher values indicating a deepening of integration. The categories (Ci) are summed, and then divided by six to give an average across all categories using the formula at this endnote.[4]

Since the data is limited to European countries, the values of IAS include the European Free Trade Area (EFTA) and the European Union. The two groupings together are referred to as the European Economic Area (EEA).[5] Effort was made to group IAS values according to membership and degree of membership. For example, Finland was a member of the EFTA from 1986, but then left this block to join the EU in 1995.

Not all EU member-states are members of the euro zone, so the IAS values for nonmembers are lower than for members. Finally the eastern expansion of the EU introduced ten new members in 2004 and two new members in 2007, but with conditions. None had the right to full free labor mobility and they were not members of the euro zone. Therefore, their IAS values are lower than full members of the EU. IAS values for nonmembers of the EFTA and EU are zero.

Relative Political Performance (measured in terms of Relative Political Extraction or RPE) is our first independent variable (Arbetman and Kugler 1997; and chapter 1 in this volume). Capable governments are able to "extract" resources from their populations. The extractive component of capacity represents efforts by a government to acquire the material resources necessary to carry out policy objectives. Since the observations are directed dyads, the first country's RPE is included in the equation.

The next independent variable is satisfaction. We operationalize satisfaction in two ways so as to capture political as well as economic dimensions. The political dimension is operationalized by the dyadic regime/institutional dissimilarity. Lemke and Reed (1996) have shown that satisfaction with a compatible regime type produces stronger peace effects. Their argument is supported by Andreski (1980), who found that military dictatorships have little incentive to engage in foreign military adventures, and Russett (1993) and Farber and Gowa (1995), who demonstrated unexpected cooperative patterns among democratic states and among narrowly defined authoritarian regimes.

Feng and Genna (2003) have also demonstrated that states with similar institutions are more integrated than states that are dissimilar. Therefore past research suggests that institutional similarity can operate as a good proxy for satisfaction. Indeed one of the major prerequisites of joining either the EU or EFTA is a state's continuing commitment to democracy. Therefore current and aspiring members need to be satisfied with this criterion.

We use Polity IV (Marshall and Jaggers 2001) data in order to measure regime similarity. We believe that it provides the superior measure and is more comprehensive than Vanhanen (2000) data.[6] Polity IV provides a composite democratic regime score for each country in our data set. We calculate a dissimilarity variable by taking the difference of score for each dyad. The larger the difference of Polity IV regime scores, the more dissimilar the pairs are. According to hypothesis three, we expect to see a negative relationship between the dissimilarity variable and the IAS.

Another dimension of satisfaction would need to estimate the economic closeness (proximity) between the pairs of states. A very large number of alternatives are available here, but we propose to use a measure of foreign direct investment (FDI) stocks between countries measured in dyads and as a ratio of total FDI stock over time using Organisation for Economic Co-operation and Development (OECD) data. Our time series is limited by the fact that this data is only available from 1981. Our rationale behind this choice is based on the assumption that the more satisfactory the relations are between pairs of countries, the more willing their respective firms will be to make long-term investment decisions in each other's economies.

We estimate our models using the following controls. The first is a Cold War dummy variable with the value of one for each dyad between 1981 and 1991 inclusively, and zero otherwise. Since the ending of the Cold War demonstrates an external shock to the international order, it may affect the pace of integration. Second, neofunctional theory stipulates that spillover occurs when integration is successful. Therefore a five-year lagged IAS value is also included. Third, each satisfaction proxy variable will operate as a control for the other. For example, when we include the institutional dissimilarity variable, both interactively with the regional leader's RPE values and independently, the FDI stock ratio variable operates as a control without interacting with the regional leader's RPE value. Finally, the models are estimated using time-series regression techniques with panel corrected standard errors.

RESULTS

Before we begin examining the results, one empirical question needs to be answered. This chapter was partially motivated by questioning the assumption that the largest economy in a region would be able to provide the carrying capacity of regional integration. In other words, does a large economic output translate to large relative political capacity?

Previous studies on global leadership of the United States focused on this assumption and its relevance for regional integration thus followed suit. Yet we question this assumption since large economic size does not necessarily translate to greater RPE. To answer this question in the European context, we included the largest economy, Germany, and the second largest, France, in each of the regression models as well as in the many unreported diagnostic models. Without exception, the French RPE variable does not demonstrate statistical significance when included with the German RPE variable. We also ran the models with each of the variables separately. The German variables offered greater explanatory value. Therefore each of the tests presented in this section uses German RPE_t in the place of RPE_d.

Table 4.1 displays the results of the three estimated models—variation of model above. The first model is our baseline because it excludes German RPE. Of the three key variables, only institutional dissimilarity is statistically significant. A state's RPE alone is not enough to foster regional integration. Also the FDI stock ratio does not help explain deepening. However, the more dissimilar a state's Polity IV score is with a European country, the lower the level of integration. What is interesting is the negative coefficient on the Cold War variable ($p = 0.145$). Contrary to what is often stated, this period in time actually had a reducing effect on integration when compared to the post–Cold War period.

Models 2 and 3 introduce Germany's RPE values. Model 2 included the interaction of the regional leader RPE variable with the institutional dissimilarity variable and therefore leaves the FDI stock ratio variable as a control. Brambor, Clark, and Golder (2006) demonstrate that examining the statistical significance of the three interaction variables' coefficients is inappropriate when attempting to determine their explanatory value. Instead all

Table 4.1. Panel Correct Standard Errors Time Series Regression Results on Integration Achievement Score for European Countries, 1981–2007

	Model 1	Model 2	Model 3
RPE_{ti}	0.005	0.021	0.011
	(0.043)	(0.041)	(0.043)
RPE_{tl}	—	−1.18	−1.56*
		(0.549)	(0.401)
Institutional Dissimilarity$_t$	−0.075**	0.237	−0.082*
	(0.029)	(0.154)	(0.030)
RPE_{tl}*Institutional Dissimilarity$_t$	—	−0.624	—
		(0.320)	
FDI Stock Ratio$_t$	−0.093	−0.035	−2.50
	(0.129)	(0.112)	(1.449)
RPE_{tl}* FDI Stock Ratio$_t$	—	—	4.28
			(2.51)
IAS_{t-5}	0.854***	0.850***	0.857***
	(0.110)	(0.110)	(0.109)
Cold War	−0.255	−0.313*	−0.306*
	(0.116)	(0.122)	(0.123)
Constant	0.678	1.38*	1.57*
	(0.301)	(0.526)	(0.585)
Wald χ^2	343.7***	646.7***	555.7***
R^2	0.685	0.699	0.697
# of groups	391	391	391
N	3,619	3,619	3,619

Notes: Unstandardized coefficients reported, standard errors in parentheses; one-tailed significance tests: ***p = 0.000, **p = 0.001, *p = 0.010.

three variables (RPE_{tl}, Institutional Dissimilarity, and their product) need to be assessed based on Germany's RPE effect on the Institutional Dissimilarity variable.

Figure 4.1 plots the marginal effect of Institutional Dissimilarity on the level of European integration as the level of German RPE increases. The graph indicates that the Institutional Dissimilarity coefficient's reducing effect increases as Germany's RPE increases. This relationship is statistically significant when German RPE holds a value greater than 0.4 (since both sides of the 95 percent confidence interval are below the zero value), which is in the range found in the data set.

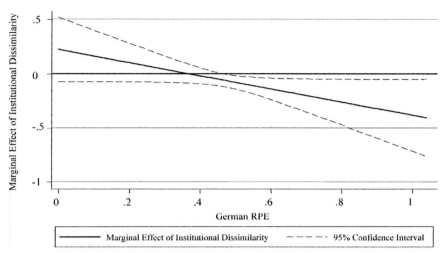

Figure 4.1.   Marginal Effects of Institutional Dissimilarity as German RPE Changes

As German capacity increases, those that wish to participate in European integration, and take advantage of German capacity, have greater institutional similarity. At the highest value of German RPE, a one-point difference in the Polity IV score between dyads will reduce the IAS value by 0.45 in the post–Cold War era. This is a 9 percent reduction in IAS value. As a result German capacity is statistically and substantively tied to greater institutional homogeneity (i.e., similar level of democracy) and therefore regional integration.

Model 3 of table 4.1 uses FDI stock ratios as a proxy for satisfaction, leaving Institutional Dissimilarity as a control variable. Again institutional dissimilarity is associated with the level of IAS in the predicted direction. Figure 4.2 illustrates the effect German RPE has on the FDI stock ratio in explaining European integration. The graph indicates that the FDI stock ratio coefficient's value increases as Germany's RPE increases. This relationship is statistically significant throughout the range of German RPE except at approximately 0.6 (since both sides of the 90 percent confidence interval are either above or below the zero value).

When German relative extraction is low (<0.6), FDI stock ratios have a negative effect on the level of European integration. When German RPE is high (>0.6), FDI stock ratios have a positive effect on the level of European integration. Moreover, the relationship is large. An increase in German RPE increases the marginal effect of a dyad's FDI stock ratio on their level of integration. At the highest level of German RPE, an increase of one percentage point in the FDI stock ratio represents a 3.33 point increase in the IAS

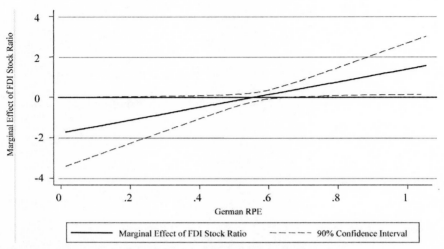

Figure 4.2.   Marginal Effect of FDI Stock Ratio as German RPE Changes

value in the post–Cold War era. This translates to a 66.5 percent increase. Therefore once again German RPE has a statistical and substantive effect on regional integration based on its effect on FDI stocks.

CONCLUSIONS

We can conclude that a state's performance alone is not important in entering into integration agreements with other European states. It will need help to tap into this resource to smooth out the policy adjustments' adverse effects. Furthermore, results show that states will more likely join when they are satisfied with conditions under integration. This means that they would prefer little institutional differentiation and greater FDI. Finally, the level of integration improves when there is a regional leader who can provide the carrying capacity some partners lack.

This last observation supports Kindleberger's argument on the important role a leader plays in the international system with the caveat that the regional leader's RPE is the key determining variable and not its mere economic size. Our findings not only support his premise at the European regional setting but also shed some light on his observation concerning the significance of followership by other states. This is indeed a delicate balance between RPE and levels of satisfaction among all parties and presents some interesting insights for policy makers.

The carrying capacity of a regional leader is an important factor in deepening regional integration, but it is a finite resource. Therefore an expansion of membership with partners that greatly lack individual capacity may stagnate the process of integration or possibly threaten it. As others have demonstrated (Arbetman and Kugler 1997), the lack of political capacity makes development harder to achieve. Since integration is often seen as an avenue of prosperity, it will take the regional leader's political capacity to help the lower achieving states. But this comes at a cost for the regional leader and its carrying capacity may not be large enough to achieve policy aims and goals.

The recent Greek debt crisis in Europe handily illustrates three of the main elements of our argument: one, that the extractive capacity of governments is important to implement policy in general, and two, that the political will and capacity of the leading states is central to the project of economic and political integration because, three, those same leading states have not allowed the European Union institutionally to have the political capacity to enforce its own standards.

When the Greek debt crisis began to rattle markets in January 2010, the European Union had just finally passed the Lisbon Treaty creating the office of the president of the European Union, a single leader to call in a time of crisis. When that phone rang this winter it was answered by Belgian Herman Van Rompuy, an anonymous consensus builder supported by German leader Angela Merkel precisely because he would not threaten the initiative of individual national leaders. When the crisis hit, the German leader got what she asked for as the markets turned to Europe's leaders in France and Germany for a response.

The crisis began to simmer in October 2009 as Greece's low RPE came to the fore. Generations of patronage-based Greek governments have won elections by handing out fiscal treats to their constituents: not enforcing tax laws for conservatives, and high public salaries and low tuitions for the left. In October, the newly elected Greek prime minister announced that the new government discovered that Greek debt levels had been higher than previously reported and submitted an updated report to the Commission (Coy, Petrakis et al. 2010 and European Commission 2010).

This event caused such stern reverberations in the markets not because it was unexpected—Greece had been warned about its numbers before, and investigations of off-books financing have been ongoing since 2004 (Chaffin and Hope 2010)—but because it occurred in the context of an institutionally and politically weak European response to the crisis. Despite keen interest in stemming the crisis, 72 percent of Greek debt was held by Eurozone banks, preventing the spread of panic to Portugal, Spain, Ireland, or Italy, and stabilizing the euro.

Germany and France disagreed on the form and type of intervention (*The Economist* 2010a; 2010b). With Germany expressing reluctance to underwrite a rescue of a southern spendthrift while tightening its own belt and France also working to keep the IMF out of any bailout, the lack of leadership intensified the crisis and Greek debt interest rates climbed and Euros shriveled (Roche 2010).

The late and reluctant leadership of Germany simply amplified the crisis because Germany is the economic anchor of the Eurozone. The argument over a proposed €35 billion of European Union support in March became a pledge of €155 billion in early May, with €35 billion from the IMF, and the European System of Central Banks backstopping Greek debt in May sales.

Finally, after markets found the May 1 effort wanting on the fear that the Bundestag wouldn't support the effort, the €750 billion European Financial Stability Facility was created with €440 billion from Eurozone states, €60 billion in ECB debt instruments, and a €250 billion IMF contribution (Reuters 2010). During this episode, the position of the German government came to be the determining factor. Without German leadership no progress would have been possible at the Eurozone side just as without the United States the IMF support would have been questionable.

Yet, despite this show of leadership on the part of Germany, one crucial factor also became evident. This crisis further adds to taxing of the EU's regional leader and that, in turn, is bound to result in slowing the deepening of regional integration in Europe. An additional factor in this regard is what eastern enlargement meant for regional integration.

The latest enlargement of the European Union increased the population of the EU by over 150 million but only added 5 percent to the Union's GDP! It is no wonder that the German government favors slowing of enlargement of the EU for the foreseeable future. Completion of the EMU and shoring up the economies of the new member-states are two important policy areas that EU leaders must acknowledge rather than extending membership to current candidate and potential candidate countries of the Balkans.

Among these countries only Turkey has a large and dynamic economy but its low per capita GDP signals nothing but danger for sharing of EU's structural and regional development funds. This country's ability to contribute significantly to EU's economic growth is not likely to be realized until 2030–2040 (Yesilada, Efird, and Noordijk 2006). In the meantime, the weaker economies of the Western Balkan states will negatively impact the ability of the regional leader to provide the needed assistance for deepening of integration.

This reality cannot be reversed by a mere growth in EU's supranational institutions' decision-making power. Despite enthusiastic comments by EU officials over how the future looks bright for the Union, the fact of the matter is that the EU is not a substitute for Germany's regional leadership role in deepening of integration. Without a political union that would substantially change the EU's RPP, member-states' RPP will be the key variable in the future success of regional integration in Europe.

NOTES

1. Charles Kindleberger first talked about the important role a leader, not a hegemon as understood by political scientists like Robert Keohane, plays in international cooperation. See Charles Kindleberger, "Dominance and Leadership in the International Economy," *International Studies Quarterly* 25, no. 2 (June 1981): 242–54, and "Hierarchy versus Inertial Cooperation," *International Organization* 40, no. 4 (Autumn 1986): 841–47.

2. A customs union is a regime established between states in which all tariffs and quotas restricting trade between the participating countries have been removed, while common tariffs and quotas are established vis-à-vis other countries. A common market goes further in removing all obstacles to trade between the countries, including such impediments as border controls and government regulations, state purchasing policies, and taxes that discriminate between the producers of one member-country and those of another. The SEA of 1987, which provided for the removal of all such obstacles to trade among EC members by the end of 1992, popularly labeled "Project 1992," represents an effort to approximate the conditions of a true common market among the EC members.

3. $IAS_t = a + \beta_1 RPE_{ti} + \beta_2 RPE_{tl} + \beta_3 S_{ti} + \beta_4 (PRE_{tl} * S_{ti}) + \gamma Controls_t + e$

Where:

IAS_t = The Integration Achievement Score in year t;

RPE_{ti} = Relative Political Extraction (proxy for Relative Political Performance) of state i in year t;

RPE_{tl} = Relative Political Extraction of regional leader l in year t;

S_{ti} = Level of Satisfaction of i in year t; and

Controls = The vector of control variables in year t.

4. $IAS = \dfrac{\sum\limits_{i=1}^{6} Ci}{6}$

5. Although Switzerland is a member of the EFTA, it is not formally a member of EEA. However it is economically connected to the EU through a separate bilateral agreement.

6. Existing long-term data sets on democracy include Munck and Verkuilen (2002a); Alvarez, Cheibub, Limongi, and Przeworski (1999) (n = 141 time table: 1950–1990); Freedom House (2000), covering all nations from 1972; Gasiorowski (1996), Political regime Change (n = 97 time table: independence-present); Hadenius (1992), (n = 132 time table: 1988); Polity IV, Marshall and Jaggers (2001) (n = 161 time table 1800–1999); and Vanhanen (2000) (n = 187 time table: 1810–1998). Three are quite comprehensive. Freedom House (2000) data measure politics rights (nine components) and civil rights (thirteen components), both as ordinal data using additive (at the level of components) and as the aggregation rule.

It is a comprehensive data set with clear and detailed coding rules. It is limited by a minimalist definition and omits participation in coding. The Polity IV is an improved and updated version of the earlier Polity III (Jaggers and Gurr 1995) and measures competitiveness of participation, regulation of participation, competitiveness of executive recruitment, openness of executive recruitment, and constraints on executive power scale and is comprehensive and reliable. The weakness is a minimalist definition that again omits participation. Aggregation procedures can be experimented with. Finally, Vanhanen (2000) measures competition and participation as interval data using a multiplicative aggregation rule. It has clear coding rules and comprehensive scope. It is limited by a minimalist definition as it omits offices and agenda setting. Appropriateness of the aggregation rule is also in question.

REFERENCES

Alvarez, Michael, Jose Antonio Cheibub, Fernando Limongi, and Adam Przeworski. 1996. "Classifying Political Regimes." *Studies in Comparative International Development* 31 (2): 1–37.
———. 1999. "ACLP Political and Economic Database Codebook" Online.
Andeski, Stanislav. 1980. "On the Peaceful Disposition of Military Dictatorships." *Journal of Strategic Studies* 3 (1): 3–10.
Arbetman, Marina, and Jacek Kugler, eds. 1997. *Political Capacity and Economic Behavior.* Boulder, CO: Westview Press.
Bicchi, Federica. 2007. *European Foreign Policy Making toward the Mediterranean.* New York: Palgrave Macmillan.
Brambor, Thomas, William R. Clark, and Matt Golder. 2006. "Understanding Interaction Models: Improving Empirical Analyses." *Political Analysis* 14: 63–82.
Bueno de Mesquita, Bruce. 1981. *The War Trap.* New Haven, CT: Yale University Press.
Chaffin, J., and K. Hope. 2010, February 16. "EU Probes Currency Swaps." *Financial Times.*
Checkel, T. 1999. "Norms, Institutions, and National Identity in Contemporary Europe." *International Studies Quarterly* 43 (March): 83–115.
Correlates of War Project2. cow2.la.psu.edu/.
Coy, P., M. Petrakis, N. Weeks, S. O'Donnell, D. Tweed, S. Reed et al. 2010. "The Bond Vigilantes Who Left Greece in Ruins." *BusinessWeek* (4167): 18–21.
Economist. 2010a. "The Cracks Spread Wide Open." 395: 63–65.
———. 2010b. "A Very European Crisis." 394: 75–77.
Efird, Brian, and Gaspare Genna 2002. "Structural Conditions and the Propensity for Regional Integration." *European Union Politics* 3 (3): 267–95.
Efird, Brian, Jacek Kugler, and Gaspare Genna. 2003. "From War to Integration: Generalizing Power Transition Theory." *International Interactions* 29: 293–313.
European Commission. 2008. "Eurostat Pocketbooks: Key Figures on Europe." *European Communities,* Luxembourg.
———. 2010. Report on Greek Government Debt. Brussels: European Commission.
Farber, Henry S., and Joanne Gowa. 1995. "Polities and Peace." *International Security* 20: 123–46.

Feng, Yi, and Gaspare Genna. 2003. "Regional Integration and Domestic Institutional Homogeneity: A Comparative Analysis of Regional Integration in the Americas, Pacific Asia, and Western Europe." *Review of International Political Economy* 10 (2): 278–309.

Freedom House. 2000. *Annual Survey of Freedom Country Scores, 1972–73 to 1999–00*. For the most recent indices, go to freedomhouse.org/ratings/index.htm.

Gasiorowski, Mark J. 1996. "An Overview of the Political Regime Change Dataset." *Comparative Political Studies* 29 (4): 469–83.

Genna, Gaspare, and Taeko Hiroi (2004). "Power Preponderance and Domestic Politics: Explaining Regional Economic Integration in Latin America and the Caribbean: 1960–1997." *International Interactions* 30 (2): 143–64.

———. 2007. "Brazilian Regional Power in the Development of Mercosul." *Latin American Perspectives* 34 (5): 43–57.

George, Stephen. 1990. *An Awkward Partner: Britain in the European Community.* Oxford: Oxford University Press.

Haas, Ernst B. 1958. *The Uniting of Europe: Political, Social, and Economic Forces, 1950–1957.* Stanford, CA: Stanford University Press.

———. 1964. *Beyond the Nation-State.* Stanford, CA: Stanford University Press.

Hadenius, Axel. 1992. *Democracy and Development.* Cambridge: Cambridge University Press.

Hix, Simon. 1994. "The Study of the European Community: The Challenge to Comparative Politics." *West European Politics* 17 (January): 1–30.

Hufbauer, Gary C., and Jeffery J. Schott. 1994. *Western Hemisphere Economic Integration.* Washington, DC: Institute for International Economics.

Jaggers, Keith, and Ted Gurr. 1995. "Tracking Democracy's Third Wave with the Polity III Data." *Journal of Peace Research* 32: 469–82.

Jensen, Michael, and W. H. Meckling. 1976. "Theory of the Firm, Agency Costs and Ownership Structure." *Journal of Financial Economics* 3: 306–60.

Kant, Immanuel. 1795. *Perpetual Peace: A Philosophical Sketch.*

Keohane, Robert. 1984. *After Hegemony.* Princeton, NJ: Princeton University Press.

Keohane, Robert O., and Stanley Hoffmann. 1991. "Institutional Change in Europe in the 1980s." Robert O. Keohane and Stanley Hoffmann, eds., *The New European Community: Decision Making and Institutional Change.* Boulder, CO: Westview Press.

Kindleberger, Charles. 1973, revised and enlarged, 1986. *The World in Depression, 1929–1939.* Berkeley: University of California Press..

———. 1981. "Dominance and Leadership in the International Economy." *International Studies Quarterly* 25 (2): 242–254.

———. 1984. "The American Origins of the Marshall Plan: A View from the State Department." Stanley Hoffmann and Charles Maier, eds., *The Marshall Plan: A Retrospective*, 7–13. Boulder, CO: Westview Press.

———. 1986. "Hierarchy versus Intertial Cooperation." *International Organization* 40 (4): 841–47.

Lemke, Doug. 1996. "Small States and War: An Expansion of Power Transition Theory." Jacek Kugler and Doug Lemke, eds., *Parity and War*, 77–92. Ann Arbor: University of Michigan Press.

Lemke, Doug, and William Reed. 1996. "Regime Type and Status Quo Evaluations: Power Transitions the Democratic Peace Proposition." *International Interactions* 22: 143–64.

Marshall, Monty G., and Keith Jaggers. 2001. *Polity IV Project: Political Regime Characteristics and Transitions, 1800–1999. Data Users Manual and the Polity IV Dataset.* Retrievable at: www.bsos.umd.edu/cidem/polity/.

Mitrany, David. 1966. *A Working Peace System.* Chicago: Quadrangle Books.

Moravcsik, Andrew. 1993. "Preferences and Power in the European Community: A Liberal Intergovernmentalist Approach." *Journal of Common Market Studies* 31 (December): 473–524.

———. 1998. *The Choice for Europe: Social Purpose and State Power from Messina to Maastricht.* Ithaca, NY: Cornell University Press.

Munck, Gerardo L., and Jay Verkuilen. 2002a. "Conceptualizing and Measuring Democracy: Evaluating Alternative Indices." *Comparative Political Studies* 35 (1): 5–34.

———. 2002b. *Regions of War and Peace.* Cambridge: Cambridge University Press.

Organski, A. F. K. 1958. *World Politics.* 1st ed. New York: Alfred A. Knopf.

———. 1968. *World Politics.* 2nd ed. New York: Alfred A. Knopf.

Organski, A. F. K., and Jacek Kugler. 1980. *The War Ledger.* Chicago: University of Chicago Press.

Pentland, Charles. 1973. *International Theory and European Integration.* London: Faber and Faber.

Reuters. 2010. "Full Text of EU Crisis Mechanism Agreement." Brussels: May 10. http://www.reuters.com/article/2010/05/10/us-eu-greece-text-idUST RE6490A820100510.

Risse, Thomas. 2004. "Social Constructivism and European Integration." Antje Wiener and Thomas Diez, eds., *European Integration Theory.* Oxford: Oxford University Press.

Roche, D. 2010. "Germany Declares War." *Euromoney.* Retrieved from stats.lib .pdx.edu/proxy.php?url = http://search.ebscohost.com/log in.aspx?direct = true& db = buh&AN = 48308203&site = ehost-live.

Russet, Bruce. 1993. *Grasping Democratic Peace: Principles for a Post-Cold War World.* Princeton, NJ: Princeton University Press.

Sandholtz, Wayne, and Alec Stone Sweet. 1998. *European Integration and Supranational Governance.* Oxford: Oxford University Press.

Tammen, Ronal, Jacek Kugler, Doug Lemke, Allan Stam, Mark Abdollahian, Carole Alsharabati, Brian Efird, and A. F. K. Organski. 2000. *Power Transitions.* New York: Chatham House.

Vanhanen, Tatu. 2000. *The Polyarchy Dataset: Vanhanen's Index of Democracy.* www .svt.ntnu.no/iss/data/vanhanen.

Yeşilada, B., Efird, B. and Noordijk, P. 2006. "Competition among Giants: A Look at How Future Enlargement of the European Union Could Affect Global Power Transition." *International Studies Review* (8), 607–22.

5

Political Performance as a Moderator of International Migration

Tadeusz Kugler, Constantine Boussalis,
and Travis G. Coan

CONTEXT

Migrations generate new opportunities in all aspects of human existence and in the long run affect the power of nations and the future of the international system. Economists have focused on the pull effects resulting from the differences in income and differential access to higher levels of social services. Political analysts have assessed the importance of human rights, instability, and the impact of differences in regime type on the decision to migrate. Much of this work is descriptive. The systematic role of the political determinants within the international migration puzzle is a growing field that is still in its infancy in terms of empirically assessed studies (Teitelbaum 2006; Hatton and Williamson 2002; Mayda 2009).

This chapter will analyze the interconnections between political capacity, economic policy, public goods, and migration. We postulate that migrants make the decision to move after they consider jointly the benefits of economic freedom (policy), access to public goods, and the government's ability to implement that freedom or good (political capacity). These three factors create the future opportunities generated by income and social security differentials. This work will systematically assess how political variations unlock access to economic opportunities to determine if this process empirically generates changes in migration flows. By investigating the interaction between the economic and political dimensions, we expect to produce a richer understanding of the underlying mechanisms that prompt general variations in international migration.

Migrations are at the heart of the continued discussions on growth both in the developed and developing world. It is to immigration that nations look as a method of increasing their labor force, revitalizing their economies, or simply taking care of their grandmothers. This study uses an empirically based analysis to show how the differing conditions and policies of receiving countries change the pull factors by which migrants evaluate their destinations. We will focus on the policies of economic freedom, public goods, and the efficiency of the government to implement those policies (RPE). It is our belief that the flows of migrations are pulled by a combination of economic and social incentives. Migrants move to countries where they have the greatest chance of lasting income gain as well as life, and these countries need to have a combination of highly efficient government and the economic and social freedom policies to create that gain. This pull effect shows more than just the interconnections of the two evaluations but also if one or the other is the key aspect. Are migrants moving toward efficient governments for that sake?

Policy is at the heart of politics. The evaluation of the policies endorsed by the political system can be the valuation of the actual differences between nations or in the lives of their populations. Yet policy is the most difficult component to construct and evaluate. Much of the study of politics has been focused on differing regimes be it communist, socialist, or the many versions of democracy. These studies are often done simply because of a lack of measurements on how the policies of a communist nation differ from Western democracies. As the political systems of the world become increasingly similar, new methods of evaluation have been developed to show differences beyond the regimes. The two independent measurements of policy we will be using are economic freedom and public goods. In addition, the implementation of policy is equally important and we will be using relative political extraction (RPE) as our government efficiency variable.

Evaluating public goods separately from economic freedom also allows for a greater degree of nuance in the research agenda. Countries are not uniform in policy with highly restricted economic systems being home to liberal social service programs or vice versa. Part of the choice of migrants is an evaluation of which part of the greater policy whole is the most important. Which is the draw for migrants: access to economic freedom, access to public goods, or some combination of the two? Better education or a better system of finance? To attempt to capture these two, often conflicting, incentives, we utilize a division between our two measurements both method-ologically and theoretically. Figure 5.1 helps illustrate these two concepts.

Economic freedom is the level of ownership and property rights, the abil-ity to move money, the stability of the monetary system, access to the financial world, and the likelihood of government interference or assistance in the actions of an entrepreneur (World Bank 2004, 2008).[1] Regulation of banks, accounting systems, currency, and the creation of stable nonbiased courts for contract disputes are all policies created by the political establish-ment. Business is based upon the foundations of government, and there-fore it is to these policies that immigrants are likely to look when evaluating countries. What are the chances of getting a loan? Is the court system simply an old boys' network? Can a foreigner own property and invest in an opportunity? All these are questions that form part of the concept and the measurements of economic freedom and are all considerations when we evaluate the pull factors of a country.

It is our belief that when given equal access to countries, a migrant will go to the place that he or she has the highest chance of gaining, first, eco-nomic success and, second, access to public goods in general. To this end, economic freedom is a key concept when it comes to the evaluation of the incentives of a nation to attract or "pull" migrants. The possibilities of eco-nomic success combined with the chance to build a business or have stable ownership over the output of one's work are powerful pulls.

Extensive research has been done on the impact of economic freedom on economic growth and the attraction of foreign direct investment (Acem-

- **Economic Freedom**
  1. Investment Freedom
  2. Business Freedom
  3. Fiscal Freedom
  4. Monetary Freedom
  5. Trade Freedom
  6. Property Rights

Economic Policy
Factor

- **Public Goods**
  1. Life Expectancy
  2. Hospital Beds/1,000
  3. Physicians/1,000
  4. Pupil to Teacher Ratio

Public Goods
Factor

Figure 5.1.   Underlying Components of Policy Factors

oglu, Johnson, and Robinson 2005). In each case, the choices of a country in terms of how it allows its population, and foreigners, to invest and to own are the critical components to whether the country has investment and the resulting economic growth. We wish to build upon this earlier work and to generalize the economic freedom argument to the field of international migrations.

Our second measurement of policy is public goods. This means access to health, education, and chance of life expectancy. Public goods can be considered as being critical to evaluations of long-term risks. Access to medical care or levels of education is something that is used either in the next generation or in the later years of one's life. Yet these are once again pull effects as migrants often think of the destination countries as the start of a new life and most importantly as the start of their children's lives.

Public goods have a direct impact on the health and well-being of residents. Public goods provision is a powerful pull, but it should be regarded as independent of economic freedom. These personal benefits are the outcomes of policy to give access to health or education, and these policies are often created due to the political pressures of the domestic population and are divorced from considerations in terms of international population pulls.

The capacity of a government to implement policy is as important as the policy itself. To this end we use relative political extraction as our measurement of the ease of implementation of policy. Arbetman and Johnson (2008) help to illustrate the theoretical underpinnings of this measurement of political efficiency, which is, that governments require resources to enact policy. RPE measures the efficiency with which governments extract those resources from the population. It does not attempt to create a measure of optimal taxation but makes the claim that, depending on economic development, the critical measure of political efficiency is how effective a government is at an action once it decides to take that action.

Efficiency is by definition the ability to meet or even exceed expected extraction capabilities. It stands to reason that if a government is able to extract efficiently, it is also able to enact policy efficiently. This theoretical statement has been heavily supported in the existing literature with extensive studies on demographical change, FDI, increasing private investment, subnational violence, and economic growth (Coan and Kugler 2008; Feng, Kugler, and Zak 2000; Feng et al. 2008; Leblang 1997; Feng and Chen 1997; Johnson 2007).

What policy the government then uses the extracted resources on is up to the government itself, and hence, what should be remembered is that a government can be very efficient at engaging in policies that are detrimental to the long-term success of a nation or province. Political capacity is inherently amoral in this regard and is not modified by the style of government or its choices. Efficiency is not limited by whether a country is a dictatorship, theocracy, or a democracy. As Arbetman and Johnson (2008,4) claim, "Governments all require resources in order to enact policies. Taxation represents willingness on the part of the population (or enforcement ability on the part of the government) to transfer resources from private individuals to the government." The combination of this variable and our abovementioned policy measurements help to craft the core of our research and our objectives. The combination of policy and a measurement of the capacity of the government to implement that policy will allow for a greater degree of understanding how people evaluate the locations of migrations and the reasons to migrate. This study therefore investigates the conditional effect of government capacity and policy on international migration patterns.

INTELLECTUAL ENVIRONMENT

Migration, in a general sense, is understood as the "permanent or semi-permanent change of residence" (Lee 1966, 49). Guided by neoclassical economic theory, contemporary political economy inquiries of migration assume that migrants are welfare-maximizing actors whose decision to migrate is governed by evaluations of conditions in their place of origin and potential destination locales as well as the costs associated with the movement (Borjas 1987, 1989).

In the context of international migration, dismal conditions in the sending country are understood as "push" effects that increase the utility of individuals to make the migration decision. The selection of the destination country is determined by an evaluation and ranking of the favorable characteristics—also known as "pull" effects—of all potential recipient nations. Lastly, migrants calculate the constraints associated with the decision to migrate to a specific locale. For example, as the distance between origin country and recipient nation increases, so does the cost of transportation. Our paper will focus on the pull factors of migration instead of the full dyadic push/pull complexity.

Migration is a complex phenomenon, and any unified explanation of migration flows is necessarily multidisciplinary. Answering the question of why people move, Richard Freeman states, "For economic gain, says the economist. Because of social networks, says the sociologist. Over short distances, says the geographer. All are right" (152). Below we discuss the theoretical justifications and empirical evidence of various economic, political, network, geographic, demographic, and cultural explanations of international migration flows.

Economic disparity between source and host country is perhaps the most commonly cited determinant of migration. Borjas (1989) argues that income maximization is a strong assumption when studying the self-selection process of potential migrants. Studies that have employed a gravity model framework propose that a migration is a positive function of income in the destination country and a negative function of income in the origin locale (Sjaastad 1962; Greenwood 1975; Borjas 1987).

It is worth noting that the income-maximization hypothesis has not been immune to criticism. Massey (1990, 64–68) argues that the effect of differences in wages between origin and destination countries on migration flows has been overstated and that economic disparity is neither a necessary nor sufficient condition of migration. Citing evidence from Katz and Stark (1986), Massey argues that since the development process is inherently a destructive process and migration decisions are determined by families and not individuals in the developing world, migration should be understood as risk minimization on the part of the family rather than income maximization of the individual. Given this, economic development in a developing nation is actually a "push" factor and therefore the economic disparity argument becomes ambiguous.

Nevertheless, the majority of systematic empirical studies support the traditional income-maximization hypothesis. In their study of migration inflows in North America, Karemera et al. (2000) find that aggregate economic output has a positive effect on immigration flows while economic development in origin countries has a negative effect on emigration. Evidence from Mayda (2009) also suggests that income levels in the recipient nation exhibit significant "pull" characteristics.

We believe that GDP per worker in a destination country is significantly and positively associated with immigration flows. In an analysis of immigration in the United Kingdom, Hatton (2005) finds a significant positive effect of income differentials on net migration. Pedersen et al. (2008) investigate migration inflows into the OECD over the period 1990–2000 and find a statistically significant nonlinear effect of economic development of the source country. That is, migration inflows are minimized when origin nations are either very poor or very rich.

As Hatton and Williamson (2005) show, immigration could be of increasing importance as the developing world reaches higher levels of prosperity. The ancient statement that people "vote with their feet" seems to be accurate only with the additional caveat that they vote with their feet but they must have enough money for the ticket. Economic progress in the poorest regions of the world could fuel massive increases in migrations as large percentages of the population of the world for the first time have enough money to have a choice to leave.

The poverty constraint is being lifted, and part of the point of this chapter is to explain the second part of those people's choices: the choice of where and why. Hatton and Williamson (2005) also discuss the effect of changing institutions on migration and how the end of the Cold War and the subsequent lifting of movement restrictions led to massive movements of populations. Ethnic Russians, for example, moved en masse from the newly formed independent states in Eastern Europe and Central Asia to the Russian Federation, a population movement caused by new political realities.

Political elements also help explain the variation in international migration flows. The effect of the regulation of migration on population movements has been a central political topic among migration researchers. Legal restrictions on movement constitute a significant constraint in the migration calculus. Consider the starkly different experience of an illegal immigrant crossing the U.S.-Mexico border to that of a European citizen moving within the Schengen Area. Similar to immigration policy, emigration restrictions can also significantly restrain population movements. In the Soviet Union, for example, emigration was a criminal offense for nonofficial movements (Borjas 1989).

Fan (2008) created an independent survey in 1998 that helps to illustrate the importance of institutions on the pull factors of migration. Within China you have a registration system (hukou) that dictates the region you are supposed to live in and the economic sector. This registration system has been used in an attempt to control population movements within China by creating a duel-class system of those who are allowed to migrate, "permanent migrants," as opposed to "temporary migrants."

The difference is directly connected to the jobs you are legally allowed to have access to as well as government services and benefits. This causes significant quality of life and income divergence between those who have the legal right to move to a new location and those who do not, creating an increasingly important class system. What is practically important about this and other associated research is that these legislative barriers are being increasingly ignored.

As the amount of "floating population" within China grows dramatically and as these people are most often in this "temporary migration" classification, it could pose a critical problem in the future. Basic economic thought would suggest that the advantage of population movement within a country is that when new economic opportunities become available the population moves to that location and this seems to be the outcome of this policy of registration. With this registration system (hukou), by limiting population movement and the employment opportunities of the population, you are limiting the expected economic growth, and this is likely to be a useful avenue of research building upon this paper.

Descriptively, therefore, legal constraints play an active role during the self-selection process of a potential migrant. There is considerable systematic empirical evidence as well to suggest that legal restrictions do indeed determine the magnitude of migration flows. Karemera et al. (2000) find strong support of a dampening effect of strict immigration policy on the size of migration flows into the United States and Canada. Mayda (2009) finds that as migration policy in the destination country becomes more lenient, the pull effects in the host country increase and the negative effects of costs such as distance become smaller. Pedersen et al. (2008) divide their sample of destination countries into two groups: countries with selective immigration policies and those that have policies based on network considerations. The authors find that there is a smaller effect of origin country illiteracy rates on inflows into host nations with selective policies. We can infer, therefore, that nations such as Canada, Australia, and New Zealand are attracting higher skilled migrants due to the requirements of their migration policies.

Research on political explanations of migration has also investigated the role of political turmoil in the origin country. A deterioration of the rule of law, be it social upheaval or an extra-legal transfer of governmental authority, has been argued as a potential "push" factor (Karemera et al. 2000). Contrary to their expectations, the authors find a statistically significant negative effect of political instability in the origin country on migration flows toward the United States during the period covered. This finding might suggest that political turmoil increases the costs of movement.

Associated with the notion of political instability is that of outright civil conflict. Here the empirical record is much more intuitive. Hatton and Williamson (2005) determine a negative effect of civil war on net migration rates over the period 1970–2000. That is, domestic conflict significantly leads to a net outpouring of citizens. We might infer from these results that the intensity of political turmoil dictates the effect on migration. Low intensity disruptions such as a coup d'etat most likely do not threaten the physical integrity of most citizens, thus there might be little reason to migrate specifically due to the political disruption. However, it is plausible to assume that civil conflicts do threaten the well-being of a significant segment of society and as such it may become reasonable to flee.

Some studies have also inquired into the effect of political freedom in the origin country. Karemera et al. (2000) find that migration flows into the United States and Canada are larger from origin countries with relatively higher political freedom scores. Pedersen et al. (2008), however, find little evidence of a relationship between origin country regime type and migration inflows in the OECD.

Another relevant theoretical argument concerning migration flows is the so-called network effect. That is, potential migrants take into account the presence of a diaspora in the host country during the self-selection process. A higher perception of familiarity with the recipient nation translates into a reduction in the cost of migration.

For example, an established network in the host nations allows for subsequent migrants of similar ilk to enjoy reduced costs associated with transportation, job acquisition, and information gathering (Cornelius 1975; Massey and Garcia-Espana 1987; Massey 1988). Pedersen et al. (2008) uncover a significant positive relationship between the stock of conationals in a given country and migration flows from the same origin country to OECD member-states. Clark et al. (2007) also find a positive effect of the "friends and relatives" effect when estimating the determinants of migration flows into the United States. Mayda (2009) also finds a positive relationship between immigrant stock from a source country and migration inflows into the OECD from the same country. At a lower level of analysis, Mckenzie and Rapoport (2007) also find that immigrant networks increase the likelihood of migration of Mexican citizens to the United States.

Demographic explanations have been put forth as well, mainly in explaining supply side dynamics. One common argument found in the literature is that as the share of young people in the source country increases, so too does the pressure to emigrate. Young individuals are more likely to emigrate since the discounted value of future earnings in the host country is larger the more time an individual can work abroad (Mayda 2009). There is considerable systematic empirical evidence that supports this theoretical expectation.

In their analysis of net migration rates in Africa, Hatton and Williamson (2003) find a positive effect of the size of the population aged 15–29 and emigration. The authors draw a historical parallel between the demographic experience of nineteenth-century European migration patterns and those of contemporary Africa. Clark et al. (2007) find a statistically significant negative effect of the size of the same age range in origin countries on the rate of immigration in the United States. Generalizing to a global sample, Hatton and Williamson (2005) also find a positive effect of the size of the youth population on emigration rates. Mayda (2009) found the demographic effect to be a considerably robust predictor of outmigration as well as empirical connections between previous levels of migration.

Much of the literature on migrations is focused on the North-South movements, named after the migrations from principally southern hemisphere countries to northern, Mexico to the United States or Africa to Europe, for example. These studies have become increasing relevant in the post-war era as movements from ex-colonial holdings to Europe have increased significantly. Following the creation of the EU and with the increased movements of population from Eastern Europe but also with population pressures from Central Asia and much of Africa, work on migration still focused on movements to the OECD. However, what we should remember is that South-South movements of populations are just as big but have had a tendency to go to countries with limited data oversight both from origin and from destination (Hatton and Williamson 2002).

The movement of people is the movement of potential. Migrations have created nations and have modified the basic core of others. Much of the history of the world has been created by population movements. The history of the New World is based upon large-scale voluntary and involuntary movements from Europe and Africa to the colonies. These movements created both nation-states and also new ethnic groups and societies.

History has been created by the incentives to move in the economic and political structures at the time. Our multiethnic world has been created by successive waves of population bringing new technologies, languages, styles, and political systems. Lalueza-Fox et al. (2004) help to illustrate the historical complexity of migrations as waves of population from vastly different regions intermingle with each other in successive waves. The analysis of DNA has been a great boon to this area of study as archaeological excavations can now help us in understanding past migration patterns. Central Asia in particular has had an incredible amount of variance and movement.

As figure 5.2 shows, over the past forty-five years the primary locations for migrants have been Western Europe, the United States of America, Australia, and other closely related countries. The primary sources of these populations have been Western and sub-Saharan Africa, central Asia, Eastern Europe, and much of Latin America. Increasingly migration has been moving toward states with high levels of economic opportunity but with limited political freedoms. The Persian Gulf region has seen huge influxes of population.

Migrations are often very difficult to measure. Illustrated in the map below, Libya has a very high proportion of migrants within its population. Much of the surrounding literature on European migration makes the case that this is caused simply by geography. Libya is part of the route toward

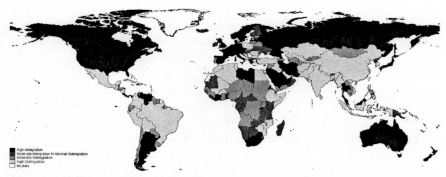

Figure 5.2.   World Migrations 1960–2010. Source: United Nations Population Division

Europe, so the high percentage of migrants is temporary as they look for methods to make it across the Mediterranean. Note also the missing nation of China: this is due to data irregularities within the UN sample and helps to explain why we have made the choice to use data from both the UN and OECD data for this study.

INTERACTIONS AND MEASUREMENTS

This chapter focuses on a number of variables as a means to explain the complex interactions between political capability and policy.

Despite a long history of study, work on migration has proven difficult to focus on empirically. Methods and measurements of the pull/push structure of migration movement or even if it exists have been discussed as international migration increased in size and velocity in the post-war period and on into the 1960s throughout most of Western Europe and the United States (Sjaastad 1962; Borjas 1987, 1989).

Measurements of population movement are often bedeviled by the origin countries having limited knowledge of the size of their own population, let alone where they end up. Further exacerbating these problems is that nature of national borders as stated policy of the national government is often at odds with the implementation of the policy on the ground. This results in countries not counting migrants, having inconsistent immigration policies, or simply ignoring their existence as politically unfeasible. This has led many of the empirically based studies to be primarily based upon small dyadic, country cross-sectional, or focused evaluations of the intake from single sources.

These data limitations as well as the interest of the researchers themselves have pushed empirical studies of migrations to focus on the OECD and in specific the United States and Europe. Zubanov (2009) shows that there is a tendency for migrations to be larger than what a local labor market may need in the long run, putting the questions of asymmetrical information and migration as a further topic of study. Hooghe et al. (2008) show that migrants are connected by culture, for example colonial ties, but that economic pressure and economic incentives in regard to the labor market are of equal or more importance.

The hypothesis that political capacity and policy preferences form a moderating relationship with immigration flows is tested using data derived from two separate sources of international migration statistics, namely the United Nations Population Division and the OECD. These measures differ both substantively and in terms of time coverage. The UN net migration indicator is available in five-year increments for the period 1960–2005 while the OECD migration variable, which measures the inflow of foreign population, is available for each year over the period 1990–2007. Given these differences, the models we employ for each of these dependent variables are not identical, although we do try to maintain theoretical consistency in all specifications. We provide a discussion on the data used in the Hatton and Williamson (2005) replication models as well as the OECD data models below.

Dependent Variable: Migration Flows

As noted above, we employ two separate dependent variables in the present study. The first attempt at explaining international migration patterns consists of a replication of the Hatton and Williamson (2005) estimation of world migration flows. These models estimate the UN's net migration indicator, which measures the difference between total outflows and inflows of citizens and noncitizens. The data is available in five-year periods between 1960 and 2005.

For the OECD sample, we use estimates of inflow of foreign population as our dependent variable. OECD member-countries themselves do not have a standardized method of counting inflows of population, and therefore the OECD has to use the slightly different country methodologies in their own estimations. For example, Ireland's data is derived from quarterly household population surveys whereas the United Kingdom uses data collected by a survey conducted at customs. Nearly all the OECD is represented from 1990 to 2008.

Independent Variables

One of the issues with these types of studies is the worry that variables have a high level of correlation. The following table helps to illustrate the limited correlations between our major variables.

Relative Political Extraction (RPE)

Organski and Kugler (1980) were the first to develop a quantitatively derived measure of government effectiveness, which they refer to as "political capacity" or, as in this chapter, political performance. The measure was further developed in Arbetman and Kugler (1997).

Table 5.1.   Correlations between Policy and RPE

	RPE	Econ Policy	Public Goods
RPE	1		
Econ Policy	0.1299	1	
Public Goods	0.2591	0.0574	1

Normative characteristics of the polity, such as political freedom, are irrelevant to the capacity of the government to implement policy effectively—they are separate processes. Indeed, Organski and Kugler's application of RPE to the analysis of wars such as the Vietnam conflict, where the North exhibited a much higher level of extractive capability vis-à-vis the South, shows that political capacity (performance) is separate from economic development and polity type.

For our purposes, we will focus on Relative Political Extraction (RPE), which is calculated as the ratio of actual government extraction to predicted extraction. The data used in this study have been collected and calculated by Marina Arbetman and Kristin Johnson. Specifically, the methodology consists of using ordinary least squares estimation to derive the level of predicted extraction. The formula is outlined in this endnote.[2]

Economic Freedom

We argue that open market policy preferences have a positive impact on the flow of immigration. We therefore control for the level of "economic freedom" for a given society. Extant empirical literature on open market policy environments tends to rely on one of two sources of information to construct indicators of economic freedom: expert opinions or factual data based on financial records and legal structures. Although there are problems associated with using both types of information, as much as possible the empirical work that follows relies on factual data. The advantage of using objective information to create an indicator of open market policies is the ability to enhance the validity of cross-country comparisons, while attempting to minimize subjectivity in the data generation process.

To construct a measure of open market environments, this study utilizes six measures of economic freedom from the Heritage Foundation—investment freedom, business freedom, fiscal freedom, monetary freedom, trade freedom, and property rights (see Beach and Kane 2007 for the methodology used to construct each indicator). These measures are available for the period 1996–2008 and are therefore only used in the OECD estimations. Each Heritage measure, as much as possible, utilizes objective information from a number of sources, and these measures have been used productively in a wide range of empirical analysis on the causes and effects of economic freedom (Steinberg and Saideman 2008).

These measures operationalize the ability to move investment capital (and products) into and out of host nations, while also incorporating the political rights necessary to protect private property and investment capital. This specification integrates the multidimensional and interactive nature of open market policies suggested in other work (La Porta et al. 1997, 1998; King and Levine 1993; Coan and Kugler 2008).

The multidimensional nature of policy environments presents the challenge of finding a suitable method to combine the underlying components. We use factor analytic techniques to combine the six Heritage measures into a single *"Policy"* scalar. Specifically, we conducted a principal components factor analysis for each of the freedom variables.[3]

Public Goods Provision

The motivation for including the coverage and quality of public goods lies in the fact that there are no subjectively derived economic policy variables that we are aware of that go as far back as 1960—the year in which the UN migration series begins. Therefore, for the Hatton and Williamson (2005) replication models we must use an objectively derived measure to approximate some form of policy preference that would be relevant to migration decisions.

We center our attention on the provision of public goods by a government as a worthy substitute. We conceptualize this indicator as reflecting a basket of certain basic *"Public Goods"* and thus including multiple dimensions, specifically health and education related. One would expect that the availability and quality of education and health care in a society would serve as a "pulling" effect in the decision calculus of a migrant. We utilize factor analysis to create a measure of the provision of public goods by a government. The underlying data of this indicator include the following variables, which were derived from the World Bank Development Indicators (WBDI) database:

Life expectancy at birth measures the expected number of years a child would live given that the present patterns of mortality remained constant throughout the newborn's life. The data are reported on five-year intervals.

Hospital beds records the number of inpatient beds (per 1,000) found in public, private, general, and specialized hospitals and health centers.

Physicians is the number of general and specialist medical practitioners (per 1,000).

Pupil-teacher ratio, primary records the number of students who are enrolled in elementary school as a percentage of the number of primary school teachers.

Pupil-teacher ratio, secondary measures the number of students who are enrolled in secondary school divided by the number of secondary school instructors.

A principal components factor analysis was conducted for each of these measures of public goods provision. Only one factor with an eigenvalue over 1 resulted from the factor analysis and all variables loaded highly on the dimension. The pupil-teacher ratio variables loaded highly but in the opposite direction when compared to the other variables, yet this is to be expected since a higher student-teacher ratio indicates a lower level of public goods provision. The lowest rotated loading was 0.73 (hospital beds) and the highest was 0.88 (doctors). Similar to the economic policy measure, we used regression scoring to compile a single variable and rescaled it to remain within the interval [0,1].[4] The public good measure is correlated only slightly with RPE ($\rho = 0.06$), which suggests that political capacity and elite preferences to provide public goods are distinct elements.

Instead of relying on a constructed index of public goods, in the OECD immigration flow estimations we control for the amount spent by a government on social services (as a percentage of GDP). These data are collected and made available by the OECD and cover the period 1980–2005.

EDUCATION-ADJUSTED INCOME DIFFERENTIAL

Following Hatton and Williamson (2005) we include a relative economic "pull" variable that is adjusted with relative education levels. We replicate the education-adjusted relative income terms offered by the authors. The income term we use is represented at this endnote.[5]

Enrollment data are derived from the Cross National Time Series Archive (Banks 2010). Hatton and Williamson (2005) test the effect of this education-adjusted income differential relative to an origin country's region and relative to the world. In unreported models we include both measurements; however, the two measures are very highly correlated. As such, we decided to include only the income term that is relative to average global values. We expect a positive relationship between the global income differential and immigration flows.

Due to limitations of yearly enrollment data, we decided to utilize a simple relative income differential among OECD countries as an economic "pull" variable for the OECD migration data estimations. That is, in those models, we are controlling for the relative performance of a member-state's economy in relation to all other OECD member-countries.

Other Control Variables

In addition to the abovementioned variables that are included in the estimations, we also account for other demographic and political variables. Regarding the demographic controls, Hatton and Williamson (2005), hereafter referred to as H&W, include the share of the total population that is between the ages of fifteen and twenty-nine in their estimation. Unfortunately, we were not able to find this variable, although we did collect the proportion of the population that is between the ages of fifteen and twenty-four. These data are available in five-year increments from 1950 to 2005.

This is not a problem for the H&W replication since the UN net migration data and many of the underlying data of the public goods measure are also in five-year intervals. On the other hand, it does pose a problem for the OECD migration flow models. Therefore, for those models we include the share of the population that is younger than fifteen years; these data were accessed at the WBDI database. We expect a positive relationship between the size of the young population and immigration flows following similar results from estimations of U.S. and sub-Saharan African migration that were also conducted by Hatton and Williamson.

Another demographic control which we include in the H&W replication models is the stock of immigrants as a share of the total destination country population. We expect a positive relationship between this variable and immigration flows as it approximates the "friends and relatives effect." Lastly, civil war years are included in the replication model. Incidence of civil strife is expected to have a negative effect on net migration since conflicts "push" many affected people into refugee status.

ESTIMATION

The influences of data have allowed for us to use two basic migration data sets. The first is constructed with the UN data and the second with the OECD. The UN has a larger number of countries and also has the necessary public goods variables, but due to the difficulties in the measurement of economic freedom, this important part of our study could only be easily conducted with the OECD data. We wanted to be able to both replicate past work and also more importantly help to illustrate the important differences between the two factors, and this is the key reason for our two slightly different models. One important consideration is that these models are focused on the pull effects, not the push. These are not dyadic models and therefore we cannot fully evaluate the flows to and from a source. For the UN sample we use the formula in this endnote.[6]

The results of the estimation of net migration using the UN sample model are displayed in table 5.2. We predict five-year averaged international net migration rates using the share of youthful population within a country (population age 15–24 as a percentage of total population), international migration stock in the destination country, incidence of civil war in the origin, income differential, destination political capacity, public goods, and the interaction between pubic goods and RPE. This model and

Table 5.2.   Regression Results for United Nations Sample

	(1) H&W Replication	(2) Public Goods	(3) RPE	(4) RPE*Public Goods
Population aged 15–24 (% total population)	0.003*** (0.001)	0.005** (0.002)	0.003*** (0.001)	0.005** (0.002)
Int. Migrant Stock (% total population)	0.003*** (0.000)	0.007*** (0.001)	0.003*** (0.000)	0.007*** (0.001)
Civil War	−0.011* (0.006)	0.002 (0.009)	−0.012** (0.006)	−0.001 (0.009)
Income Differential (education-adjusted)	0.014*** (0.002)	0.029*** (0.004)	0.015*** (0.002)	0.029*** (0.004)
RPE			0.003 (0.005)	
Public Goods		−0.008 (0.016)		
RPE (centered)				0.001
(0.013) Public Goods (centered)				−0.011 (0.017)
RPE*Public Goods (centered)				0.036* (0.021)
Time FE	Yes	Yes	Yes	Yes
Country FE	Yes	Yes	Yes	Yes
Constant	−0.072*** (0.017)	— −0.125***	— −0.075***	−0.137*** (0.042)
Observations	897	361	858	351
Number of countries	145	131	142	128
R-squared	0.108	0.270	0.109	0.295
F test	15.042	11.786	12.375	9.928
Prob >F	0	0	0	0

Standard errors in parentheses. *** $p<0.01$, ** $p<0.05$, * $p<0.1$

the following are both additionally constructed with fixed effects for tie and country.

The parameters of the independent variables are in the expected direction. The shares of young population, migration stock, and most importantly income differential are significant at traditional levels and in the expected direction. Our results suggest that political capacity as operationalized by RPE does not have a statistically significant direct effect on migration flows. Rather, we observe a significant conditional relationship of political capacity and public goods provision on net migration.

A graphical representation of the interaction between RPE and public goods is displayed in figure 5.3, with solid lines representing statistically significant regions of the moderating variable. The results suggest that in destination countries with low levels of political capacity, net immigration materializes as public goods provision increases. The variance explained by the fully augmented model is relatively high ($R^2 = .295$) suggesting that the model adequately fits the observations of international net migration for the period studied.

Our second model of international migration rates, which utilizes data from the OECD, is offered in this endnote.[7]

The results of the estimation of immigration inflows into the OECD are presented in table 5.3. As shown in column 2, the share of young people in the destination country has a significant negative effect on immigrant inflows. This is the expected result since a larger number of youth reduces

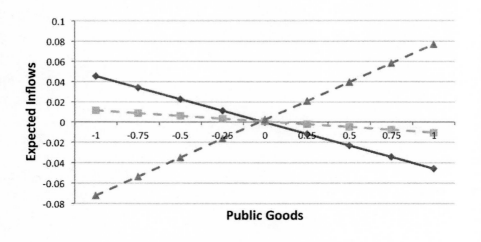

Figure 5.3.   Net Migration and the Interaction between Political Capacity and Public Goods Provision

Table 5.3.   Regression Results for OECD Sample

	(1) *RPE*Public Goods*	(2) *RPE*Econ Policy*
Population aged 0–14 (% total population)	0.000 (0.000)	−0.000* (0.000)
GDP per capita Ratio	0.013*** (0.002)	0.016*** (0.002)
RPE (centered)	−0.001 (0.001)	0.001 (0.001)
Public Goods (centered)	0.000*** (0.000)	
RPE*Public Goods (centered)	0.000 (0.000)	
Econ Policy (centered)		0.002 (0.001)
RPE*Econ Policy (centered)		0.006** (0.002)
Time FE	Yes	Yes
Country FE	Yes	Yes
Constant	−0.011*** (0.003)	−0.002 (0.004)
Observations	353	228
Number of countries	27	22
R-squared	0.370	0.478
F test	8.972	10.893
Prob >F	0	0

Standard errors in parentheses. *** $p<0.01$, ** $p<0.05$, * $p<0.1$

the demand for foreign labor. The economic performance of an OECD country relative to other member-states has a statistically significant positive effect. Migrants seem to be targeting the highest performers among the developed nations.

Regarding the effect of political capacity, we do not find a conditional relationship between RPE and public goods provision on expected inflows. Rather, the interaction between relative political extraction and economic policy is significant and in the anticipated direction. Figure 5.4 displays this interaction graphically. As the economic policy of the destination country

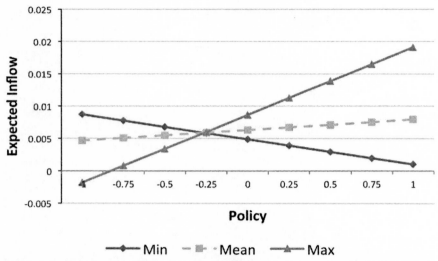

Figure 5.4.   Immigration Inflows into the OECD and the Interaction between Political Capacity and Economic Policy

liberalizes, expected inflows among receiving nations with high political capacity increase while those of low-performing countries decrease.

The above table helps to show a higher degree of importance and influence from the interaction between RPE and economic freedom with a higher level of statistical significance ($p<0.05$) and a higher degree of variance (R^2 adjusted $= .0.478$). The combination of the two samples leads to future work as both types of policy do have some supporting evidence that they are important, but the dynamics of that importance is of ongoing concern. What is interesting is that the age dynamics of population are not relevant but that GDP ratio is. As in the previous model neither Policy nor RPE is significant, and it is only with the interaction that we gain some understanding.

CONCLUSIONS

This chapter has empirically shown that migrations seem to be influenced by the interconnection between policy and political performance and supports our original theory that the incentive structure that unlocks economic success and to a degree public goods is a critical component of migration. This helps support the previous literature and provides evidence that people do, in fact, move for economic reasons and also lends support to our theoretical argument that the ability to invest and grow helps to create that pull incentive.

In both the OECD and UN samples, the GDP ratio and Income differential are also important characteristics showing that money and the ability to make money is an expected part of the evaluation process for migration. This is, to the best of our knowledge, unique as the effect of economic freedom on migration has yet to be tested. This chapter also finds evidence for the argument that public goods provision, when combined with the ability to implement policy, leads to higher levels of immigration.

Previous studies have found little evidence of a welfare effect on migrant flows due to their focus only on public goods alone. We argue that previous inquiries into the pull effects of public goods have ignored a crucial piece of the puzzle. That is, the effectiveness of government to extract resources with the objective of implementing national goals moderates the role that public goods play in the migration calculus.

Our study has established a link between the performance of governments in destination countries and the magnitude of immigration inflow. Future investigations of the effect of political capacity on migration will benefit from dyadic analyses of the determinants of actual flows between origin and destination. By conducting the analysis in such a fashion, classic explanations of migration such as distance can be accounted for.

International migrations will continue to increase going forward in the twenty-first century. As developed nations begin to experience the consequences of demographic transitions, migration is likely to become a norm. How these flows of population can be attracted, therefore, is as important as the basic demography of countries.

NOTES

1. Each of the components of Economic Freedom is generated by using data from a number of sources, including the World Bank, the International Monetary Fund, the U.S. Department of Commerce, Economist Intelligence unit, and the Office of the U.S. Trade Representative. For instance, to create the "investment freedom" variable used in this analysis, researchers scanned official reports from the above sources to examine questions such as whether there is a foreign investment code that defines the countries' investment laws and procedures, whether there are government restrictions on foreign exchange, and whether foreign firms are treated the same as domestic firms under the law. Researchers then define a rubric to place each nation on a 100 point scale, where 100 indicates the highest level of investment freedom (again, see Beach and Kane 2007 for the methodology used to construct each indicator).

$$\frac{Tax}{GDP} = \beta_0 + \beta_1(time) + \beta_2(\frac{Mining}{GDP}) + \beta_3(\frac{Agriculture}{GDP}) + \beta_3(\frac{Exports}{GDP}) + \epsilon$$

2. The predicted values of this estimation are then used as the denominator of the general RPE formula which is specified as:

$$RPE = \frac{\text{Actual Government Revenue}}{\text{Predicted Government Revenue}}$$

Values of RPE which equal one signify that the government has met its expected extractive capability. When the ratio is above one, this indicates that the government has exceeded anticipated extraction levels—the sign of a highly capable political establishment. Similarly, when RPE is less than one, the government is unable to meet its expected extraction levels and is thus considered to be lacking effectiveness.

3. The primary purpose of PCA is data reduction. Thus, the result of PCA is fewer variables, with less overlap and higher reliability between the variables. Varimax rotation was used to create more interpretable results, through maximization of the variance of the factor loadings. It is important to note that we experimented with alternative factor analytic methods—the results were similar in all cases, with a single component emerging with an eigenvalue over 1. Cronbach's alpha indicates that the scale is reliable by traditional standards (alpha = .90). As expected, only one factor with an eigenvalue over 1 emerged and all six variables loaded highly on the single dimension in the same direction—the rotated loadings ranged from a high of .89 (property rights) to a low of .64 (monetary freedom), with most variables over .80. After extracting the factor, we used regression scoring to produce a single indicator and, in order to ease interpretation, rescaled the variable to range between 0 and 1. The *Policy* measure is only marginally correlated with *RPE* (? = .22), and thus one may be confident that *Policy* is measuring a dimension of political choices that is independent from government capacity.

4. The scale of this variable seems to be reliable given the high Cronbach's alpha (0.76).

5. $IncomeDiff_{it} = \frac{Ypc_{it}}{Ypc_{wt}} - \frac{Epc_{it}}{Epc_{wt}}$

Where t is a given year, i signifies the country of interest and w represents the average world value. Ypc is GDP per capita and Epc is the sum of Secondary and University enrollment per capita.

6. $Migration_{it} = \beta_0 + \beta_1 RPE_{it} + \beta_2 RPE*Policy + \beta_3 PopAge_{it} + \beta_4 MigrationStock_{it} + \beta_5 CivilWar_{it} + \beta_6 IncomeDif_{it} f + \gamma FE_R + \lambda FE_T + \epsilon_{it}$

7. $Migration_{it} + \beta_0 + \beta_1 RPE_{it} + \beta_2 RPE*Policy + \beta_3 PopAge_{it} + \beta_6 GDPperCapita + \gamma FE_R + \lambda FE_T + _{it}$

REFERENCES

Acemoglu, D., S. Johnson, and J. Robinson. 2005. "Institutions as the Fundamental Cause of Long-run Growth." NBER wp 10481. *Handbook of Economic Growth.* Elsevier, North-Holland.

Arbetman, Marina, and Kristin Johnson. 2008. "Relative Political Capacity Empirical and Theoretical Underpinnings." Paper presented at International Studies Association.

Arbetman, Marina, and Jacek Kugler. 1997. *Political Capacity and Economic Behavior.* Boulder, CO: Westview Press.

Banks, Arthur S. 2010. "Cross-National Time-Series Data Archive." Databanks International. Jerusalem, Israel; www.databanksinternational.com.

Beach, W. W., and T. Kane. 2007. *Methodology: Measuring the 10 Economic Freedoms.* Washington, DC: The Heritage Foundation.

Borjas, G. J. 1987. "Self-Selection and the Earnings of Immigrants." *American Economic Review* 23 (3): 531–53.

———. 1989. "Economic Theory and International Migration." *International Migration Review* 23 (3): 457–85.

Clark, X., T. J. Hatton, and J. G. Williamson. 2007. "Explaining U.S. Immigration, 1971–1998." *The Review of Economics and Statistics* 89 (2): 359–73.

Coan, T. G., and Tadeusz Kugler. 2008. "The Politics of Foreign Direct Investment: An Interactive Framework." *International Interactions* 34 (4): 402–22.

Cornelius, W. A. 1975. *Politics and the Migrant Poor in Mexico City.* Stanford, CA: Stanford University Press.

Fan, C. Cindy. 2002. "The Elite, the Natives, and the Outsiders: Migration and Labor Market Segmentation in Urban China." *Annals of the Association of American Geographers* 92 (1): 103–24.

———. 2008. *China on the Move: Migration, the State and the Household.* New York: Routledge.

Feng, Y., and Chen Baizhu. 1997. "Political Capacity and Private Investment." Marina Arbetman and Jacket Kugler, eds., *Political Capacity and Economic Behavior.* Boulder, CO: Westview Press.

Feng, Y., J. Kugler, S. Swaminathan, and P. J. Zak. 2008. "Path to Prosperity: The Dynamics of Freedom and Economic Development." *International Interactions* (34) 4: 423–41.

Feng, Y., Jacek Kugler, and Paul Zak. 2000. "The Politics of Fertility and Economic Development." *International Studies Quarterly* 44 (4): 667–93.

Foley, C. F., A. D. Mihir, and J. R. Hines Jr. 2004. "A Multinational Perspective on Capital Structure Choice and Internal Capital Markets." *Journal of Finance* 59 (6): 2451–88.

Freeman, R. 2006. "People Flows in Globalization." *Journal of Economic Perspectives* 20 (2): 145–170.

Greenwood, M. J. 1975. "Research on Internal Migration in the United States: A Survey." *Journal of Economic Literature* 13 (2), 397–433.

Gwartney, J., R. Lawson, and R. G. Holcombe. 1999. "Economic Freedom and the Environment for Economic Growth." *Journal of Institutional and Theoretical Economics* 155: 643–63.

Hatton, T. J. 2005. "Explaining Trends in UK Immigration." *Journal of Population Economics* 18 (4): 719–40.

———. 2003. "Demographic and Economic Pressure on Emigration out of Africa." *Scandinavian Journal of Economics* 105(3): 465–486.

Hatton, Timothy, and Jeffrey Williamson. 2002. "What Fundamentals Drive World Migration?" National Bureau of Economic Research Working Paper No. 9159.

Hatton, T. J., and J. G. Williamson. 2005. "What Fundamentals Drive World Migration?" G. J. Borjas and J. Crisp, eds., *Poverty, International Migration and Asylum,* 15–38. Hampshire, UK: Palgrave Macmillan.

Heming, Li, P. Waley, and P. Rees. 2001. "Reservoir Resettlement in China: Past Experience and the Three Gorges Dam." *The Geographical Journal* 167 (3): 195–212.

Hooghe, Mark, Ann Trappers, Bart Meuleman, and Tim Reeskens. 2008. "Migrations to European Countries: A Structural Explanation of Patterns, 1980–2004." *International Migration Review* 42 (2): 476–504.

Johnson, K. 2007. "Sub National Capabilities and Internal Conflict." Unpublished doctoral dissertation, Claremont Graduate University, Claremont, CA.

Karemera, D., V. I. Oguledo, and B. Davis. 2000. "A Gravity Model Analysis of International Migration to North America." *Applied Economics* 32 (13): 1745–55.

Katz, E., & O. Stark. 1986. "Labor Migration and Risk Aversion in Less Developed Countries." *Journal of Labor Economics* 4, 131–149.

King, G., and J. Honaker. 2005. "What to Do about Missing Values in Time Series Cross-Section Data." Unpublished manuscript.

King, G., J. Honaker, A. Joseph, and K. Scheve. 2001. "Analyzing Incomplete Political Science Data: An Alternative Algorithm for Multiple Imputation." *American Political Science Review* 95: 49–69.

King, Robert G., and R. Levine. 1993. "Finance, Entrepreneurship, and Growth: Theory and Evidence." *Journal of Monetary Economics* 32 (3): 513–42.

Kishlansky, M., P. Geary, and P. O'Brien. 2003. *Civilization in the West,* Fifth Edition. New York: Longman.

Kugler, Tadeusz, and J. Kugler. 2010. "Political Demography." Robert A. Denemark, ed., *The International Studies Compendium.* Hoboken, NJ: Wiley-Blackwell.

Kugler, Tadeusz, and S. Swaminathan. 2006. "The Politics of Population." *International Studies Review* 8 (4): 581–96.

Lalueza-Fox, C., M. L. Sampietro, M. T. P. Gilbert et al. 2004. "Unraveling Migrations in the Steppe: Mitochondrial DNA Sequences from Ancient Central Asians." *Proceedings: Biological Sciences* 271 (1542): 941–47.

La Porta, R., F. Lopez-de-Silanes, A. Shleifer, and R. Vishny. 1997. "Legal Determinants of External Finance." *Journal of Finance* 52 (3): 1131–50.

———. 1998. "Law and Finance." *Journal of Political Economy* 106 (6): 1113–55.

Leblang, David. 1997. "Political Capacity and Economic Growth." Marina Arbetman and Jacek Kugler, eds., *Political Capacity and Economic Behavior.* Boulder, CO: Westview Press.

Lee, E. S. 1966. "A Theory of Migration." *Demography* 3 (1): 47–57.

Massey, D. S. 1988. "Economic Development and International Migration in Comparative Perspective." *Population and Development Review* 14 (3): 383–413.

———. 1990. "The Social and Economic Origins of Immigration." Annals of the American Academy of Political and Social Science 510: 60–72.

Massey, D. S., and F. Garcia-Espana. 1987. "The Social Process of International Migration." *Science* 237: 733–38.

Mayda, A. M. 2007. "International Migration: A Panel Data Analysis of the Determinants of Bilateral Flows." *CEPR* Discussion Paper No. DP6289.

———. 2009. "International Migration: A Panel Data Analysis of the Determinants of Bilateral Flows." *Journal of Population Economics* 23 (4): 1249–74.

Mckenzie, D., and H. Rapoport. 2007. "Network Effects and the Dynamics of Migration and Inequality: Theory and Evidence from Mexico." *Journal of Development Economics* 84 (1): 1–24.

Organski, A. F. K., and Jacek Kugler. 1980. *The War Ledger*. Chicago: University of Chicago Press.

Pedersen, P., M. Pytlikova, & N. Smith. 2008. "Selection and Network Effects— Migration Flows into OECD Countries 1990–2000." *European Economic Review* 52 (7), 1160–1186.

Schneider, F., and B. Frey. 1985. "Economic and Political Determinants of Foreign Direct Investment." *World Development* 13: 161–75.

Sjaastad, L. 1962. "The Costs and Returns of Human Migration." *Journal of Political Economy* 70 (5, part 2): 80–93.

Steinberg, D.A., and Stephen M. Saideman. 2008. "Laissez Fear: Assessing the Impact of Government Involvement in the Economy on Ethnic Violence." *International Studies Quarterly* 52(2): 235–259.

Teitelbaum, M. S. 2007. "Demography and American Immigration." In R. Ueda, ed., *A Companion to American Immigration*, 275–288. Oxford, UK: Blackwell Publishing Ltd.

The World Bank. 2004. *Doing Business in 2004*. Washington, DC: The World Bank Publications.

———. 2005. *World Development Report 2005: A Better Investment Climate for Everyone*. Washington, DC: The World Bank Publications.

———. 2008. *Doing Business in 2008*. Washington, DC: The World Bank Publications.

———. 2010. *World Development Report 2010: Development and Climate Change*. Washington, DC: The World Bank Publications.

Zubanov, Nikolay. 2009. "Too Many, Too Fast? Dynamics of Net Migration in OECD, 1984–2001." *Applied Economics Letters* 16 (6): 597–602.

6

Oil . . . Path to Prosperity or Poverty?

The Effects of Political Performance in Africa

Marina Arbetman-Rabinowitz and Kristin Johnson

CONTEXT

A general consensus on development has emerged in recent years that the fastest route to both economic and human development is through economic growth. In Africa, the vehicles for generating this growth are limited by lack of infrastructure, low levels of education, HIV, and political instability to name a few. Consequently, external resources are deemed critical for most countries in Africa to galvanize economic growth, either through FDI, borrowing, or foreign aid.

Discoveries of vast oil resources in Africa appeared to present a solution to the growth and therefore development issue for a number of countries in western and central Africa. Multiple interests including international organizations, multinational corporations, and foreign governments are converging to invest in this new "gold rush." In contrast to a substantial literature on the "resource curse," the World Bank indicated in late 2007 that this gold rush was accompanied by a turnaround in economic growth in Africa (World Bank 2007). With a third of the global oil discoveries and an anticipated 20 percent of global production capacity in the next five years, these tremendous oil resources have been touted as the path to prosperity for many African nations (Ghazvinian 2007).

At the same time, the United Nations Millennium Development Project's refocus on abject poverty prompted the reinvigoration of efforts to deal with it in a global context. This project highlights the differences between economic growth and human development, which although intertwined have different goals, cultural implications, and long-term consequences. In this context, the World Bank has revitalized the original goal of resource transfers of .07 percent of GDP from the most developed to developing countries as a strategy for eliminating poverty.

To date, most OECD countries have failed to realize these goals. More recently, concerns surrounding the global economic downturn beginning in 2008 have resulted in diminishing levels of foreign aid, with estimates in declines ranging from 30 to 45 percent for Africa (Mendoza, Jones and Vergara 2009; UNCTAD 2009). What will be the effect, if any, of this change in the flow of money for economic growth and development?

One of the most perplexing issues surrounding these efforts is a general failure to demonstrate substantial improvements in human development as a consequence of these various efforts at growth. Explanations for this range from a failure to transfer adequate resources, to poor institutional development, to the phenomena referred to as the resource curse or paradox of plenty. However, the fundamental assumption that growth leads to development remains almost unchallenged. The domestic political context in which human development emerges, and in fact the role of politics in both growth and human aspects of development, are typically ignored in the analysis.

We remedy this gap in the literature and evaluate two parts of the development puzzle in this chapter. First, we look at the contribution of external resources, oil wealth, and politics to the overall accumulation of wealth within societies. Then we look at these same factors in light of human development. Our findings are striking. Unlike the prevailing literature, we find that economic growth does not translate into corresponding increases in human development. External resources and oil do in fact prompt growth, but the failure of that growth to translate into increases in the wellbeing of a population is not surprising. We find that first the political mobilization of a population and then the political efficiency of the government are key levers in increasing human development.

This chapter is organized as follows: the initial section reviews existing work on economic growth, investment, oil, and development. The second section tests the relationship between growth, investment, and oil. The third and fourth sections examine the relationship between economic and human development and elaborate on the results.

INTELLECTUAL ENVIRONMENT: ECONOMIC GROWTH, INVESTMENT, AND OIL

Mineral wealth is often considered an asset that opens doors for economic growth and provides opportunities for social development to countries with few development prospects. Recent discoveries of oil throughout central and western Africa have renewed hopes of generating rapid economic growth and eliminating poverty in large parts of the world's poorest continent. Africa is relevant for this analysis since one-third of the world's new oil discoveries since the year 2000 have taken place in this continent. "Of the 8 billion barrels of new oil reserves discovered in 2001, 7 billion were found there. In the years between 2005 and 2010, 20 percent of the world's new production capacity is expected to come from Africa" (Ghazvinian 2007, 1). Countries highlighted as important oil producers include Nigeria, Angola, Gabon, Equatorial Guinea, Sao Tome and Principe, and more recently Chad and Sudan; new discoveries stretch from additional deposits in Sudan to Ghana, the Congo, and Uganda (see appendix 6.1, map of Africa). Therefore, policy makers keep wondering if oil will be the key to a better life for these populations.

A body of empirical literature maintains that countries endowed with mineral resources perform worse than less "lucky" ones.[1] For instance, Sachs and Warner (1997) report that countries with exports concentrated in the natural resource sector tend to grow relatively slowly, on average, by about 1 percent per year during the period 1970–1989. Understanding the causes of this empirical regularity has not been that easy. Despite evidence that overall growth occurs with oil-exporting African countries, a rich literature has emerged on the existence of the paradox of plenty (Karl 1997) or the notion more commonly referred to as the resource curse (Auty 1993). The paradox of plenty describes the condition in which a country's economy is characterized by tremendous resource wealth; however, this resource wealth does not translate into actual gains for the well-being of the population. The resource curse occurs when reliance on exports of a particular nonrenewable primary commodity is likely to impede rather than stimulate long-term economic growth.

The reasons for these limitations on growth include arguments of a trade-off between investments in mineral and other sectors of the economy including agriculture and manufacturing. Compounding this problem is the thesis referred to as Dutch Disease, which identifies a tendency for real exchange rates to appreciate overtly in response to positive shocks such as newfound natural resources, which in turn lead to a contraction of the tradable sector, fostering deindustrialization as a response (Sachs and Warner 1995). Furthermore, national economies become susceptible to boom and bust cycles as a consequence of changes in international demand and prices. More politically oriented explanations of this argument include the assessment that governments with weak institutions reroute public investments instead of investing in human capital gains realized from resource extraction (Ross 2003).

On the other hand, there is a large consensus among economists that economic growth and development are driven by factors that include investment, the accumulation of human capital, and the ability to innovate (Pritchett 2000). A number of insights that have particular relevance for Africa are gleaned from these approaches to economic growth. Differences in rates of growth based on levels of development demonstrate that developed countries evidence slow long-term growth, while developing countries are characterized by rapid and volatile changes in growth rates, with huge variations around general trends (Prichett 2000).

Historically, developed countries demonstrate that economic growth put to good use facilitates development. If the lessons from developed countries could be easily extrapolated to Africa and economic growth is a panacea for poverty, the story of Africa's development would have had a quick and happy ending. Instead Africa is characterized by extensive poverty and a lack of institutional development.

Strong institutions that develop over time are often identified as integral to the ability to attract and utilize investments effectively (Rodrick 2000). In Africa in particular, enormous challenges have emerged in the attainment of investment and in the accumulation of human capital. Initially, there have been few reasons for investors to target African countries outside of the acquisition of primary commodities.

The primary barriers to investment, even in profitable commodities, include poor institutional development, political instability, and nearly nonexistent infrastructure. Moreover, poor institutional development in Africa has often been attributed to colonial legacies that have been carried over as postcolonial economic models.[2] While this approach did generate some greater degree of growth, a number of countries focused their efforts on primary commodity exports; changes in international prices and demand dramatically impact their domestic economies.[3] Countries that have successfully adopted this approach to date seem to be ones that have primarily exported oil, for example Nigeria.

The discussion above highlights the difficulties in determining if oil and mineral revenues generate improvement in overall quality of life for populations when they are the driving factor in economic growth. Certainly, export-oriented growth models enjoy a mixed record, with the Asian "tiger" economies touted as successes and Latin American countries experiencing a parallel contraction. Countries choosing development strategies that rely on primary commodity exports are particularly subject to the boom and bust cycles identified above.[4]

Despite the difficulties faced in the establishment of export-based economic growth, oil is seen as a panacea for development in a number of African countries. This is based both on the empirical record of successful economic growth for oil-producing economies in Africa, and on the notion that oil development can coincide with institutional development.

Growth is often identified as the best means in the long run for alleviating poverty; however, the distributional effects of wealth and the structure of growth influence the degree of poverty reduction. Oil booms create a massive infusion of capital into societies resulting in tremendous short-term economic growth, which is why the World Bank and others identify Africa as in the process of turning around. Figure 6.1 illustrates the difference in mean GDP per capita between oil- and non-oil-producing African countries.[5]

We do not argue that oil discovery does not correlate with economic growth, but suggest that the long-term problem is that if growth does not translate into development, these countries will stagnate. Moreover, the pattern of non-oil-producers in Africa has been slow but steadily positive toward development once the per capita GDP starts taking off. Countries with greater resources have an opportunity to accumulate more wealth and start the process of development earlier, but the empirical evidence tells us that this is not always the case.

The assumption that oil is the resource that will bring wealth is also suspicious for many authors. Serious criticism of variable selection and a lack of contextual examination have resulted in a reassessment of whether or not oil resources are likely to bring a boom or bust for Africa in the long term (Bannon and Collier 2003). Furthermore, most recent work on the resource curse suggests that oil, unlike other primary commodities, is an inelastic resource, not subject to boom and bust cycles (Basedau 2005).

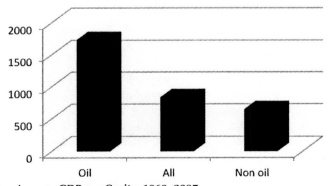

Figure 6.1.   Average GDP per Capita, 1960–2007

A number of scholars are returning to macroeconomic assessments of the possibilities of economic growth by looking at the likely future oil development will have for Africa's growth, arguing that the increased wealth from oil may allow states to exercise control over populations without relying on tax revenue, but is also likely to facilitate long-term investment and growth.[6] (See appendix 6.2, for a comparative table of diverging economic problems and indicators.) By far, the most salient component of recent claims that oil will alleviate many of Africa's problems relies on the notion that if oil-producing countries are able to develop strong or capable institutions, they will be able to adequately manage oil returns and maintain growth. The issue that remains unclear is if this growth translates into development.

Most economists contend that oil is the best chance for poverty reduction in Africa, primarily because it affords countries a massive and immediate acceleration in growth (Basedau 2005). Still, others argue that oil exports represent an example of countries with widening poverty gaps, where the overall level of wealth in a country increases while the population becomes poorer (for an extensive overview of this argument see Ross 2003). Countries without the infrastructure to absorb resources, accounting capabilities, or transparency will lose track of resources, face resource diversion, and are more susceptible to distribution of resources along clientalist or patronage networks.

While initial arguments along the lines of resource looting were made in studies of the relationship between oil and conflict (Ross 2003), oil has been demonstrated to be a nonlootable resource. Unlike diamonds or precious metals, oil is difficult to transport and contain, particularly in sufficient quantities to make looting profitable. Oil companies provide fairly comprehensive security, and to date, looting of oil resources has been limited to small quantities for private use and would be more appropriately described as pilfering (e.g., Nigeria, where small holes are drilled in existing pipelines for energy use at an individual scale for household energy needs).

Not all countries in Africa share in the oil resource wealth. Investment and foreign aid projects are the primary external resources these countries receive. However, as indicated in the preceding section, Africa does not possess many of the attributes required to make investment attractive. For these countries, foreign aid is a primary tool for increasing economic growth. However, foreign aid shares some of the criticisms of other external revenue streams. Foreign aid is often politically driven and conditioned on either targeted programs or objectives, or even to realize profits for companies from the donor country. A notable example is Japanese foreign aid to small Pacific Island states such as Vanatu or Tuvalu, where foreign aid has been used to construct massive docks to service Japanese fishing fleets. The consequence is little or no real investment in the actual "infrastructure" of these countries in a way that benefits citizens. Foreign aid is also subject to boom and bust cycles and is often limited or unavailable when it is most needed, for example during economic downturns. A recent study by UNCTAD (2009) identifies contractions in foreign aid that accompany global recessions, up to 40 percent. Despite the significantly smaller amounts of revenue received through foreign aid compared to oil resources, the same institutional components and constraints impact its effective use.

The dilemma in addressing the growth versus development issue in Africa is illustrated by the debate on growth-led vs. poverty-focused development strategies as better suited in the long run for African countries (Hayami and Akiyama 2003; Thurlow and Wobst 2006). One of the largest relevant discussions is found in the resource curse literature surrounding redistributive strategies of oil wealth as a mechanism to limit growing poverty and inequities in oil-producing countries.

The more compelling argument for a relationship between oil and poverty lies in two dimensions: one is that oil allows a small majority to retain power and obtain sufficient resources to quash dissent from a deprived population. Despite a record of reasonable economic growth, Nigeria for periods of time fits this model. In seeking to realize immediate returns from oil profits, countries will become heavily indebted. Countries that are higher credit risks are more likely to receive shorter terms on loans from private, government, and international lenders.

In many of these instances, countries did not possess sufficient resources to realize the returns from resource extraction and were saddled with high levels of debt without a means to service it. In others, initial revenues were directed toward debt service, with increased capacity required to generate additional income for the national government. An examination of early oil-exporting countries in Africa (Nigeria and Angola both initially financed oil extraction through high levels of borrowing) also fits this model. Recent oil exploration and development have been based significantly less on borrowing and to a much greater degree on investment. In either case, returns realized from oil development do not trickle down to the population or culminate in human capital increases.

INSTITUTIONAL DEVELOPMENT AND POLITICAL PERFORMANCE

Institutional development can constitute an important component of the management of oil revenue windfalls. Many countries in Africa lack the institutions to even absorb, much less distribute, the tremendous increases in revenues. Positive examples, such as Botswana's investment in roads, health care, and infrastructure with mining revenues, demonstrate that

good institutional development can facilitate the transformation of resource revenues into infrastructure that can assist in long-term development goals. Initial evidence demonstrates that institutional development in
oil-producing countries may also facilitate long-term growth efforts.[7]

Institutional development remains a significant component of a country's ability to function and attract investment. A number of both economic
and political measures are used in order to try to capture the degree institutions have formed; arguably institutions emerge over time as a confluence
of historical and cultural influences. Existing measures of institutional performance include measures of corruption (for example the Corruption Perception Index) intended to reflect legitimacy and trust in institutional
function[8] or stability in policy choices (Banks 2002). Institutions also capture the intersection of politics and economics, functioning as well as the
existing political structure is able to make the most of, maintain, and
enforce rules.

The inclusion of politics has resulted from the general conclusion that
there are political constraints on economic growth. Intuitively and theoretically, this is demonstrated by the ability of governments to implement a
desired set of policy choices: governments can only implement policies to
the degree they either can get consent from a population or can coerce a
population. Early and rough measures for institutional development
include degree of democratization, policy stability and certainty, and corruption. Each of these approaches runs into the problem that they assume
particular forms of government will be superior in terms of implementing
policies.

An alternate means of measuring institutional development relies on
evaluation of the overall capabilities of governments. Relative political
extraction captures both the intersection of politics and economics and the
ability of governments to implement a desired set of policies given a country's level of development (Organksi and Kugler 1980; Arbetman and
Kugler 1997). This measure avoids the normative components assumed in
measures based on democracy or Western values, and instead assesses if a
country is able to extract the resources anticipated based on economic
endowment.

An additional important assessment of institutional development can be
found in the complementary indicator relative political reach (RPR) (Arbetman 1990; Arbetman and Kugler 1997), which measures the extent to
which the government can mobilize its population by assessing if they are
willing to abide by the rules and be part of the official labor sector. The
measure looks at the size of the workforce compared to the average profile
of similar countries to gauge the degree of labor activity that occurs outside
the purview of the government.

MODEL AND METHODOLOGY

In this chapter, we test two models, one looking at the determinants of economic development and the second looking at the determinants of human development. Our thesis is that the determinants of growth are not the same as the determinants of development, although policy makers often equate them. Whether or not politics or economics matter more in terms of wealth accumulation is an open and oft-debated question, one that is critical to the question of how to develop. Development requires both economic growth and an increase in the quality of life; Africa constitutes a development challenge. Traditional development strategies, including external inflows of resources and increases in overall wealth, fall short of promised development gains for the countries under examination. We approach this in two ways. First, we evaluate the role of external and internal influences on GDP per capita growth. Then, we look at these same influences and the accumulation of wealth in the context of human development.

The two theoretical models we propose, based on the current literature, are:

(1) Economic Development = oil + political extraction + political reach + income flows + error
(2) Human Development = oil + political extraction + political reach + income flows + error[9]

AFRICA: OIL AND ECONOMIC GROWTH

One of the most important issues to note at the outset in the evaluation of these models is that this chapter is not intended to explain economic growth[10]; instead our goal is to evaluate the influence of both internal and external factors on the accumulation of wealth within Africa and the role of these same factors in the distribution of resources throughout a population. These external and internal factors can more readily be described as external resources and internal political characteristics of a country.

In recent decades, oil-producing countries in Africa have demonstrated higher GDP per capita growth than non-oil-producing countries. In our sample, at constant 2000 values, the average oil-producing countries' GDP per capita is $1,735.06, compared to non-oil-producing countries' average of $648.11. Overall GDP per capita rates of growth differ by 21 percent, with oil-producing countries demonstrating increases of 4.2 percent contrasted to 3.7 percent for non-oil-producers.

Given the preceding statistics, our findings, in table 6.1, are not surprising. The strongest predictors of higher per capita wealth are financial: high levels of foreign aid and high levels of foreign direct investment. The resource curse seems not to apply: oil production is positively related to overall increases in wealth per person. Most countries in Africa do not possess the ability to galvanize their economies with their existing resources, with the exception of countries with high value primary commodities such as oil. It is interesting to note that politics is marginally significant in predicting per capita GDP, while economics seems to be the strongest predictor.

Differences emerge when the sample is divided between oil and non-oil-producers. Non-oil-producing countries constitute nearly 70 percent of the sample, with oil-producing countries making up the remaining 30 percent. In each subsample, the influx of external resources is positive and significantly related to increases in GDP per capita. For oil-producing countries, once FDI has been established, the main predictors of per capita wealth are foreign aid and oil production; investments are not that important. While it may seem counterintuitive that foreign direct investment is not significant, consider that in oil-producing countries foreign direct investment is concentrated in the oil sector and most often only occurs at the onset of oil discovery and during initial infrastructure development and extractive phases.

Following the initial production of oil, revenues realized from the oil sector overwhelm foreign direct investment. Equatorial Guinea is a good example; following the 1996 discovery of oil in the country FDI increased dramatically, only to be eclipsed in 1999 by the realization of substantive revenues from oil production. By 2004, Equatorial Guinea ranked third in Africa in terms of crude oil production (Vidal 2004), and the GDP per capita in the country was among the top ten countries in the world (IMF 2008). It is interesting to note that although RPE is still significant, RPR is not. In the richest African countries, mobilizing the population will not contribute to economic development but relative political extraction will.

The scenario changes when we focus on non-oil-producing countries. For the poorest in Africa, political extraction is not significant but political reach becomes highly significant. This argument is congruent with the argument made by Organski and Kugler (1980): at very low levels of development the population needs to be mobilized before they can start the path to development (see figure 6.2). Also, the poorer the country is, the higher the marginal effect of foreign aid and FDI.

Table 6.1 summarizes the relationship between institutional capabilities and influences on economic development between oil- and non-oil-producing countries.

$$GDP \text{ per capita} = RPE + RPR + Year + Income \text{ Inflows} + Oil \text{ Production} + Error$$

Table 6.1. Economic Development and Oil Production

Dependent Variable GDP per Capita	Model 1: Whole Sample	Model 2: Oil Producers[1]	Model 3: Non-Oil-Producers
Political Extraction	111.38*	343.41*	65.65
	(56.00)	(137.57)	(43.78)
Political Reach	177.75*	− 271.32	**331.62****
	(79.42)	(200.23)	(59.56)
Year	6.37*	12.46	**8.40****
	(2.61)	(7.05)	(1.94)
Investment: FDI	**500.46****	299.73	**491.56****
	(105.31)	(231.99)	(85.66)
Foreign Aid	**3.52****	**8.13****	**2.09****
	(0.58)	(1.55)	(0.42)
Oil Production	**0.92****	**0.57****	807.04
	(0.06)	(0.11)	(301.05)
Constant	− 1254.39*	− 24123.25	− 16812.82**
	(5189.52)	(14054.23)	(3855.03)
Adjusted R. Sq.	.1649	.1117	.0915
Sample Size	1529	500	1029

** Significant at the .0001 level
* Significant at the .005 level

1. Countries included in the oil producers subsample (model 2) produce at least 0.2 barrels of oil per day.

Foreign Aid per capita is consistently significant across sample and sub-samples. Foreign aid is a complement to revenues realized from oil. In long-term oil-producing countries such as Nigeria, declines in other sectors of the economy such as agriculture and manufacturing accompany growth in the oil sector. This phenomenon is detailed extensively in the preceding section of the chapter in the discussion of the resource curse. High levels of foreign aid per capita may assist in offsetting, at least in terms of GDP per capita levels, some of this contraction. A simpler explanation may lie in the politics of foreign aid. Governments make decisions surrounding the transfer of resources to further political objectives, which can include both the goals of securing access to resources and increasing development. Either way, foreign aid constitutes an influx of resources into a national economy, increasing the wealth per person.

African countries lie primarily in the left-hand portion of the distribution illustrated in figure 6.2. Looking at the variables that foster economic devel-

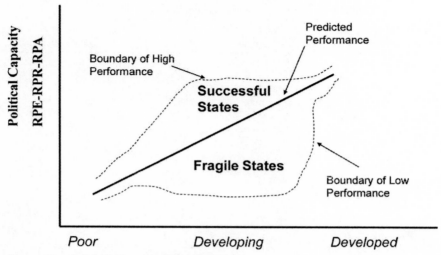

Figure 6.2. Political Capacity and Development

opment, on average, the inference is that the more financial flows into the country, of any kind, the higher the probability of wealth accumulation. If this is correct then the resource curse is a fantasy. The critical next question becomes why many African countries, regardless of oil production, do not seem to be getting out of abject poverty. What triggers allow countries to escape poverty and increase development? Are the same factors that increase wealth accumulation also critical to increases in human development?

AFRICA: GROWTH AND DEVELOPMENT

In order to address the effects of these same variables on human development, or to see if these gains are evident in the well-being of the population enjoying oil resources, we need to begin by measuring human development.

Development studies have shifted in recent years from an emphasis on overall wealth and wealth per capita levels to quality of life indicators. The emphasis on morbidity and mortality in populations arguably is more nuanced than one that either looks at the percentage of populations at or below a national poverty rate or at the average wealth per person. While there are a few wealth-based assessments (e.g., the Millennium Development Indicators inclusion of the percent of populations residing at or below a dollar a day), emphasis has shifted to factors that constitute human development in a physical sense, or assess the extent to which the basic needs of a population are met.

Existing measures of quality of life focus on two dimensions: physical and social indicators reflecting a societal total, and/or the experience of life enjoyed by an individual. The first approach relies on objective data, viewing quality of life as something that happens to an individual or as the effect of environmental and other factors on physical reality. This approach evaluates quality of life as a collective unit for a society rather than focusing on the experience of an individual; in other words, quality of life defined in this sense is a multidimensional phenomenon rather than an individual human experience. Initial studies of physical quality of life measures in political science are found in Morris's (1979) book *Measuring the Condition of the World's Poor: The Physical Quality of Life Index*, subsequently used in studies by Dixon and Moon (1985), London and Williams (1988), and Bradshaw and Tshandu (1990). More recent efforts include the Human Development Index (HDI) and indicators identified as significant as part of the United Nations Millennium Development Project.

Human development measures often include quality of life components that address basic needs in addition to other facets of individual experience. Educational access and completion and access to health care and other services are often identified as important components of human development. There is tremendous overlap between both physical and social indicators of quality of life and indicators of human development. Multiple indicators for physical quality of life are difficult to come by, particularly in developing countries due to poor data availability.

Indicators that measure basic survival, including access to improved water, availability of health care, immunizations, and frequency of disease, are difficult to collect in countries with substantial rural populations or are available only when self-reported by countries, often with questionable accuracy, or reported by international aid agencies that may only be present in particular parts of a country or for limited durations.

An additional obstacle to researchers is the vast differences in intervals of data collection: indicators such as literacy or infant mortality may be available on a nearly yearly basis, while immunization rates may be reported every five years in some countries and in others sporadically or not at all. The relationship between each of these indicators and other indicators of physical quality of life compound the measurement problem. Many may indirectly or directly reinforce each other.

We were unable to utilize HDI given the scope of our study so we utilize infant mortality levels, as they are both readily available for the duration of the series and highly correlated (=.82) with the Human Development Index. Infant mortality levels are also a better measure than many of the

Table 6.2.   Principal Components Analysis: Factor Loadings

Variable	Factor 1	Uniqueness
Literacy	−0.95123	0.09516
Infant Mortality	0.95112	0.09538
Life Expectancy	−0.95250	0.09275
Birth Rates	0.92465	0.14503
Fertility Rates	0.95014	0.09724
Education %	−0.90614	0.17891

extant measures of physical well-being because they capture near immediate influences on the economic well-being of populations (where other indicators demonstrate a significant lag in registering) (World Bank Working Paper 36, 2006). We note in the principal components analysis below that across measures, patterns of basic needs variance are similar, demonstrated across a few of the most readily available basic needs indicators for Africa.

The principal component analysis reveals that it is likely that one factor does (particularly given the 4.9 difference value) determine the pattern of relationships between variables, assuming the uniqueness or variance in measures not captured by the components to be zero. The initial component above has an eigenvalue far larger than the other components, indicating that variance in the data can largely be explained by one component. The substantial drop in the eigenvalue evident in the second component indicates that while there is a possibility of a second significant component, it is likely that components 2 through 6 are sampling noise. This also suggests that the use of any of these variables as proxies is appropriate.

For the reasons stated above, the concept of human development is accurately measured by infant mortality. We assert that an increase in overall wealth is a key facet for development in poor polities, albeit not a panacea. The ability of a population to realize increases in human development requires more than money. This assertion is borne out by discussions of a

Table 6.3.   Principal Component Factor Eigenvalues
(principle component factor; 1 factor retained)

Factor	Eigenvalue	Difference	Proportion	Cumulative
1	5.29554	4.95135	0.8826	0.8826
2	0.34419	0.13811	0.0574	0.9400
3	0.20608	0.09386	0.0343	0.9743
4	0.11222	0.08673	0.0187	0.9930
5	0.02549	0.00900	0.0042	0.9973
6	0.01648	.	0.0027	1.0000

resource curse, structural adjustment policies and failures, and the continuing failure to observe increases in wealth translating into increases in the well-being of populations. Solutions to the development question vary from political to economic, with shifting arguments surrounding everything from institutional development and democratization to economic restructuring, micro-lending, and oil stabilization funds.

Therefore, and given our results in terms of increases of wealth, consideration of the other side of the paradox of plenty issue lies with the issue of human development.

Our findings, in table 6.4, show that politics and not economics is the main determinant of human development. These results explain why so often (and it does not matter how much foreign investment a country receives) the outcome in terms of development does not seem to match the investment. Economic aid has a positive effect on human development when looking at the overall results but has a negative effect when focusing on oil-producing countries. International organizations can take stock of this information when deciding how to direct their resources.

Regarding the political variables, both RPE and RPR have the expected signs when analyzing the whole sample, although RPR has a lower standard error. When the sample is divided between oil and non-oil-producers, a political story unfolds. Oil-producing countries seem to have lost much of the leverage to foster human development; RPE is not significant but RPR is. It is in the countries that have no oil and are at much lower level of economic wealth where politics can really make an impact, especially if foreign aid is properly utilized. This result indicates that the drivers to development are very much dependent on internal factors.

Equation 2: Infant Mortality = RPE + RPR + Year + Income Inflows + Oil Production + Error

Efficient governments that are able to enact their policy preferences are much more likely to effectively impact development. Essentially, governments need to be both horizontally (reach) and vertically (extraction) capable in order to facilitate development efforts. As posited in the previous section, political mobilization seems to be a precursor to efficiency, but existing in conjunction is an important part of ameliorating low levels of human development.

The most substantial influence is the political reach variable. Theoretically, this is very consistent with levels of development in Africa. In order for a government to deliver services and aid, they need to be able to distribute, advertise, and generally be relevant in the population's daily lives. Governments lacking political reach are unable to provide access or information to a population that can make real differences. One of the largest

Table 6.4. Human Development and Oil Production

Dependent Variable *Infant Mortality*	*Model 1:* *Whole Sample*	*Model 2:* *Oil Producers*[1]	*Model 3:* Non-Oil-Producers
Political Extraction	−6.23* (1.95)	5.45 (3.36)	−9.17** (2.41)
Political Reach	**14.86** (2.76)	−15.87* (4.89)	−16.89** (3.27)
Year	−1.35** (0.091)	−.609** (0.17)	−1.54** (0.11)
Investment: FDI	2.56 (3.66)	4.49 (5.67)	−0.009 (4.71)
Foreign Aid	−0.058** (0.02)	0.075* (0.037)	−0.095** (0.023)
Oil Production	−0.019** (0.002)	−0.012** (0.0028)	−473.66* (167.31)
Constant	2821.87** (180.51)	−1310.53** (343.55)	3195.76 (212.09)
Adjusted R. Sq.	.1847	.106	.2241
Sample Size	1529	500	1029

** Significant at the .0001 level
* Significant at the .005 level

1. Note, we define oil producers as the countries that produce more than 0.2 barrels of oil per day on average.

challenges in addressing poverty and development challenges in Africa is getting the population to "listen" to the government.

In terms of development for Africa, these findings are striking. Increasing economic resources externally is not a solution that will result in measureable differences in the quality of life throughout Africa. The solution to the development puzzle lies in political capacity: first in terms of political mobilization, and then in terms of political extraction. In the case of human development, the resource curse seems to stand; the oil-producing countries have very few levers to induce change.

CONCLUSIONS

Oil has been a blessing and a curse for developing countries. Economic growth gives African countries with oil resources the opportunity to offer better living conditions to their population. However, the story of Africa is the story of missed opportunity. Oil and mineral exporters need to be mindful of capitalizing on their good luck, making sure that the gains spill over to the rest of the system, while at the same time making sure they avoid problems often found with Dutch Disease.

Missed opportunity is the curse of oil development, where human development improvements do not follow the same positive path as economic growth. In fact, the standard tools used to facilitate growth from external sources seem to make human development worse.

It is clear that we cannot address human development in a vacuum. Increasing the overall resources per individual is the most important component in increasing human development. For countries that possess resources, governance becomes incredibly important. Economic development and human development issues require consideration in conjunction with each other. This in part explains the contradictory discussions surrounding the resource curse, and illustrates the challenge in both managing wealth and attempting to escape the trap of poverty. Governance or political performance becomes critical when countries are on the precipice of the development trap—those that have a mobilized population are likely to realize real gains, while those that do not are not likely to achieve an increase in quality of life for the population.

There is a bleak side to this picture: without mobilizing the population, countries without resources appear to be growing from a base of economic development that is simply too low to facilitate gains from either aid or investment. Without the necessary domestic capacity to utilize international resources, development efforts are likely futile. These countries are likely to remain in a development trap—evidenced by poverty and failure to meet the basic needs of the bulk of the population. The most salient and immediately obvious conclusion from these models is that politics is a critical companion for development.

NOTES

1. See also Leite and Weidman (1999), Bravo-Ortega and De Gregorio (2005), Auty (1990), and Gelb (1988).

2. Ali and Elbadawi (2002) identify two approaches to managing economies under colonial powers: in the first approach populations and industries are subsidized heavily in the hope that they eventually will become efficient (long-term colonizers); the second includes economies based on an "extract and export model" (the short-term colonizers). Adoption of the first approach by a number of African countries resulted in inefficient industries and social programs that could not be supported in the long term.

3. Twelve of the world's twenty-five most mineral-dependent states, and six of the most oil dependent, are classified by the World Bank as Highly Indebted Poor

Countries. Furthermore, it has been established that oil production is correlated with higher debt and increase in oil exports. Some of the reasons for this correlation are: an increase of direct investments, fiscal irresponsibility, and increased volatility of oil prices.

4. Telling examples include bauxite production in Caribbean countries, where discoveries of additional bauxite resources coupled with a decline in global demand during the 1970s were disastrous for countries that had made borrowing and expenditure decisions based on projections of continued growth in bauxite consumption. An additional parallel example is the production and extraction of copper in Mongolia, which enjoyed a period of unprecedented economic euphoria prior to the 2008 financial crisis, only to experience severe economic contraction as international demand fell.

5. GDP per capita data averages are calculated from GDP in 1990 constant dollars. The data are from the Penn World Tables (Summers and Heston 2000) and the World Development Indicators.

6. The trends show that oil exporters are performing slightly better than non-oil exporters in overall GDP growth, 5.3 percent for the last compared to 4.8 percent for total Africa (Jerome 2007).

7. For example, the oil stabilization fund in Norway.

8. Contract Intensive Money is often used as an indicator of trust and performance of institutions, as it does indicate willingness of a population to trust enforcement mechanisms and property rights within a given society.

9. Where
Economic development = GDP per capita (constant 2000 dollars)
Political extraction = level of rpe
Political Reach = level of rpr
Year = Temporal control
Income flows: Investment = FDI/GDP and Aid = foreign aid per capita
Oil = Oil production in barrels per day
Human Development = Infant Mortality Rates

10. Note that the adjusted R2 in all three models is below 20 percent. Also note that there are no lagged variables included.

REFERENCES

Abouharb, M. R., and A. L. Kimball. 2007. "A New Dataset on Infant Mortality Rates 1816– 2002." *Journal of Peace Research* 44 (6): 743–54.

Ali, Abden Gadir. 2000. "Can the Sudan Reduce Poverty by Half by the Year 2015?" Arab Planning Institute.

Ali, A.G., and I. Elbadawi. 2002. "Poverty in the Arab World: The Role of Inequality and Growth," in Ismail Sirageldin (ed.), *Human Capital: Population Economics in the Middle East*. The American University in Cairo Press (An Economic Research Forum Edition): pp. 62–95.

Arbetman, Marina. 1990. "The Political Economy of Exchange Rate Fluctuations." PhD diss., Vanderbilt University.

Arbetman, Marina, and Kristin Johnson. 2008. "Relative Political Capacity Empirical and Theoretical Underpinnings." Paper presented at International Studies Association.

Arbetman, Marina, and Jacek Kugler. 1997. *Political Capacity and Economic Behavior*. Boulder, CO: Westview Press.

Arbetman-Rabinowitz, Marina, and Kristin Johnson. 2007. Relative Political Capacity: Empirical & Theoretical Underpinnings. Claremont Political Economy Workshop. Unpublished manuscript.

Auty, R.M.. 1990. *Resource-Based Industrialization: Sowing the Oil in Eight Developing Countries*. New York: Oxford University Press.

———. 1993. *Sustaining Development in Mineral Economies: The Resource Curse Thesis*. London: Routledge.

Banks, Arthur S. 2002. Cross-National Time-Series Data Archive. Databanks International.

Bannon, Ian, and Paul Collier, eds.. 2003. *Natural Resources and Violent Conflict— Options and Action*. Washington, DC: World Bank.

Basedau, Matthias. 2005. "Context Matters—ReThinking the Resource Curse in Sub-Saharan Africa." GIGA Working Paper No.1.

Beck, Nathaniel & Jonathan N. Katz. 2003. "Modeling dynamics in time-series-cross-section political economy data." Working Papers 1304, California Institute of Technology, Division of the Humanities and Social Sciences.

Bennell, P. 2003. The impact of the AIDS epidemic on schooling in sub-Saharan Africa. Paper presented at the Association for the Development of Education in Africa ADEA Biennial Meeting, Grand Baie, Mauritius, December 3–6.

Bradshaw, York W., and Zwelake Tshandu. 1990. "Foreign Capital Penetration, State Intervention, and Development in Sub-Saharan Africa." *International Studies Quarterly* 34 (2): 229–251.

Bravo-Ortega, Claudio, and Jose de Gregorio. 2005. "The relative richness of the poor? Natural resources, human capital, and economic growth." *Policy Research Working Paper Series* 3484, The World Bank.

Dixon, William, and Bruce Moon. 1985. "Domestic Political Conflict and Basic Needs Outcomes: An Empirical Assessment." *Comparative Political Studies* 22 (2): 178–98.

Feng, Yi, Jacek Kugler, and Paul Zak. 2000. "The Politics of Fertility and Economic Development." *International Studies Quarterly* 44: 667–93.

Gelb, Alan. 1988. *Oil Windfalls: Blessing or Curse?* New York: Oxford University Press.

Ghazvinian, John. 2007. *Untapped: The Scramble for Africa's Oil*. Orlando, FL: Harcourt Books.

Hayami, Yujiro, and Suzanne Akiyama 2003. From the Washington Consensus to the post-Washington Consensus: Recent Changes in the Paradigm of International Development Assistance. Foundation for Advanced Studies on International Development.

Heston, Alan, Robert Summers, and Bettina Aten. 2000. Penn World Table, Center for International Comparisons of Production, Income and Prices at the University of Pennsylvania.

IMF. 2008. Government Finance Statistics 2008. Washington, DC: International Monetary Fund.

Jerome, Afeikhena. 2007. "Managing Oil Rent for Sustainable Development and Poverty Reduction in Africa." UNU-WIDER Jubilee Conference, Thinking Ahead: The Future of Development Economics.

Karl, Terry Lynn. 1997. *Paradox of Plenty—Oil Booms and Petro States*. Berkeley: University of California Press.

Kutner, Michael, Chris Nachtsheim, and John Neter. 2004. Applied Linear Regression Models, 4th edition. New York: McGraw-Hill.

Lay, Jann, and Mahmoud Toman Omar. 2005. "The Resource Curse at Work: A Cross Country Perspective with a Focus on Africa." Mattias Basedau and Andreas Mehmet, eds., *Resource Politics in Sub-Saharan Africa*. Hamburg: Institute of African Affairs.

Leite, Carlos, and Jens Weidman. 1999. "Does Mother Nature Corrupt? Natural Resources, Corruption, and Economic Growth." *International Monetary Fund Working Paper*. 99/85.

London, Bruce, and Bruce A. Williams. 1988. "Multinational Corporation Penetration, Protest, and Basic Needs Provision in Non-Core Nations: A Cross National Analysis." *Social Forces* 66 (3): 747–773.

Mendoza, Ronald, Ryan Jones, and Gabriel Vergara. 2009. "Will the global financial crisis lead to lower foreign aid? A first look at United States ODA." *Fordham Economics Discussion Paper Series* dp2009–01, Fordham University, Department of Economics.

Moon, Bruce E., and William J. Dixon. 1985. "Politics, the State, and Basic Human Needs: A Cross National Study." *American Journal of Political Science* 29: 661–94.

Morris, Morris David. 1979. *Measuring the Condition of the World's Poor: The Physical Quality of Life Index*. London: Cass.

NCHS. 2005. National Center for Health Statistics 2005. The Centers for Disease Control. http://www.cdc.gov/nchs/.

Organksi, A. F. K., and Jacek Kugler. 1980. *The War Ledger*. Chicago: University of Chicago Press.

Pritchett, Lant. 2000. "Understanding Patterns of Economic Growth: Searching for Hills among Plateaus, Mountains, and Plains," *World Bank Economic Review*, 14 (2).

Rodrick, Dani. 2000. "Institutions for High-Quality Growth: What they are and how to acquire them." *Studies in Comparative International Development* 35 (3): 3–31.

Ross, Michael L. 2003. "The Natural Resource Curse: How Wealth Can Make You Poor." Ian Bannion and Paul Collier, eds., *Natural Resources and Violent Conflict—Options and Action*. Washington, DC: World Bank.

Sachs, Jeffrey D., and Andrew M. Warner. 1997. "Sources of Slow Growth in African Economies." *Journal of African Economies* 6 (3): 335–76.

Shin, Doh C. 1979. "The Concept of Quality of Life and the Evaluation of Developmental Effort: Some Applications to South Korea." *Comparative Politics* 11 (3): 299–318.

Summers, Alan, and Michael Heston. 2000. Penn World Tables.

Thurlow, James and Peter Wobst. 2006. "Not All Growth is Equally Good for the Poor: The Case of Zambia." *Journal of African Economies* 15 (4): 603–625.

UNCEA (United Nations Economic Commission for Africa). 2004. Africa: Statbase. United Nations: New York. http://new.uneca.org/acs/home_acs.aspx

UNCTAD. 2007. *UNCTAD Handbook of Statistics 2007*. United Nations Conference on Trade and Development. New York: United Nations.

UNCTAD. 2009. *UNCTAD Handbook of Statistics 2009*. United Nations Conference on Trade and Development. New York: United Nations.

UNICEF. 2005. The State of the World's Children 2005—Childhood under threat. http://www.unicef.org/publications/index_24432.html.

United Nations Development Project. 2007. The Human Development Index.

Vidal, John. 2004. "The Oil Grab." *The Guardian*, 8 October 2004.

World Bank. 2007. The World Development Indicators. Washington, DC: World Bank.

World Bank and International Finance Corporation. 2002. "Treasure or Trouble? Mining in Developing Countries." Washington, DC: World Bank, Mining Department.

World Development Indicators. 2008. devdata.worldbank.org/dataonline.

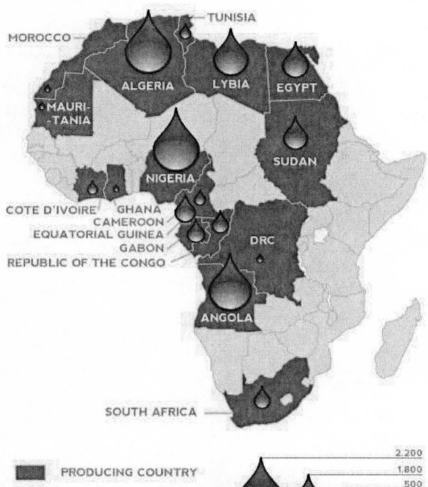

Appendix 6.1.   Oil Resources in Africa. Source: Catholic Relief Services, www.crs.org

Appendix 6.2. Diverging Economic Problems

GDP Growth	1998–2004	2005	2006(e)	2007(p)	2008(p)
Total Africa	4.0	5.2	6.3	6.0	6.0
Net Oil exporters	4.5	5.9	6.0	7.4	6.3
Net Oil importers	3.6	4.7	5.1	4.7	4.7
CPI Inflation					
Total Africa	10.0	8.8	9.1	9.2	9.5
Net Oil exporters	11.6	9.4	5.7	5.3	5.3
Net Oil importers	8.8	8.4	12.0	12.7	12.9
Fiscal Balance					
Total Africa	− 2.0	2.4	3.2	2.7	2.0
Net Oil exporters	− 0.8	7.0	8.2	7.3	6.4
Net Oil importers	− 3.1	− 1.9	− 2.3	− 2.2	− 2.4
Trade Balance					
Total Africa	1.8	6.7	7.8	7.6	6.6
Net Oil exporters	7.5	20.3	21.3	20.6	19.4
Net Oil importers	− 3.4	− 6.2	− 6.5	− 6.2	− 6.8

Source: Jerome 2007

Appendix 6.3.   Sample, Variables, and Data Sources

The sample includes fifty-three African countries for the period 1960–2007. Panels are incomplete for Eritrea, Comoros, and Canary Islands.

VARIABLES AND DATA

GDP per Capita: GDP per capita is measured in constant 2000 dollars. The base series used is from the World Bank (2008). In order to complete the series, overlapping series including the World Development Indicators (1960–2005), Penn World Tables (Heston, Summers and Aten 2000), and national sources. For complete reference see general appendix.

RPE: RPE is estimated by the actual value of extraction divided by the predicted level of extraction for a given country in a given year. In this case, a regional estimation (including all fifty-three African countries) for the time period included was estimated using a model for developing countries and omitting the control for oil. For more information on the estimation of RPC, see Organski and Kugler (1980), Arbetman and Kugler (1997), and for the specific data set used Arbetman and Johnson (2008).

RPR: RPR is estimated by the actual working population divided by the predicted size of the workforce controlling for level of economic development and demographic distribution. Economically Active Population (EAP) data is from the International Labor Organization (ILO), WDI, and national sources where data was lacking. For complete reference see general appendix.

Year: 1960–2007 Year is a temporal control.

Oil: Oil is the crude oil production in thousands of barrels per day. The data is from INDEXMUNDI.com/energy; UN online sources; IEA Oil Information 1999/1998 edition; *Oil Economist Handbook,* 5th edition, volume 1; Table of BP Statistical Review of the World Industry 1961, 1971, 1981, 1989; BP Statistical Review of World Energy Historical Data 1965–2007. Where data was lacking we used national sources.

Infant Mortality: Infant mortality is the rate per thousand that babies less than a year old die. The base data set was developed by M. R. Abouharb and A. L. Kimball (2007). We supplemented using national sources, WDI Human Development indicators, UNICEF (2005), NCHS (2005), and UNCEA (2004) and national sources.

Investment: Investment is the ratio of FDI/GDP. The data was obtained from UNCTAD (2007), Bennell (2003), the IMF Country Reports' Statistical Annexes. Where data was lacking we used national sources.

Foreign Aid: Foreign aid is foreign aid per capita from the World Development Indicators (2008) online data set.

Appendix 6.4. VIF and Robust Regression as Diagnostics

Variance Inflation and Decomposition (VIF) calculates how much collinearity increases the variance of a coefficient using an index (Kutner, Nachtsheim, and Neter 2004). In other words, the square root of the VIF indicates how much larger a standard error is than it would be if all variables in an estimation were uncorrelated. Generally, a VIF of higher than 10 indicates significant problems with multicollinearity, although Kutner at al. suggest that a value of 5 is still excessive In this case, the VIF values are well below 5, demonstrating little problem with multicollinearity in the estimation. Robust regression works by estimating the original model, running Cooks values on observations, dropping any that exceed 1, and re-estimating the model (Beck and Katz 2003). Robust regression is used as it is a good check on if particular observations have excessive leverage on the results or if outliers are driving the findings.

From table 6.1: GDPCAP = f(RPR, RPE, FDI, Oil, Aid, Year

Variable	VIF	1/VIF
RPR	1.11	0.896911
RPE	1.09	0.914092
FDI	1.14	0.873584
Oil Production	1.12	0.895995
Aid	1.06	0.939620
Year	1.05	0.955490
Mean VIF	1.10	

Linear regression, correlated panels corrected standard errors (PCSEs)

Group Variable: code — Number of obs = 1529
Time variable: year — Number of groups = 48
Panels: correlated (unbalanced) — Obs per group: min = 10
Autocorrelation: no autocorrelation — avg = 31.85417
Sigma computed by casewise selection — max = 45
Estimated covariances = 1176 — R-squared = 0.1649
Estimated autocorrelations = 0 — Wald chi2(6) = 148.67
Estimated coefficients = 7 Prob > chi2 = 0.000 — Prob > chi2 = 0.000

GDPcap	Coef.	Panel-Corrected Std. Err.	z	P>|z|	[95% Conf. Interval]	
RPE	111.3813	58.47525	1.90	0.057	− 3.228105	225.9907
RPR	177.7538	87.99185	2.02	0.043	5.292945	350.2147
FDI	500.4619	188.0258	2.66	0.008	131.9381	868.9858
AID	3.527589	1.321573	2.67	0.008	.93735396	.117825
Oil Product	.9270852	.1074997	8.62	0.000	.71638951	.137781
Year	6.375545	1.870065	3.41	0.001	2.710285	10.0408
cons	− 12564.39	3656.069	− 3.44	0.001	− 19730.16	− 5398.631

Appendix 6.4.   (Continued)

From table 6.2: Human Development (Infant Mortality) = f(RPR, RPE, FDI, AID, Oil Prod, Year)

Variable	VIF	1/VIF
RPR	1.11	0.896911
RPE	1.09	0.914092
FDI	1.14	0.873584
Oil Production	1.12	0.895995
Aid	1.06	0.939620
Year	1.05	0.955490
Mean VIF	1.10	

Number of gaps in sample: 3
xtpcse inf_mort var10 rpr2_af year fdi_gdp aidcap_cous oilp, rhotype(dw)
Number of gaps in sample: 3
Linear regression, correlated panels corrected standard errors (PCSEs)

Group variable: code	Number of obs = 1529
Time variable: year	Number of groups = 48
Panels: correlated (unbalanced)	Obs per group: min = 10
Autocorrelation: no autocorrelation	avg = 31.85417
Sigma computed by casewise selection	max = 45
Estimated covariances = 1176	R-squared = 0.1879
Estimated autocorrelations = 0	Wald chi2(6) = 1399.95
Estimated coefficients = 7	Prob > chi2 = 0.0000

Inf Mort	Coef.	Panel-Corrected Std. Err.	z	P>|z|	[95% Conf. Interval]	
RPE	−6.227413	1.131984	−5.50	0.000	−8.44606	−4.008766
RPR	−14.86167	1.909889	−7.78	0.000	−18.60499	−11.11836
FDI	2.564955	4.045589	0.63	0.526	−5.364253	10.49416
AID	−.0577317	.0146992	−3.93	0.000	−.0865416	−.0289219
Oil Product	−.0191433	.0013738	−13.93	0.000	−.0218358	−.0164507
Year	−1.354743	.0695711	−19.47	0.000	−1.4911	−1.218386
Cons	2821.87	138.4967	20.38	0.000	2550.421	3093.318

III

SUBNATIONAL PERFORMANCE

7

Following the Wisdom of Elders

Instability in China

Kristin Johnson, Marina Arbetman-Rabinowitz,
and Siddharth Swaminathan

CONTEXT

China's rapid rise as a global economic power has generated concerns about its internal stability. Whether or not China can maintain political and economic stability is of great interest not only to great powers but developing nations as well. Scholars have approached the stability question from many different directions. Brockmann, Delhay, Yuan, and Welzel (2008) look at the expectation gap in China's emerging middle class. Reilly (2006) focuses on income inequality while Yang (2007) looks at political and social dislocation and Pei (1995) tackles the important question of democratization. Whatever the perspective, internal stability is the foundational concern.

In order to pin down the nature of internal instability in China, we will use a subnational approach. Scholars have concluded that political violence within China generally is a local phenomenon, thus amenable to a subnational analysis (Wallace 2010). This analytical technique is appropriate due to the relative levels of autonomy in provinces and the relevance of local political entities as salient political units in the distribution of goods despite the authoritarian and centralized nature of the Chinese government (Hoggard 1967; Kolaweski 1981; Yep and Fong 2009; Wallace 2010). At a minimum, this approach complements more aggregate studies of internal violence in China, providing insights into variance in provinces with otherwise similar profiles.

The Chinese case presents a dilemma: qualitative and empirical observations indicate that increasingly severe violence is concentrated in rural areas, primarily between subsistence-level farmers or peasant populations and local authorities. But existing theoretical work—including economic theories of civil conflict (Collier and Hoeffler 2001), gaps in political authority (Fearon and Laitin 2003), relative deprivation theory (Gurr 1970), and urban social mobilization and revolution (Downs 1989)—fails to adequately explain this process. In part, it is likely that these theoretical approaches lack explanatory power due to the localized nature of conflict in China. They do not explain how local government officials destroy means of livelihood nor do they explain how a lack of measures for political redress or economic compensation exacerbates violence between individuals and local leaders.

We posit that the concept of social exclusion (Li 2009; Burchardt, Le Grand, and Piachaud 2002), where particular populations lack access to social opportunities, resources, or entitlements in a given society, better explains violence in China. Social exclusion is difficult to operationalize, and historically suffers from a lack of comparability across populations. We argue that Relative Political Reach provides a nonnormative and comparable measure of social exclusion: in regions where government involvement in the daily lives of the population is low, the social structure provided by the government and institutions is unable to furnish or yield expected benefits and services to the population. In the context of China, this is particularly important. Social and cultural mobilization historically serves as a key facet of social organization in China.

Our analysis includes controls for associated explanatory factors of internal conflict including political extraction, urban population, income per capita, and prior levels of conflict in a region. We find a significant negative relationship between political reach and the severity of violence in a province.

The results suggest that China would be well served by following policy objectives of its historic leaders: do not neglect the rural and peasant populations. Despite claims to the contrary, including a 1994 tax reform, trends in Chinese policy have been to reward and increase rewards to provinces where economic success is evident (World Bank 1998; Yep and Fong 2009). In anticipating and minimizing violence, China's policy makers should listen to the wisdom of their elders and increase the relevance of the government in the places where it is least present.

INTELLECTUAL ENVIRONMENT

Numerous studies of political violence and instability have identified aspects of political or economic exclusion as contributing factors to the choice to engage in conflict. Gurr's (1970) work on relative deprivation argues that the gap between rising expectations and realized gains explains the choice of individuals to engage in conflict; however, this theory more accurately describes inclusion failures other than the process of exclusion. Ethnic, religious, and identity-based conflicts are often attributed to institutional or political exclusion based on politicized identity and/or geographic underrepresentation (Toft 2003).

Studies focusing on the relationship between political repression and democracy and conflict cite a lack of access to political voice and goods provided by the state as integral to the choice to rebel (Moore 2000; Saxton 2005). Each of these arguments is composed of, at least in part, the notion that aspects of exclusion from social networks, political access, or economic resources contribute to political violence and instability. Despite our intent to explain political violence on a smaller scale than many of the studies listed above, the common element of exclusion is where our focus is centered. We find that theories of social exclusion provide a sound explanation for the motivation for violence across populations.

A relatively new theory, social exclusion has its roots in studies examining increasing inequality in the United States and Western Europe in the 1970s (Sen 1997; Silver 1994, 2007). Generally, the concept of social exclusion refers to a gap in the extension of social, political, or economic rights to a population (Silver 1994), the lack of or dissolution of social or cultural bonds (Loury 1999; Sen 1997), or a lack of access to economic resources (Rodgers, Gore, and Figueiredo 1995). Traditionally focusing on either the social dislocation caused by disruptions in social networks, specific discrimination as the result of policy or institutional practice, or established hierarchies that concentrate economic deprivation within particular populations, social exclusion is often criticized for its conceptual slipperiness (Rodgers, Gore, and Figueiredo 1995).

More recent work suggests that social exclusion is often a multidimensional and dynamic process composed of various aspects of each of the above characteristics (Silver 2007). For example, a lack of access to political rights can result in a failure to realize resources or affect policy; a lack of access to economic resources can result in political irrelevance or social exclusion as a product of lack of funds for schooling, health care, or other social services. These relationships emphasize only a few ways in which social, political, and economic exclusion can have ripple effects.

Social exclusion can be distinguished from repression in several ways. First, studies of repression tend not to be comparative across populations and instead focus on the ability of individuals to influence or make appeals to the government. Repressed populations experience the government as extremely relevant in the regulation of behavior and suppression of desired activities. Socially excluded populations experience a lack of involvement by the government in their daily lives. Social exclusion is typically an externality, resulting as a consequence of other policy decisions.

Conversely, repression is typically overt or intentioned exclusion and can exist as a consequence of ongoing rivalry between competing groups. In other words, social exclusion precludes building social capital and networks that build cultural cohesion and civic engagement. Social exclusion can result in apathy and disengagement or, when livelihoods are more directly threatened, small-scale violence.

Attempts to operationalize the concept of social exclusion are often based on normative assessments that rely on the composition of a particular society's political culture or on the particular type of exclusion (political rights, lack of access to social services, etc.) within a society. While useful for specific analysis, this renders the concept difficult to use in cross-national comparisons and across studies. We argue that the concept of relative political reach (RPR) captures the assumptions behind theories of social exclusion. RPR is a relative measure that indicates the degree to which the government is involved in the daily lives of a population.

We suggest that populations where the government is not relevant or present in a meaningful daily way are experiencing social exclusion across multiple dimensions; they do not have access to the benefits and services provided by the government, they often have little say in the formulation of policy, and their social networks are not integrated into local governmental institutions. Even within states, RPR should be somewhat varied, particularly in countries with high regional variance in economic or other development. Due to its relative nature, values of RPR are inherently comparative and provide a useful tool for beginning comparisons of social exclusion. In this paper, we posit that in Chinese provinces where RPR is lower, violence is more likely to occur.

VIOLENCE IN CHINA

Political instability and violence in China have long been recognized as appropriately examined at the subnational level (Kolaweski 1981). The relative levels of autonomy in provinces, vast size of China, and differences in provincial economies and populations justify assessment of violence from this level of analysis (Hoggard 1967; Kolaweski 1981; Yep and Fong 2009; Wallace 2010). For example, five of China's thirty-one provinces are designated as "autonomous regions" where the regional cultural practices and language are afforded protected status.[1] In addition, despite centralization, tax efforts and transfers from the central government to provinces are not equitably distributed (World Bank 2002; Shih and Qi 2007).

China is characterized by a transfer system that has historically made allocation decisions based on considerations other than population and apparent need, with a structure that passes along deficits to subnational governments. Essentially, the central government requires provinces to administer required and often unfunded programs without accounting for the necessary allocation.

In this system, provinces are faced with tough choices: either raise rents in other ways or become increasingly politically savvy to extract a greater number of transfers in the future. In some instances the fiscal stress on provinces is untenable because standard expenditures exceed standard collections. The 1994 tax reform intended to compensate provinces for shortcomings in the elaborate transfer system by changing existing tax structures to include rebates for value-added, consumption, and resource taxes (Fan, Kanbur, and Zhang 2009). However, these reforms failed to reach their desired goals. In studies of 1995 and 2000 subsidies, the World Bank found that there is a consistent and established relationship that continues between the level of revenue collection and subsidies received from the central government (Shinn and Zhang 2009).

In a study of land conflicts among peasant populations in China, Yep and Fong (2009) find that localities that fail to attract sufficient numbers of transfers are more likely to seek rents by terminating land leases and offering the land for sale. For example, in 2005 in Guangdong province, only 27 percent of budgetary revenue was available for satisfying mandated policies, compared to a more average 46 percent in Shangdong (Yep and Fong 2009).

Not surprisingly, Guangdong province also generates large revenues from land lease abrogation; in 2005 they generated 1,584 million yuan, or approximately 232 million U.S. dollars, to cover revenue shortfalls (Yep and Fong 2009). Wallace (2010) suggests that this trend slightly declined in the mid-2000s as the Chinese government recognized that increasing threats to security are located in rural areas characterized by a lack of transfers. However, the process in which the reach of provincial government impacts violence is still largely unexamined.

RELATIVE POLITICAL REACH AS A MEASURE OF SOCIAL EXCLUSION

The mobilization or reach of the government is likely to be the most important facet in explaining conflict in China. Provinces where the government is more directly involved in the daily lives of the population are less likely to experience extensive upheaval when resource shortfalls occur. Individuals may still experience disenfranchisement, but an active and mobilized population that deems itself politically relevant will seek redress through government channels as well as secure alternate social support and services from provincial governments.

Measuring social mobilization has been a challenge for researchers. Relative political reach measures the degree to which the population accepts the presence of government in their lives; societies characterized by little trust in government and elites are more likely to actively avoid the government, cutting out involvement in economic and other interactions. Human resources in a population are important not only because they will produce more in terms of increasing national power but also because they can be mobilized to support the agendas of policy makers, including the choice to go to war or to make significant economic reforms (Arbetman 1990).

Relative political reach measures the degree the government is involved in economic activities of the population relative to the expected degree of involvement given the education and employment of the population. The conceptual groundwork for this measure can be found in Organski (1958) and was initially modeled and expanded by Arbetman (1990) with operationalization and model refinements by Arbetman and Johnson (2008a, 2008b, 2009).

In a context where the population trusts the government, the involvement of government decreases transaction costs and provides benefits in the form of services and social organization that outweigh imposed costs including taxation. In China, regions with low levels of political mobilization can also be described as regions experiencing high levels of social exclusion.

Application of the logic of social exclusion to urban violence in Latin America lends empirical support to our theoretical extension of the concept and the relationship between rising levels of exclusion and the occurrence of violence (Berkman 2007; Koonings and Kruijt 2007). In China, political mobilization is also a cultural phenomenon; populations that exist outside the formal sector are also excluded from the political hierarchy and many benefits including education, health care, and other social welfare programs.

At the moment, violence is not an overwhelming concern in China, although trends in the region are of increasing instability. Understanding the contributing factors can facilitate the design and implementation of proactive policies. These policy considerations merit particular emphasis as China experiences political and economic change.

We model the effect of social exclusion on the severity of violence by hypothesizing that governments with high political mobilization will be able to control instability. We utilize relative political reach as an indicator of social exclusion. To test this proposition, we use the model in this endnote.[2]

CONCEPTS

Violence

Violence is defined as the number of deaths from conflicts between individuals and military, police, or public safety officials in a province.[3] Violence or the severity of conflict can be measured in numerous ways. Categorical assessments that include other forms of instability such as riots, demonstrations, strikes, and other forms of protest are available for limited time series and are weighted aggregate measures that have not been collected at the subnational analysis. The methodology used by the traditional source typically requires a higher incident threshold in order to be calculated (Taylor and Jodice 1983; Banks 2002; Goldstone et al. 2000).

Other existing measures of violence rely on assessments of number killed in combat (excluding nonmilitary fatalities) but are again nationally aggregated data that report selected years. These sources include the Correlates of War intrastate conflict data from the University of Michigan, which includes conflicts where at least one thousand have died, and the new Armed Conflict Database from the Peace Research Institute that includes aggregated data where more than twenty-five deaths have occurred.

In order to obtain provincial-level data over time, we adopted the Armed Conflict Database description for conflict. National sources, including government statistical reporting; news sources; and human rights organizations were used to locate the province or state in which the violence occurred and the total number of deaths. Inclusion required at least two separate media reports of casualties. Where numbers conflicted, the more reliable source was utilized or, barring a difference in information quality, casualties for a province were averaged. Precedents to this measure and approach for provincial-level conflict in China can be found in multiple studies including Hoggard (1967) and Kolaweski (1981), which used compilations of Facts on File, the *London Times*, Keesing's Contemporary, and the *New York Times* Index to form their data sets.

The total number of deaths in a province per year is the most appropriate dependent variable in this context, avoiding the difficulties accrued in establishing minimal levels of conflict for inclusion. Several advantages are garnered from this approach as well. First, this operationalization of civil conflict, since it is inclusive of lower levels of violence, is consistent with an examination of the relationship between micro-level behavioral explanations and the occurrence of civil conflict. In addition, assessing trends over time allows for smaller changes to be recognized. Finally, evaluation of lower levels of conflict makes much more sense in a subnational context, where the overall numbers of deaths in regions are much more likely to be small.[4]

Urban Population

Two theoretical traditions informed the debate on the urban or rural populations in civil conflicts. First, some contend that rural populations are less subject to the purview of government control and are more able to mount opposition efforts. Second, scholars of social mobilization and revolution argue that social movements and revolutionary efforts are born in urban environments.

In 1980, 19.6 percent of China's population was urban; by 2007 this number had reached 41.4 percent (WDI 2008). Compared to developed countries where urbanization ranges from 80 percent to 95 percent, the level of urbanization in China is low, but the increase in the past twenty years has been substantial. We include a measure of the percentage of urban population in order to determine where instability is located in China and to control for the potential effect of this demographic shift.

Political Reach

For China, we estimate political reach in the following way:

$$\text{EMPLOYED/POP} = \text{SECONDARY ENRL/POP} + \text{BUREAUCRACY/} \\ \text{POP} + \text{AGE014/POP} + \text{GDPperCapita}[5]$$

where political reach is the actual employed population/predicted employed population.

In estimating the size of the likely employed labor force, some issues are important to consider. First, the percentage of the population with secondary education is likely to be reflected in employment. Secondary education constitutes an important level of human capital accumulation for formal employment in factories, manufacturing, and other services. Secondary education is important for the development of a skilled labor force that can perform tasks that require higher skilled training, written communication, and other basic skills. Thus, in developing countries, the employed population is likely larger where a higher percentage of the population is highly educated. This is particularly reflected in the fact that this type of employment occurs almost exclusively in the formal sector.

The size of the bureaucracy or number of government employees is also an important control for the political reach of the government. Large numbers of government employees also increase the size of the employed population, although in terms of productivity they might be considered underemployed but still under the purview of the government.

Political reach is a relative indicator; for this sample the range of RPR levels is from .7 to 1.3. Generally speaking, the higher the level of RPR, the greater the degree of political mobilization on the part of the government.

Political Extraction

We use a relative measure of political extraction as our control for state strength and to emphasize the importance of state capacity to realize transfers to minimize violence. Preceding research has found that states with higher levels of political extraction are likely to experience less severe conflict (Benson and Kugler 1998; Johnson 2007; Arbetman-Rabinowitz and Johnson 2009). A number of previous studies on civil conflict suggest that the strength of a province is important in explaining violence, particularly because weak provinces present both a lower opportunity cost to rebellion and in these areas there is more likely to be an authority gap.

Political extraction measures each of these situations. The transfer of resources from individuals to governments represents a willingness to relinquish individual wealth to the government, demonstrating either an acceptance of that government as legitimate on the part of the population or at least a tacit acceptance of the coercive mechanisms of the government.

In the case of China, the following model is used at the provincial level following RPE models used extensively at the national level:

$$\text{Tax revenue/GDP} = \text{Year} + \text{Exports/GDP} + \text{Agriculture/GDP} + \text{Oil} + \text{Error}^6$$

with the value for political extraction being the actual level of tax revenue divided by the predicted level.

This simple model for the estimation of RPE is appropriate in the context of China. Initially, there is substantial variance in revenue collection between provincial governments. A choice is required between the use of either revenues or fiscal transfers as the dependent variable. Revenues better represent the ability of a province to mobilize the available economic resources of the population. In addition, despite the 1994 tax revision that was meant to address disparity in resource allocation, subsidies are highly correlated with revenue collected from a given province rather than population size or level of poverty, reflected in data reported by the World Bank on fiscal transfers in 1995 and 2000 (Zhang, Li, and Cui 2005).

The temporal domain is important to control for in the case of China. Our analysis covers a period of substantive economic change within the country, including reforms and the expansion and development of industry in a number of areas. Differences between rural and urban areas have increased, and the economies of different regions have been influenced by variance in economic development strategies. In addition, tax reforms have impacted some regulations surrounding revenue collection, making it critical that we control for revenue extraction over time.

We also control for some key structural aspects of provincial economies. Provinces that are either exporting goods or extracting oil are able to realize revenues that do not require a politically capable government to increase fiscal pressure on the population.

Finally, we control for the agricultural contribution to provincial productivity. Agricultural goods are harder to tax, particularly when they are produced at subsistence levels by peasant populations.

GDP per Capita

GDP per capita is an important control as it describes the employment climate of the region. Most of the extant literature on civil conflict identifies income per person as the most critical explanatory factor in defining the opportunity cost of conflict (Collier and Hoeffler 2001; Fearon and Laitin 2003). We note that this measure is used in the two studies cited here at the national level rather than disaggregated to regions; however, it remains an important control in identifying the relative level of investment individuals have in the system. We use GDP per capita in constant 2000 dollars.[7]

Prior Conflict

The existing literature also establishes a robust relationship between levels of conflict in previous years and the current year (Fearon and Laitin 2003; Collier and Hoeffler 2001). We control for the difference in level of conflict from the prior year to the current year, capturing, instead of intensity, the relative change in conflict levels from year to year. We expand on the theoretical and empirical aspects of our estimations in the following section.

ESTIMATION AND RESULTS

The negative binomial model is the most appropriate model given the distribution of our data. The dependent variable, violence, is clustered in values in the lower ranges and zero inflated. Violence is a rare event, and modeling infrequently occurring values that occur independently of each other is appropriate for this estimation technique (Miaou and Lum 1993; Greene 2008, 2008). While it may seem that controlling for change in levels of violence violates this assumption, in fact the nature of our data is consistent with this. An examination of violence within provinces demonstrates that there are not consistent patterns between a single opposition group and the government in a particular locality. In fact, violence outbreaks are independent of each other, but are causally likely to be related (for example the land abrogation practice discussed in detail at the outset of the chapter). It is important we control for the change in violence; however, the model is appropriate as the data do not violate the model assumptions.

Our statistical results are recorded in this endnote.[8] We also report ordinary least squares (OLS) estimations for robustness checks and as a means of providing easily interpretable diagnostic checks on our model.

The results are consistent with our theoretical expectations. The fact that GDP per capita is barely significant and the coefficient is quite small indicates that there is little support for economic models of civil conflicts in China. The argument that economic growth insulates China from domestic violence is clearly limited. Between 1980 and 2007 China's GDP per capita in constant 2000 US$ grew 862 percent, and at the same time the intensity of violence has increased. We can conclude that for the case of China, explanations of instability using wealth as a proxy for the opportunity cost fail to offer a valid explanation.

We find no support for either theories of urban-based social revolution or theories maintaining that rural areas provide sanctuary for opposition groups. The fact that China is a rural country rapidly urbanizing does not have any influence on the level of violence since the measure of urban population is not significant. It should be noted that the process of urbanization is happening across all provinces to some degree.

The significant positive correlation between prior conflict and violence indicates that social exclusion in some areas may be persistent, suggesting systemic policy failures on the part of regional governments. We emphasize that while conflict may occur in the same province, it does not indicate that the same subpopulation is the epicenter of the instability. That persistence may indicate that during the tenure of a specific government, political mobilization may be lacking and therefore policies to minimize domestic instability could not be implemented.

Political extraction is not significant in our models, suggesting that violence is not a product of institutional inefficiency or gaps in authority. The strength of provincial governments can be an influential factor in mitigating violence, and this result is inconsistent with our previous research on subnational violence (Johnson 2007; Arbetman-Rabinowitz and Johnson 2008). We suspect that the nature of political violence in China explains our findings. Violence in China occurs between distinct and separate subsets of the population and authorities rather than as a collective opposition enterprise.

In instances where violence is a product of social exclusion, transfers from the central government are less salient than the political mobilization that provides conduits for redress. While we note in our discussion of prior conflict that spates of violence occur in provinces, these are not continued conflicts between a single opposition group and the government. Essentially, the nature of political violence in China explains the lack of results; out of the thirty-one provinces in China, more than seventeen have experienced significant violence (more than fifty deaths) in a single year. Simple correlations between the political reach and political extraction variables indicate that the level of correlation is very low (6.02 percent).

Our results support our hypothesis that higher levels of social exclusion contribute to the severity of violence. Political Reach is negative and significant (-12.14); for every unit increase in political reach, there is a 12.14 decline in the number of deaths in a given province year. In the case of a country as diverse and populous as China, particularly given levels of regional autonomy, emphasizing the role regional governments can play in eliminating practices of social exclusion is a priority. This result is very consistent with theories and empirical work on state building, where the political mobilization and reach of the government are both necessary and sufficient aspects of creating functioning political and economic institutions (Herbst 2000; Englebert 2000; Bates 2009).

Ethnic divisions in China, exemplified by increasing conflict between Uyghur populations and authorities in the province of Xinjiang in 2008 and 2009, are often by products of social exclusion. China does have five autonomous regions; however, the bulk of the Chinese population, 91 percent, is ethnically Han Chinese. We can argue that ethnic conflicts are the politicized product of social exclusion, rather than inherent to identity. In fact, even those attributing conflict to ethnic divisions identify the lack of inherent indigenous or native rights to land and the management of these lands as the root causes of conflicts.

CONCLUSIONS

To satisfy the short-term demands of policy and meet standards of living, provincial governments in China are compromising the social cohesion and wealth of future generations.

This chapter offers insights into the study of conflict at the subnational level in China as a process of social exclusion. Some evidence of social exclusion is clear simply from observations; policies that pass down debt and require towns to abrogate land lease agreements in order to realize revenues are a prescription for violence and fomenting rebellion.

Traditional policies of redistribution and social mobilization, cornerstones of China's historical political apparatus, are the best mechanism for ensuring stability in the long term. In other words, as China continues its radical economic growth initiatives and continues to transform economically and socio-politically, it would be well served to remember the peasant populations and maintain the political agenda of the past.

The temptation to invest in primarily revenue-generating regions may result in the creation of two Chinas—one mobilized, prosperous, and growing and one demobilized and dissatisfied. In addition, the government would be well served by substantially revisiting policies that decentralize and pass along deficits. Perhaps this is the most telling finding from this analysis.

Local governments forced to implement mandates without funding will pass the cost along to populations least likely to be politically relevant. Conflict becomes a product of being pushed out of the system further. Differentiation between urban and rural populations is not the solution in this context. While a systematic review of our violence data suggests that these are the locations in which violence is occurring, this is a product of social exclusion, not of rural residence.

In addition, China should pay attention to regions that are experiencing violent outbreaks. While these are not concentrated in single opposition efforts, what they do indicate is more widespread dissatisfaction with the existing system. Provinces that experience some level of conflict are more likely to be characterized by violence in the future. In terms of long-term stability for outlying regions and populations, this observation does offer a prescriptive approach for China's future stability. Looking into the future, China should also pay attention to levels of political reach in urban areas. A number of studies cite the emerging gender gap in China and the difficulty China faces with an estimated twenty-four million young urban men likely to remain single and potentially dissatisfied.

The results also have important implications for work on political performance. The results of this chapter demonstrate that political reach can effectively be used as an indicator of political mobilization. Intuitively, this makes sense: a population has to view the government as relevant in order to engage institutions in seeking social change. Governments seeking to increase their political capacity face a number of challenges. It may be that governments would be best served by creating incentives to increase the percent of the population employed in the formal sector of the economy. Individuals then incur the benefits of social inclusion as they begin to also make individual resource transfers to the governments, decreasing the opportunity cost of participation.

NOTES

1. China's autonomous regions include: Tibet, Ningxia, Xinjiang, Inner Mongolia, and Guangxi.

2. $\text{Violence}_{pt} = \text{RPE}_{pt} + \text{RPR}_{pt} + \text{Urban Population}_{pt} + \text{GDP per capita}_{pt} + \text{Prior Conflict}_{pt-1} + \text{Error}$

where:

$t = 1980–2007$

$p = \text{province } 1 \ldots 31$

$\text{RPE}_{pt} = \text{Relative political extraction of a province (see below)}$

RPR_{pt} = Relative political reach of a province (see below)
Urban Population$_{pt}$ = percentage of urban over total provincial population
GDP per Capita$_{pt}$ = Income per person in constant US$
Prior Conflict$_{pt-1}$ = Difference in conflict (t-1)-t

3. For additional information on the reliability of sources for the violence variable, see appendix 3 in Johnson 2007.

4. In order to avoid the inclusion of an excessive number of zeros, when in question, deaths for provinces at 0 levels of violence are coded as .001.

5. Several issues, *China National Statistics Yearbook*, China Statistics Press, National Bureau of Statistics of China.

6. See general appendix for variable definitions and sources.

7. See general appendix for variable definitions and sources

8. See table 7.1.

Table 7.1.   China: Political Capacity and Violence

Dependent Variable: Violence	OLS Model (N = 472)	Negative Binomial Model (N = 472)
Political Extraction	− 0.78	− 0.22
	(1.57)	(0.42)
Political Reach	− 33.46***	− 12.14***
	(6.97)	(2.48)
Urban Population	− 7.00**	− 0.91
	(2.10)	(0.60)
GDP per Capita	0.012***	0.001*
	(0.002)	(0.0008)
Prior Conflict	0.78***	0.064***
	(0.02)	(0.01)
Constant	33.71***	12.10***
	(7.18)	(2.70)
Adjusted R SQ.	.77	.57 (Pseudo)

*p<.05, **p<.01, ***p<.001

REFERENCES

Arbetman, Marina. 1990. "The Political Economy of Exchange Rate Fluctuations." PhD diss., Vanderbilt University.

Arbetman, Marina, and Kristin Johnson. 2008a. "Relative Political Capacity Empirical and Theoretical Underpinnings." Paper presented at International Studies Association.

———. 2008b. "Power Distribution and Oil in the Sudan: Will the Comprehensive Peace Agreement Turn the Oil Blessing into a Curse?" *International Interactions*. 34 (4): 382–401.

———. 2009. "Oil . . . Path to Prosperity or Poverty? Political Reach and Capacity in Africa." Paper presented at the Annual International Studies Convention, New York, February 2009.

Banks, Arthur S. 2002. Cross-National Time-Series Data Archive. Databanks International.

———. 2006. Cross National Times Series Data Archive.

Bates, Robert. 2009. *The Logic of State Failure: Learning from Late-Century Africa*. New York: Routledge.

Benson, Michelle, and Jacek Kugler 1998. "Power Parity, Democracy, and the Severity of Internal Violence." *The Journal of Conflict Resolution* 42 (2): 196–209.

Berkman, Heather L. 2007. "Social Exclusion and Violence in Latin America and the Caribbean." Inter-American Development Bank Research Department Working Paper No. 613.

Bhalla, Ajit, and Frederic Lapeyre. 1997. "Social Exclusion: Towards an Analytical and Operational Framework." *Development and Change* 28 (3): 413–33.

Brockmann, H., J. Delhay, H. Yuan, and C. Welzel. 2008. "The China Puzzle: Declining Happiness in a Rising Economy." World Values Survey Working Paper. Available at: margaux.grandvinum.se/SebTest/wvs/new_index_publications.

Burchardt, Tania, Julian Le Grand, and David Piachaud. 2002. "Degrees of exclusion: Developing a dynamic, multidimensional measure." In John Hills, Julian Le Grand, and David Piachaud (eds.), *Understanding social exclusion*. Oxford: Oxford University Press, pp. 30–43

Collier, Paul, and Hoefler, Anke. E. (2001). "On the incidence of civil war in Africa." *Journal of Conflict Resolution*, 46 (1): 13–28.

de Haan, Arjan, and Simon Maxwell. 1998. *Poverty and Social Exclusion in North and South*. Brighton: University of Sussex, Poverty Research Unit.

Downs, Charles. 1989. *Revolution at the Grassroots: Community Organizations in the Portuguese Revolution*. Albany: State University of New York Press.

Englebert, Pierre. 2000. "Pre-Colonial Institutions, Post-Colonial States, and Economic Development in Tropical Africa." *Political Research Quarterly* 53 (1): 1–30.

Fan, Sheggan, Ravi Kanbur, and Xiaobo Zhang. 2009. *Regional Inequality in China: Trends, Explanations & Policy Responses*. New York: Routledge

Fearon, James D., and David D. Laitin. 2003. "Ethnicity, Insurgency, and Civil War." *American Political Science Review* 97 (1): 75–90.

Figeroa, Aldolfo. 2002. "Social Exclusion and Rural Underdevelopment." Paper prepared for the workshop Social Exclusion and Poverty Reduction in Latin America, organized by the World Bank, Washington, D.C., May 26–27.

Goldstone, Jack A., Ted Robert Gurr, Barbara Harff, Marc A. Levy, Monty G. Marshall, Robert H. Bates, David L. Epstein, Colin H. Kahl, Pamela T. Surko, John C. Ulfelder, and Alan N. Unger in consultation with Matthew Christenson, Geoffrey D. Dabelko, Daniel C. Esty, and Thomas M. Parris. 2000. *State Failure Task Force Report: Phase III Findings*. McLean, VA: Science Applications International Corporation (SAIC).

Greene, William. 2008. *Econometric Analysis*. Upper Saddle River, New Jersey: Prentice Hall.

Gurr, Ted Robert. 1970. *Why Men Rebel*. Princeton: Princeton University Press.

Herbst, Jeffrey. 2000. *States and Power in Africa*. Princeton, NJ: Princeton University Press.

Hoggard, G. A. 1967. Comparison of reporting for the New York Times Index, Asian Recorder and Deadline Data: Chinese interactions, January through October, 1962. Mimeo.

Johnson, Kristin. 2007. "Sub National Capabilities and Internal Conflict." PhD diss., Claremont Graduate University, Claremont, CA.

Koonings, Kees, and Dirk Kruijt. 2007. *Fractured Cities: Social Exclusion, Urban Violence and Contested Spaces in Latin America*. New York: Macmillan.

Li, Linda Chelan. 2009. "Decision-Making in Chinese Local Administrative Reform: Path Dependence, Agency and Implementation." *Public Administration and Development* 29 (1): 79–87.

Loury, Glenn C. 1999. "Social Exclusion and Ethnic Groups: The Challenge to Economics." Annual World Bank Conference on Development Economics.

Miaou, S., and H. Lum. 1993. "Modeling vehicle, accidents and highway geometric design relationships." *Accident Analysis and Prevention* 25 (6): 689–709.

Moore, Will. 2000. "The Repression of Dissent: A Substitution Model of Government Coercion." *Journal of Conflict Resolution* 44 (1):107–12.

Organski, A. F. K. 1958. *World Politics*. Knopf: New York.

Pei, Minxin. 1995. "'Creeping' Democracy in China." *Journal of Democracy* 6 (4): 65–79.

Reilly, Benjamin. 2006. *Democracy and Diversity: Political Engineering in the Asia Pacific*. Oxford: Oxford University Press.

Rodgers, Gerry, Charles Gore, and Jose B. Figueiredo, eds. 1995. *Social Exclusion: Rhetoric, Reality, Responses*. Geneva: International Institute for Labour Studies.

Saxton, Greg. 2005. "Repression, Grievances, Mobilization and Rebellion: A New Test of Gurr's Model of Ethnopolitical Rebellion." *International Interactions* 31 (1): 87–11.

Sen, Amartya. 1997. "Inequality, Unemployment and Contemporary Europe." *International Labour Review* 136 (2): 155–72.

Shih, V., and Z. Qi. 2007. "Who Receives Subsidies? A Look at the County Level in Two Time Periods." V. Shue and C. Wong, eds., *Paying for Progress in China*. London: Routledge.

Silver, Hilary. 1994. "Social Exclusion and Social Solidarity: Three Paradigms." *International Labour Review* 133 (5–6): 531–78.

———. 2007. "The Process of Social Exclusion: The Dynamics of an Evolving Concept." CPRC Working Paper 95.

Taylor, Charles, and David Jodice. 1983. *World Handbook of Political and Social Indicators*. New Haven, CT: Yale University Press.

Toft, Monica Duffy. 2003. The Geography of Ethnic Violence: Identity, Interests, and the Indivisibility of Territory. Princeton, NJ: Princeton University Press.

Wallace, Jeremy. 2010. "Cities and Stability: Directing Urbanization, Defining Unrest, and Distributing Transfers in China." PhD diss. chapter.

World Bank. 2006. *China: Revitalizing the Northeast—Towards a Development Strategy.* Washington, DC: World Bank.

The World Development Indicators 1998. Washington DC, The World Bank. http://devdata.worldbank.org/dataonline.

The World Development Indicators 2002. Washington DC, The World Bank. http://devdata.worldbank.org/dataonline.

The World Development Indicators 2008. Washington DC, The World Bank. http://devdata.worldbank.org/dataonline.

Yang, Fenggang. 2007. "Cultural Dynamics in China: Today and in 2020." *Asia Policy* 4: 41–51.

Yep, Ray, and Carolin Fong. 2009. "Land Conflicts, Rural Finance and Capacity of the Chinese State." *Public Administration and Development* 29 (1): 69–78.

Zhang, W., X. Li, and H. Cui. 2005. *China's Inter-Census Survey in 2005.* Beijing: National Bureau of Statistics.

8

Will Foreign Aid Help Curb Terrorism in Pakistan?

Ayesha Umar-Wahedi and
Marina Arbetman-Rabinowitz

CONTEXT

Pakistan's descent toward a failed state has been exacerbated by growing violence, instability, and terrorist activities alongside severe economic dislocations. With constant news of explosions, suicide bombings, and politically motivated shootings, terror seems to have engulfed the entire nation.

The rapid spread of terrorism across the country has become a severe concern for not only the people and government of Pakistan but also the international community. Since the terrorist attacks of 9/11, more than $15 billion has poured in aid to Pakistan from the United States alone. The Obama administration approved another $7.5 billion in October of 2009, with a further commitment of five years of funding (Paul 2009). Secretary of State Clinton reiterated the offer during her visit to Pakistan in July of 2010.

With huge financial support pouring in, the inevitable question is: will foreign aid be successful in curbing political instability and terrorist activities in Pakistan, or is it the improvement in the political capabilities of the Pakistani government that is the key to stabilizing the region? Over recent years there have been concerns regarding the Pakistani government "keeping the Taliban at bay just enough to persuade American benefactors to keep their wallets open, thereby ensuring a lifeline for the country's mangled economy" (Paul 2009). These assessments stem from reports that document misspent funds along with cases where the funds may have directly landed in hands of the insurgent groups, thus worsening the problem of terrorism.

Pakistan is a country with a complex administrative set-up of four provinces, a capital territory, FATA (Federally Administered Tribal Areas), and de facto jurisdiction over Azad Kashmir and Northern Areas. Pakistan's provinces and regions have separate ethnic identities, languages, culture, and traditions.[1] This political fragmentation makes Pakistan an ideal breeding ground for terrorist activities. Aside from the ethnic divisions, Pakistan is also faced with tensions along the Shia/Sunni, secular/Islamist, urban/rural, educated/uneducated, native/muhajir (migrants from India at the time of partition) divisions, some of which have resulted in violent incidents.

FATA, which has been at the heart of instability in recent years, is a complex entity that has only been nominally controlled by the federal government of Pakistan. "FATA is composed of autonomous tribal agencies, and possesses isolated villages surrounded by rugged mountainous terrain—all of which create obstacles for administration by government" (Demkiv 2009). Moreover, FATA is one of the poorest regions in the country, with no infrastructure or political structure. To make matters worse, there is a significant Taliban presence, with the "Taliban serving as a de facto political and administrative authority in FATA" (Demkiv 2009). Hence, we argue that securing FATA is the most important policy goal with ramifications for the stability of the entire country.

Over recent years, the number of suicide bombings has risen significantly, and the spreading influence of Islamic militants across FATA, Baluchistan, and parts of Khyber-Pakhtun-Khwahas places the viability of Pakistan as a country at risk. The situation in FATA is particularly difficult since an authority vacuum has opened the door to the Taliban and Al-Qaeda to create a safe haven. Some have argued that Islamabad's lack of authority in FATA is the most important factor in pushing Pakistan toward a failed state status (Demkiv 2009). This grave picture focuses the question on whether political and economic disenfranchisement is one of the main contributing factors of the rapid spread of violence in Pakistan, and more specifically in FATA, and whether international or domestic forces will be able to contain this downward spiral through provision of aid.

A country with a turbulent past and a multitude of economic, political, and social challenges, Pakistan has experienced a severe worsening of its political and economic climate over the past decade. Neighboring Afghanistan has exported their own political problems and opened drug trafficking routes. The problems with India could reignite at any time, although there is evidence that both parties are engaged in an informally agreed-upon hiatus.

Being a nuclear power with an unstable leadership history and plagued by poverty, insurgency, and terrorism, Pakistan's future is a substantial cause of concern for the international community. Thus exploring the underlying causes of instability in Pakistan is a timely and critically important issue. Using data at the subnational level for Pakistan, this chapter is an attempt to search for levers to overcome one of the main bottlenecks for development—instability—and more fundamentally to address the question of whether economic aid is the answer to moderating the effects of domestic terrorism.

INTELLECTUAL ENVIRONMENT

There is an observable lack of institutional development in Pakistan. This in turn explains why economic development has lagged behind China or India. Even during periods of respectable economic growth, it has occurred without development. In this chapter we explore whether political instability and terrorism are the manifestations of the lack of political capacity.

We also argue that building capacity without a productive economic base might not be enough. If this is the case, external capital may be important, but is it the same in all provinces or are there distinctions to be made? Given these questions we will evaluate how external and internal forces of capacity building in Pakistan can foster stability, and how this may vary from province to province.

The economic consequences of foreign aid have been investigated extensively by scholars, without a unanimous agreement on the universal effects of the transfer of resources. Clearly foreign assistance has both political and social effects according to most scholars, but how much, where, and when remain open questions. According to neoclassical economic theory, aid contributes to growth by adding to the available stock of savings and investment.

In the simplest neoclassical growth models, for example, "the role of foreign savings of all kinds is to augment domestic savings to increase investment and thus accelerate growth" (Perkins et al. 2001, 414). However, there is a lack of robust findings on the impact of aid on economic development. Studies have reported diverse findings from a positive impact of aid on growth to aid being detrimental to growth and development, and from aid improving institutions to the destabilizing impact of aid on institutions.

In a foundational study that formed the basis of World Bank aid policies, Burnside and Dollar (2000, 2004) provided evidence that aid, in the presence of sound institutions, leads to economic growth in developing countries; however, in weak institutional settings, aid does not contribute to growth. This view is shared by a large number of analysts who argue that aid inflows in countries that lack institutional capacity do not lead to reform and instead may have negative consequences (Burnside and Dollar 2004; Collier 2004). In an earlier study Easterly (2003) questions the claim that aid can buy growth.

Others argue that "aid might be particularly associated with weak governance, possibly because aid inflows reduce the need for governments to tax the governed or enlist their cooperation" (Rajan and Subramanian 2007, 9). Similarly, a large number of studies have attempted to research the aid and growth connection; however, there is no unanimous agreement in literature on the impact of aid on growth. The study put forth by Oechslin (2006) provides a rationale for such differences in findings of the empirical literature and also forms the theoretical model for our study.

Collier (2004) revisits the issue of failures in development as a result of conflict, where conflict pertains to civil war. This study suggests a different approach at fostering stability and promoting economic development. Collier's approach calls for a wide range of instruments "including governance templates, trade preferences, strategies which squeeze the finances of rebel groups, and military interventions, besides increased aid" (Collier 2004).

Easterly (2001) investigates the issue of aid, growth, and development in Pakistan, which has depended on foreign aid for funding its development programs since its conception. He held that economic growth was not enough to bring about economic development and stability. This pattern was particularly relevant for Pakistan where periods of increases in economic growth did not translate into development despite both foreign aid and government programmatic support (Easterly 2001). Furthermore, the foreign aid programs as well as government initiatives did not have an impact on social progress. Thus, he concluded that "the Pakistan case illustrates the principle that the social payoff to foreign aid is low in a polarized society" that is divided along ethnic lines.

Another strand of literature looks at the connection between institutions and economic development. The proponents of this view argue that the quality of economic and political institutions is a major determinant of economic performance (North 1990; Rodrik et al. 2004; Acemoglu et al. 2001; Bardhan 2004).

The literature on economic consequences of aid fails to address the question if aid also plays a stabilizing role in politically volatile and violence prone settings, such as Pakistan. Before turning to that critical issue, however, first it is important to explore the theoretical foundations of terrorism. Multiple definitions of terrorism exist, but they do not make clear distinctions between terrorism, resistance, and military hostilities (Krueger and Maleckova 2003).

There are two central commonalities among the contemporary definitions of terrorism. The first is that "terrorism involves aggression against noncombatants" and the second stipulates that "the terrorist action in itself is not expected by its perpetrator to accomplish a political goal but instead to influence a target audience and change that audience's behavior in a way that will serve the interests of the terrorist" (Victoroff 2005; Badey 1998; Laqueur 1999). Several theorists have attempted to explain the causes of terrorist behavior using rational choice framework, explanations such as insanity/sociopathy, game theory, and other behavioral theories. A detailed assessment of these theories is provided by Victoroff (2005), who finds a great deal of heterogeneity in terrorist behavior.

According to Krueger and Maleckova (2003), the literature on the economics of crime provides evidence for the link between poverty and crime; however, a similar link has not been observed in the case of violent crimes as well as hate crimes. Similarly the literature on terrorism, which is akin to crime, has not provided clear evidence for the connection between terrorism and poverty. Studies on terrorism do provide some credence to the argument that the motivation to participate in terrorism is not economic gain but to bring about political change (Landes 1978; Sandler, Tschirhart, and Cauley 1983; Krueger and Maleckova 2003). According to this view, terrorism may have greater payoffs for those who are highly educated (Krueger and Maleckova 2003).

Guillaumont (2007) argues that one channel through which economic instability affects growth is by "triggering political instability that sometimes can lead to armed conflict, which is a very important cause of economic decline" (14). This view is rejected by Krueger and Maleckova (2003), who find no link between poverty, violence, and terrorism. In fact, they argue that aid geared toward fighting terrorism may create perverse incentives for recipients.

According to this study, economic theory does not provide satisfactory evidence for economic deprivation as a root cause of terrorism. Moreover, Krueger and Maleckova (2003) argue that terrorists are motivated by the passionate support for their cause and therefore "eradication of poverty and universal secondary education are unlikely to change these feelings. Indeed, those who are well-off and well-educated may even perceive such feelings more acutely" (123). We argue that the lack of political rather than economic opportunities may better explain the causes of terrorist motivations in Pakistan, and more specifically in FATA, and the solution may very well lie with politics. Governments that are politically capable should be able to control or minimize the uprising of terrorism.

Some have argued that "neither social background, educational opportunity or attainment seem to be particularly associated with terrorism" (Taylor 1988). Similar arguments are also put forth by Graham (2010) when analyzing whether aid can help stop terrorism. He states that not enough is known about the links between underdevelopment, poverty, and terrorism; therefore it is not known how effective aid can be in fighting terrorism.

We argue that it is important to explore the links between underdevelopment, foreign aid, and terrorism in the case of Pakistan for the following reasons. First, even if poverty is not an explanation for the causes of terrorism, it may provide some evidence for settings such as FATA that become safe havens for terrorist organizations. Secondly, improvement in the economic climate as a result of foreign aid in regions where terrorists were able to find support from the local population may result in creating stakeholders in the system who respond unfavorably to the terrorist causes.

This may discourage the "Robin Hood model of terrorism" where the primary motivation of terrorism results from the economic deprivation of fellow countrymen (Krueger and Maleckova 2003). Exploring the effectiveness of aid in Pakistan and especially FATA is essential, where terrorists have "capitalized on abject poverty" that plagues the tribal belt of Pakistan (Haqqani and Jawad 2008). According to Mr. Haqqani, Pakistan's ambassador to the United States, and Mr. Jawad, Afghanistan's ambassador to the United States:

> People who are well fed are not desperate. People who have confidence in public education do not turn toward political madrassas to educate their children. People who have good jobs do not shelter terrorists. In other words, prosperity is one of the most important predictors of political stability, which in turn is the single most critical element in the containment of fanaticism and terrorism. (Haqqani and Jawad 2008)

Since the terrorist attacks of 9/11, Pakistan has seen a dramatic increase in foreign aid due to its strategic importance in the war on terror. Yet little is known of the links between aid, underdevelopment, institutional capacity, and terrorism. Thus in this chapter we explore the effectiveness of aid in fighting terrorism in Pakistan, using subnational data from 1990 to 2008.

Although there is no agreement about the economic basis for terrorism, there is an understanding about the political rationale. A population mobilized by the government will be less likely to align with illegal activities. In the same way, a government that can efficiently extract resources from the population, for redistribution, will be less prone to creating pockets of resistance. This has very important implications for FATA, which is politically, legally, and administratively different from the rest of the country, so much so that "laws framed by the National Assembly of Pakistan do not apply in the FATA unless so ordered by the President, who is empowered to issue regulations for the tribal areas" (GAO 2008).

This political vacuum in FATA is a result of an administrative system distinct from the rest of the country—the Frontier Crimes Regulation (FCR). The Pakistan government retained the FCR codified by the British in 1901. The strategy was not intended to disenfranchise the FATA population but to recognize and reward the tribal structure with degrees of autonomy (GAO 2008). Subsequently, a wide range of approaches to stabilize FATA have proved futile, including military options, development aid, and diplomatic efforts. The region continues to be known as a global terrorism hub. We argue that any approach toward fostering security and stability in FATA will not be effective unless the basic political needs of FATA are met and the Pakistan government is able to secure legitimacy in the area.

THEORETICAL FOUNDATIONS

Our study follows the theoretical model put forth by Oechslin (2006), which argues that political instability is a "potential explanation for why foreign aid is frequently ineffective with respect to economic performance." In this regard he deviates from the existing literature on growth and aid, which primarily investigates "the impact of aid on growth via capital accumulation," and instead analyzes the role of aid in improving institutional quality as well as assesses the issue of "aid-induced instability" (Oechslin 2006, 5).

The model is based on a dynamic game theoretic framework in which the author first considers the choices available to the regime or the "ruler" of whether or not to invest in good institutions. The analysis suggests that "economically weak states may strongly fail to enhance private economic activity through the provision of good institutions" (Oechslin 2006, 16). To analyze whether good institutions utilize aid and increase stability, the impact of economic aid on the choices of the "ruler" is introduced to the game theoretic model. The assumption is that there are limited checks on the executive power of the ruler; however, the regime itself is weak and prone to insurgencies—a case that applies to Pakistan. The model put forth by Oechslin does not demonstrate the universal ineffectiveness of aid, but rather outlines a set of conditions of the recipient countries under which aid may not only be ineffective but perhaps also harmful.[2]

The policy implications of this study suggest that more foreign assistance may make matters worse for countries with the following characteristics: countries that are prone to insurgencies and have conditions such as the "presence of rough terrain which allows insurgents to form their movement without being destroyed at an early stage." Under these circumstances, foreign aid may actually degrade the political climate, he argues (Oechslin 2006, 20).

This condition seems to apply especially to FATA, where the rough terrain and a porous border between Pakistan and Afghanistan have been the greatest impediments to the elimination of terrorist groups or capture of their leaders. And it continues to provide "a physical and symbolic enclave for al Qaeda structure and its subsidiary organization, the Taliban" (Demkiv 2009).

A second case in which aid may be harmful would occur when there is an inequitable distribution of resources or the control of local assets without local participation or benefit. This condition seems to directly apply to the resource-rich, yet sparsely populated province of Baluchistan where dissatisfaction with the federal government's distribution of or control over resources has resulted in several insurgent movements. This is a major challenge to the success of development initiatives, as seen in case of the Gwadar port project in Baluchistan. The administrative and economic control of the Gwadar port project, an undertaking with huge development implications made possible by Chinese investments, has turned into a major dispute between Islamabad and Baluch nationalists.

Very few analyses are conducted empirically at the provincial level, but in this chapter, using data at the subnational level for the period 1990–2008, we explore the impact of foreign aid, political capacity, and federal transfers on the levels of terrorism.

A POLITICAL PERFORMANCE MODEL OF TERRORISM

The goal of this analysis is to evaluate how successful foreign aid has been at fostering stability in Pakistan and also to analyze the impact of domestic aid (transfers from central government) as a stabilizing or destabilizing force. The main element of interest is to understand how external powers can help control the level of instability, or whether it is the domestic forces that are a key to solving this problem. The formula for understanding this phenomenon is found in this endnote.[3]

Although drawing from Oechslin's formal model, we put part of his theoretical arguments to the test by using data on Pakistan provinces and extending the analysis to the regions of FATA and Islamabad. From Oechslin, we test the idea that foreign aid reflects more money in the hands of the regime and the subsequent distribution of those resources producing wasteful rent seeking activities and instability. Oechslin also posits that since the quality of government institutions is endogenous, large inflows of resources destroy the equilibrium, resulting in aid-induced instability. We test this proposition by using the determinants of political capacity, viz. RPR and RPE, as measures of quality of government capacity and analyzing the impact of aid and political capabilities of the government on terrorism in each province.

VARIABLES DESCRIPTION AND DATA SOURCES

This chapter posed a major challenge in data collection. The level of granularity of information required at the provincial level and for the tribal areas required investigative skills. Finding information about the disbursement of international aid by region and sometimes tracing projects to individual geographic areas required the use of many different sources. The data on terrorism is more readily available by region.

Although Pakistan has fiscal information for the four provinces, there is practically no information for FATA and the other territories. Therefore calculating the individual components for RPE and RPR required some triangulation with other information; for example, when regional GDPs were not available, we used agricultural production trends.

Several definitions of terrorism and/or terrorist-related violence exist, but this analysis is based on the U.S. Department of Defense definition: terrorism is "the calculated use of unlawful violence or threat of unlawful violence to inculcate fear; intended to coerce or to intimidate governments or societies in the pursuit of goals that are generally political, religious, or ideological" (International Terrorism and Security Research n.d.). It is important to note that terrorism is unique from other forms of crime where analysts have found some evidence that "poverty and lack of education are connected to illegal activity"; such evidence is lacking in the literature on terrorism (Krueger and Maleckova 2003).

An excellent survey of measurement issues around terrorism is provided by Frey and Luechinger (2005). The data is from the Global Terrorism Database (GTD) produced by the National Consortium for the Study of Terrorism and Responses to Terrorism, a United States Department of Homeland Security Center of Excellence. GTD reports the total number of fatalities as well as the total number of nonfatal injuries from terrorist incidents in Pakistan from 1970 to 2007. Data from South Asia Terrorism Portal (SATP), compiled using news sources, is used for robustness checks. The *Terror* variable is compiled by province and region from the data presented by the geographical position of the incident; the sum of the number of casualties and injuries per incident is used as a proxy for the level of terrorism.

Two sources of aid are considered in this chapter: international and national. International aid information at the subnational level is not extensive, although foreign sources of donations are often discussed as a lever for development in developing countries. The primary source considered reliable for *Aid* is the Development Assistance Database (DAD), established by the government of Pakistan. This measure of aid has been used in other Pakistan-related studies such as the Pakistan Index report from the Bookings institution that tracks variables of reconstruction and security (Campbell and O'Hanlon 2009). The aid data is provided in three categories, viz. committed, disbursed, and expended.[4] For robustness checks we use data on foreign grants available through the Pakistan Statistical Yearbooks from 1990 to 2008.

One of the ways that the central government allocates funds to the provinces is through *Federal Tax Assignments*. Oechslin's (2006) framework also utilizes this variable, stating that poor economies have a low ability to generate tax revenues, hence, the need for assistance. Federal transfers to the provinces have been a steady source of revenue for the provinces, although the average is around 4 percent of their GDP, as well as a source of contention and disagreements regarding the distribution.

The "financial dependence of provinces on the federal government is indicated by the quantitative importance of federal transfers in the form of federal tax assignments and current grants in the total revenue receipts of the provinces" (Qureshi 1991). Grants from the federal government to the provinces, also reported by the Pakistan Statistical Yearbooks, would have been a better choice because they amount to larger transfers (average of 16 percent of the provincial GDP with a standard deviation of 30 percent), but the data is unavailable for FATA and any study that focuses on terrorism in Pakistan should not exclude FATA. Federal Tax Assignment and Transfers measures are presented as ratios to GDP.

The motivation of using GDP per capita as a control variable comes from its use as an explanatory variable for the cost of conflict. Conflict theories, in general, support the thesis that as the economic well-being of the population increases, the probability of conflict decreases (see the chapter on China in this volume for a more extensive review of the theoretical reasons for this control variable). For the purpose of this study we use GDP per capita in constant U.S. dollars for each province. This data was obtained from the World Bank Pakistan office.

As stated in chapter 1, measuring the political performance of subnational governments presents several challenges that are not encountered in the estimation of political performance across countries. Pakistan Statistical Office produces fiscal information at the provincial level, but it is not so readily available for the territories. Furthermore, the transfers and other monetary resources that FATA receives have been administered by the central government for a long time but in the last years that administration has been spearheaded by the Northwest Frontier Province (NWFP), leaving no trace in the national accounts.

The most important control variable to include in this estimation is the amount of revenues subnational governments receive, so estimations based on several sources as well as the new information that now appears on the

$$TotRev.Gdp_{at} = \beta_0 + \beta_1 Year_{at} - \beta_2 Agr.Gdp_{at} + \beta_3 Min.Gdp_{at} + \varepsilon$$

$$RPE_{at} = \frac{Totrev.GDP_{at}}{Predicted\ Tot\ rev.GDP_{at}}$$

Figure 8.1. Relative Provincial Political Capacity Based on the Economic Endowment of Provincial Governments

FATA website has been used. Like the cross-national measure of political capacity, relative provincial political capacity is based on the economic endowment of provincial governments. The measure captures how regional governments are performing based on their economic endowments, or in other words, whether provincial governments are performing in terms of resource extraction to anticipated levels based on their economic endowments. The formula is found in figure 8.1.

Conceptually, political reach reflects the degree to which the population accepts the presence of government in their lives: societies characterized by little trust in elites or government are more likely to actively avoid the government, cutting out involvement in economic and other interactions. This variable tends to be of utmost importance in developing countries where the number of people—not the amount of money—that escapes government scrutiny tends to be larger than in developed countries. The political reach formula is in figure 8.2.

Provinces that have institutions that are relatively more efficient should be able to minimize the outbursts of terrorism. Empirically we test this proposition by using RPR, RPE, and Relative Political Performance (RPP), represented by the interaction term: RPR*RPE. Data to construct the RPE and RPR variables are available from the Pakistan Statistical Yearbooks and the Pakistan Labour Force Surveys (FBS 1989–2008).

Finally, in our analysis we will also use an interactive term RPP = RPE*RPR to gauge the influence that these two aspects of government's capacity—mobilization and extraction—empower each other in affecting the severity of terrorist incidents.

MODEL AND ANALYSIS

In this chapter we argue that a capable government that is able to mobilize its population and extract resources to implement its desired policies will

$$Labor.Pop_{at} = \beta_0 + \beta_1 Gdpcap_{at} - \beta_2 Unemploy_{at} + \beta_3 Liter_{at} - \beta_4 Young_{at} + \varepsilon$$

$$RPR_{at} = \frac{Labor.Pop_{at}}{Predicted\ Labor.Pop_{at}}$$

Figure 8.2. Political Reach

have more chances of minimizing the existence of terrorism in its country. We also test the competing theories: (1) the theories that argue that foreign aid or transfer of economic resources in general will give governments the flexibility to improve the welfare of the population and as a result curb terrorism and (2) from Oechslin the argument that given large inflows of money, governments may not spend productively or may even produce wasteful rent seeking activities, fueling conflict over the distribution of resources among provinces and political factions.

Following the first argument about aid, we expect transfers to help curb terrorism since the distribution of these resources is geared toward increasing the future revenue base of individuals by giving them more present economic opportunities. What is good for the people is good for the government. The opposing view, following Oechslin, also is a plausible scenario; instead of pushing the province into a steeper growth path, the extra money may produce friction among the different factions and fuel conflict over appropriations regardless of the quality of the investments.

When it comes to the effect of good governments, there is consensus that efficient institutions facilitate the path to development and stability. As explained in the previous section, the expectation is that the higher the relative political capacity of the provincial governments, the more internal stability is generated. Using the average wealth of the population as a control variable responds to the same assumption that a more endowed region will have less incentive to turn to terrorism as a "way out" from poverty.

This study draws on a provincial data set from 1990 to 2006 on Pakistan. Since the data available at the subnational level is limited, the methodology utilized is ordinary least squares (OLS) as a first approach to these exploratory results. However, as more data becomes available, future analysis on the connection between aid, political capacity, and terrorism will lend itself to more complete and sophisticated statistical methods and these should render more robust findings based on a larger data set. The results are found in table 8.1 in this endnote.[5]

The results in table 8.1 are unexpected. They show that for the case of Pakistan, disbursed foreign aid has *no* effect on controlling terrorist incidents. Although Oechslin (2006) points out that the money that comes from foreign governments and nongovernmental organizations is counterproductive, in our test those distinctions seem to be irrelevant.

The variable that has the strongest effect is Federal Tax Assignments, that is, the central government can influence violence by administering transfers to the affected areas. The policy implications for the international community are significant. International organizations whose objective is to curb terrorism would be better off directing their resources elsewhere. The results also show that the number of terrorist incidents is more pronounced in more affluent areas. This result can be masking the fact that most incidents are clustered in urban areas.

A similar analysis with the same sample but using a more restrictive dependent variable produced the results in table 8.2 at this endnote.[6] Deaths from terrorist incidents show similar results but now politics starts to emerge as a cause of violence. RPR is significant and so is the interactive term.

The results from tables 8.1 and 8.2 confirm that international aid does not curtail terrorist acts, not even in the case of the more violent situation involving deaths. Domestic transfers have a positive effect on curbing incidents and death from terrorism. The model, using deaths as a dependent variable, shows politics as a dissuasive element for violence. The lesson seems to be that strong political ties between the national and subnational governments are a far more effective condition in combating terrorism than providing the provinces with foreign aid.

The third table looks at all terrorist incidents in Pakistan over time.[7] These results indicate that it is political capacity or politics that has an effect on terrorist incidents.[8] The more the government mobilizes its population and extracts resources, the more they control terrorist incidents. The interactive term (RPC = RPE*RPR) shows that both political variables have simultaneous influence on the level of terrorist incidents, compounding the magnitude of the effect.

POLICY IMPLICATIONS

The goal of this analysis was to look at the effectiveness of foreign aid in curbing terrorism in Pakistan. Using provincial data from 1990 to 2008, the preliminary evidence from this analysis showed counterintuitive results. When viewing the results from only the four provinces, international money—when channeled domestically—seems to makes a difference. Hence it is reasonable to expect that economic forces can drive stability in the provinces.

However, once we include FATA in the picture, the results show that no matter how much money pours in, politics is the driver of stability in FATA. The implications are that when the political situation is very unstable, it does not matter how much money is received in the affected area; if the political situation does not improve, those resources will be wasted. If, on the other hand, the instability is not extreme, then domestic resources and foreign aid can be distributed through domestic channels to improve the situation.

Inclusion of FATA in our analysis shows that economics does not seem to matter; politics makes the difference. Hence we argue that unless there is an improvement in political performance, more money, whether foreign or domestic, would be ineffective in stabilizing the tribal belt of Pakistan.

This finding is consistent with the recognition that "FATA residents do not have access to political parties and political parties are forbidden from extending their activities into the agencies of FATA" (GAO 2008). The most important implication is that securing FATA is the key to stability and halting the spillover of terrorism to the rest of the country. To that end, the first step is filling the political and administrative void in FATA. Only after the Pakistan government establishes its legitimacy in FATA can we expect that foreign aid money will foster stability and prosperity in what has been called the most dangerous region in the world.

In this chapter we tested whether politics or economics is the substantial driver of the efforts to curb instability and terrorism in Pakistan. Because of Pakistan's complex ethnic and geographic structure, our analysis uses data disaggregated by the four provinces, the tribal belt, and the capital territory. We argue that domestically channeled money to the provinces, excluding FATA, will make a difference in curbing terrorism. However, the first step toward stabilizing FATA is capacity building.

Foreign or domestically channeled money to FATA will not make a difference unless the government has reach over the population in the dangerous tribal belt. Without adequate capacity building, it is very likely that aid money to FATA will be misspent and will produce no results. An unstable FATA can in turn destabilize the entire country. The stakes could not be higher and yet the concept of effective governance seems lost in the fog of war.

NOTES

1. Punjab is the most populous province with almost 60 percent of the country's population (The Atlantic Council of the United States, February 2009). Subsequently Punjabis have dominated the government, military, and bureaucracy of the country. The economic and political disparity between Punjab and the other three provinces has been a historical cause of grievances. This disparity plays out still further when it comes to the division of resources among the provinces. As a result, the resource-rich province of Baluchistan, with only 5 percent of the country's population and the largest province by area, has been subject to various separatist movements. The recent riots and protests mainly by the non-Pakhtuns in NWFP, resulting from the renaming of NWFP to Khyber-Pakhtunkhwa, also point to the ethnic complexities of the region.

2. For example, one of the cases he presents is:

Aid effectiveness with threats of insurrection . . . the more interesting case in which the incumbent ruler may be forced out of power along the equilibrium path. As a first step, it is convenient to parameterize the distribution function of the private costs of rioting as F (x) = ρH(xpmin), where H(x) is a continuous distribution function with a finite density h(x) for all x > 0.10 Hence, the probability of a successful insurrection is given by p(t + a) = F (τ + α / pmin) = ρH (τ + α). Note that ρ is a natural measure for the ruler's political strength. A lower ρ corresponds to a situation in which the ruler is more entrenched since the cost of replacing him is frequently high or a large fraction of the population is required to force him out of power. (18)

3. $Terrorism_{pt} = \alpha_0 - \beta_1\ Political\ Capacity_{pt} - \beta_2 Economic\ Aid_{pt} + \epsilon$
Where t denotes the year and *p* is the province/region index.
In more detail:
$Terrorism_{pt} = \alpha_0 - \beta_1\ RPE_{pt} - \beta_2 RPR_{pt} + \beta_3 RPC_{pt} - \beta_4\ Foreign\ Aid_{pt} - \beta_5\ FedTax$
$Assign_{pt} - \beta_6 GDPCap_{pt} + \epsilon$

4. Commitment is "a firm obligation expressed in writing and backed by the availability of the necessary funds for a particular project, program, sector, trust fund or to support the domestic budget." Disbursement is "the placement of resources at the disposal of the government, or a 1st level implementing agency. The Disbursement Date is the date at which those funds were made available." Expenditure is "the actual spending of funds by the 1st level implementing agency to pay for project-related goods and services OR the placement of resources by the 1st level implementing agency at the disposal of a 2nd level implementing agency." (Development Assistance Database 2010)

5. See table 8.1.

Table 8.1. OLS on Terrorist Incidents for All Pakistan Provinces and Islamabad, excluding FATA, 1990–2007

Source	SS	df	MS	Number of obs = 51	
				$F(6,44) = 4.12$	
Model	375345.338	6	62557.5563	Prob>F = 0.0023	
Residual	668544.701	44	15194.1978	R-squared = 0.3596	
				Adj. R-Squared = 0.2722	
Total	1043890.04	50	20877.8008	Root MSE = 123.26	

terrorGTD	Coef.	Std. Err	t	P>|t|	[95% Conf. Interval]	
disbursedusd	− 1.68e-07	2.07e-07	− 0.81	0.421	− 5.86e-07	2.50e-07
fedtaxassi~p	− 2739.74	1210.389	− 2.26	0.029	− 5179.118	− 300.3619
gdpcapusco~t	.8117896	.2664983	3.05	0.004	.27469761	.348882
rpe	− 295.2702	701.7841	− 0.42	0.676	− 1709.623	1119.083
rpr	− 694.7101	732.2261	− 0.95	0.348	− 2170.415	780.9946
rpc	584.9931	689.3244	0.85	0.401	− 804.249	1974.235
_cons	265.5958	777.3241	0.34	0.734	− 1300.998	1832.19

6. See table 8.2.

Table 8.2. OLS on Deaths from Terrorist Incidents for All Pakistan Provinces and Islamabad, excluding FATA 1990–2007

Source	SS	df	MS	Number of obs = 51
Model	38201.0196	6	6366.83661	F(6,44 = 2.93 Prob>F = 0.0173
Residual	95768.3921	44	2176.55437	R-squared = 0.2851 Adj. R-squared = 0.1877
Total	133969.412	50	2679.38824	Root MSE = 46.654

killgtd	Coef.	Std. Err	t	P>|t|	[95% Conf. Interval]	
disbursedusd	−4.86e-08	7.85e-08	−0.62	0.539	−2.07e-07	1.10e-07
fedtaxassi~p	−790.8261	458.111	−1.73	0.091	−1714.088	132.436
gdpcapusco~t	.1869842	.1008649	1.85	0.070	−.0162958	.3902641
rpe	−413.141	265.613	−1.56	0.127	−948.4489	122.1669
rpr	−537.0434	277.1348	−1.94	0.059	−1095.572	21.48509
rpc	468.0033	260.8973	1.79	0.080	−57.80059	993.8072
_cons	468.4741	294.2036	1.59	0.118	−124.4544	1061.402

7. See table 8.3.

Table 8.3. OLS on Terrorist Incidents for All Pakistan Provinces and Islamabad, including FATA, 1990–2007

Source	SS	df	MS	Number of obs = 58
Model	309760.318	6	51626.7197	F(6,51) = 2.24 Prob>F = 0.0544
Residual	1177671.56	51	23091.5992	R-squared = 0.2083 Adj. R-squared = 0.1151
Total	1487431.88	57	26095.2961	Root MSE = 151.96

terrorGTD	Coef.	Std. Err.	t	P>|t|	[95% Conf. Interval]	
disbursedusd	−3.41e-08	2.47e-07	−0.14	0.891	−5.29e-07	4.61e-07
fedtaxassi~p	−1996.072	1402.017	−1.42	0.161	−4810.739	818.5942
gdpcapusco~t	.3290221	.2146893	1.53	0.132	−.1019846	.7600289
rpe	−1425.327	615.6445	−2.32	0.025	−2661.285	−189.3694
rpr	−1758.54	670.7803	−2.62	0.012	−3105.187	−411.8922
rpc	1557.606	642.8153	2.42	0.019	267.1003	2848.111
_cons	1677.857	612.6436	2.74	0.008	447.9238	2907.79

8. Similar results are found when the dependent variable is deaths from terrorist incidents. The same variables are significant, although the results are slightly stronger (Adjusted R2 = .12).

REFERENCES

Acemoglu, D., S. Johnson, and J. A. Robinson. 2001. "The Colonial Origins of Comparative Development: An Empirical Investigation." *American Economic Review* 91 (5): 1369–401.

Arbetman, M., and J. Kugler. 1997. *Political Capacity and Economic Behavior.* Boulder, CO: Westview Press.

The Atlantic Council of the United States. 2009, February. *Needed: A Comprehensive U.S. Policy Towards Pakistan.*

Badey, T. J. 1998. "Defining International Terrorism:A Pragmatic Approach." *Terrorism and Political Violence* 10: 90–107.

Baloch, S. 2008. "A Lesson To Be Learnt." *DAWN,* August 5.

Bardhan, P. 2004. *Scarcity, Conflicts, and Cooperation: Essays in Political and Institutional Economics of Development.* Cambridge: MIT Press.

Burnside, C., and D. Dollar. 2000. "Aid, Policies, and Growth." *American Economic Review* 90 (4): 847–68.

———. 2004. "Aid, Policies, and Growth: Revisiting the Evidence." The World Bank, Policy Research Working Paper Series 3251.

Campbell, J. H., and M. O'Hanlon. 2009. *Pakistan Index: Tracking Variables of Reconstruction and Security.* Washington, DC: Brookings.

Collier, P. 2004. *Development and Conflict.* Oxford: Centre for the Study of African Economies.

Demkiv, A. 2009. "Pakistan's FATA, Transnational Terrorism and the Global Development Model." *Journal of Global Change and Governance* 2 (1).

Development Assistance Database. 2010, February 25. (G. o. Pakistan, Producer, and Economic Affairs Division, Pakistan.) Retrieved February 25, 2010, from www.dadpak.org/.

Easterly, W. 2001. "The Political Economy of Growth Without Development." *World Bank* 1–53.

———. 2003. "Can Foreign Aid Buy Growth?" *Journal of Economic Perspectives* 17 (3): 23–48.

FBS. 1989–2008. *Pakistan Labour Force Surverys.* Islamabad: Federal Bureau of Statistics, Pakistan.

———. 2007. *Pakistan Statistical Yearbook 2007.* Islamabad: Federal Bureau of Statistics, Pakistan.

———. 2008. *Pakistan Statistical Yearbook.* Islamabad: Federal Bureau of Statistics, Pakistan.

Frey, B., and S. Luechinger. 2005. "Measuring Terrorism." A. Marciano and J.-M. Josselin, eds., *Law and the State: A Political Economy,* 142–81. Cheltenham: Edward Elgar.

GAO (U.S. Government Accountability Office). 2008. *Combating Terrorism: The United States Lacks Comprehensive Plan to Destroy the Terrorist Threat and Close the*

Safe Haven in Pakistan's Federally Administered Tribal Areas. Publication Number: GAO-08-622, Washington D.C. Retrieved from http://www.gao.gov/products/ GAO-08-622.

Gill, K., ed. 2000. Institute for Conflict Management. Retrieved February 15, 2010, from South Asia Terrorism Portal: www.satp.org.

Graham, C. 2010. "Can Foreign Aid Help Stop Terrorism?" *Brookings Review*, April 13.

Guillaumont, P. 2007. "Aid Works Best in Vulnerable Countries." *Poverty in Focus* 14.

Haqqani, H., and S. T. Jawad. 2008. "Pakistan and Afghanistan Unite Against Terrorism." *Wall Street Journal*, September 26.

International Terrorism and Security Research. n.d. Retrieved April 2, 2010, from Terrrorism Research: www.terrorism-research.com.

Krueger, A. B., and J. Maleckova. 2003, Fall. "Education, Poverty and Terrorism: Is There a Causal Connection?" *Journal of Economic Perspectives* 17 (4): 119–44.

Landes, W. 1978. "An Economic Study of U.S. Aircraft Hijackings, 1961–1976." *Journal of Law and Economics* 21 (1): 1–31.

Laqueur, W. 1999. *The New Terrorism: Fanaticism and the Arms of Mass Destruction*. New York: Oxford University.

North, D. C. 1990. *Institutions, Institutional Change and Economic Performance*. Cambridge: Cambridge University Press.

Oechslin, M. 2006, November. "Foreign Aid, Political Instability and Economic Growth." Institute for Empirical Research in Economics Working Paper No. 310, 1–34.

Paul, K. 2009. "About Those Billions." *Newsweek*, October 21.

Perkins, D. H., S. Radelet, and D. L. Lindauer. 2001. *Economics of Development*. New York: W. W. Norton.

Qureshi, S. K. 1991, Winter. "Trends and Patterns in Federal-Provincial Fiscal Flows in Pakistan: A Preliminary Analysis." *Pakistan Development Review*.

Rajan, R., and A. Subramanian. 2007. "Does Aid Affecr Governance?" *American Economic Review* 97 (2): 322–27.

Rodrik, D., A. Subramanian, and F. Trebbi. 2004, July. "Institutions Rule: The Primacy of Institutions over Geography and Integration in Economic Development." *Journal of Economic Growth* 9 (2): 131–65.

Sandler, T., J. T. Tschirhart, and J. Cauley. 1983, March. "A Theoretical Analysis of Transnational Terrorism." *American Political Science Review* 77 (1): 36–54.

START. 2009. A Center of Excellence of the U.S. Department of Homeland Security. Retrieved April 30, 2010, from Global Terrorism Database: www.start.umd.edu.

Taylor, M. 1988. *The Terrorist*. London: Brassey's Defence Publishers.

Victoroff, J. 2005, February. "The Mind of the Terrorist—A Review and Critique of Psychological Approaches." *Journal of Conflict Resolution* 49 (1): 3–42.

Appendix 8.1.   Variable Description and Source

Variables	Description	Sources
Disbursed-USD	Aid Money Disbursed (USD)	DAD—Development Assistance Database, Pakistan
KillGTD	number of fatalities from terrorism	GTD—Global Terrorism Database
WoundGTD	number of non-fatal injuries from terrorism	GTD—Global Terrorism Database
TerrorGTD	KillGTD + WoundGTD	GTD—Global Terrorism Database
GDP/CAP	provincial GDP per Capita	World Bank—Personal Communication
FedTaxAssign/GDP	Federal Tax Assignments /GDP	White Paper
Grants/GDP	Foreign Grants channeled domestically/GDP	Pakistan Statistical Yearbook
GDP	provincial Gross Domestic Product	World Bank—Personal Communication
RPR	Relative Political Reach	using data from Pakistan Labour Force Surveys
RPE	Relative Political Extraction	using data from Pakistan Statistical Yearbook
RPC	Relative Political Capacity = RPR*RPE	Pakistan Statistical Yearbook; Pakistan Labour Force Survey
Terror-SATP	number of fatalities + injuries from terrorism	SATP—South Asia Terrorism portal

9

Provincial Politics and the Attraction of FDI in India and China

Tadeusz Kugler, Travis G. Coan,
and Constantine Boussalis

CONTEXT

Interest in understanding the correlates of foreign direct investment (FDI) has grown considerably over the past several decades. A number of theoretical and empirical models have been introduced in the economics literature that highlight the benefits of attracting FDI, particularly for developing nations (Dunning 1981). For underdeveloped economies, an inflow of foreign capital—particularly from developed nations—facilitates a transfer of knowledge and technological spillovers with the potential to jump-start economic development (Mansfield and Romeo 1980).

The vast majority of such studies rely on national-level data, analyzing variation in FDI flows across nations. While cross-national studies are no doubt useful, past research has paid insufficient attention to the significant variation in FDI within nations. This chapter attempts to move the literature in this direction.

Investing significant material resources in a foreign country is a risky enterprise. Political systems are designed to best serve domestic constituents and rarely are the interests of foreign investors placed above the exigencies of domestic politics. In order to mitigate the potential negative implications of risk, FDI has traditionally moved between nations with similar legal, political, and societal structures (Kaufmann, Kraay, and Mastruzzi 2003, 2008; De Soto 1989, 2000).

Expanding investment opportunities throughout the developing world are changing the global investment environment (World Bank 2005, 2007). While much of the world's FDI continues to flow between highly developed nations, the percentage flowing to less-developed nations is increasing at a steady rate (World Bank 2007). These shifts highlight the opportunities and challenges facing both domestic governments and international investors in a highly integrated global environment.

In order to address variation in FDI at the subnational level, we focus attention on India and China—two emerging markets with enormous economic potential. Both India and China are fortunate to have massive populations, substantial resources, and a considerable amount of untapped potential. Further, these emerging markets have made significant steps in liberalizing their economic systems and allowing for FDI inflows (For example, Indian net FDI inflows have grown from US$73 million in 1991 to US$22 billion in 2008 [World Bank 2010]).

Chinese FDI inflows increased from approximately US$3 billion to more than US$94 billion for the same period. The natural economic advantages of these countries, however, raise important political questions. Do India and China have the government capacity to realize their economic potential? How is government capacity distributed across the provinces of these nations? Does variation in government capacity help to explain variation in regional FDI flows?

We address these questions by examining the spatial distribution of FDI and relative political capacity (RPC) across Indian and Chinese provinces.[1] Using panel data during the period 2000–2005, we examine the relationship between RPC and FDI at the provincial level. Our empirical results suggest an inverted U-shape relationship between investment and capacity, supporting the presence of an optimum level of capacity at the provincial level.

INTELLECTUAL ENVIRONMENT

There is a well-established literature at the national level on the potential drivers of FDI. General explanations tend to focus on two different—though not mutually exclusive—paths: one based on economics and the other on political explanations. This section will briefly review each explanatory framework, with particular attention paid to the empirical literature. Although most empirical studies on the correlates of FDI focus attention at the national level, we will also provide a brief overview of FDI at the subnational level in India and China.

Economic Explanations

Most economic studies on the drivers of FDI flows begin with measures that attempt to proxy market size. The variables typically used to capture the effects of market size include population (Wei 2000; Feng 2003), GDP, and GDP per capita (Chakrabarti 2001). Theoretically, measures of market size fall into the more general category of "location related factors" described in Dunning's (1981) classic ownership, location, and internalization (OLI) framework.

Each measure attempts to provide an indicator of a particular geographic region's consumer base and thus provides a rough indicator of the profitability associated with a particular foreign investment (Banga 2003). Empirically, Chakrabarti (2001) demonstrated that measures of market size offer one of the only robust predictors of FDI flows at the national level.

In addition to market size, many studies argue that economic growth explains shifts in FDI flows. A number of studies argue that economic growth facilitates additional business opportunities, changes the economic incentive structures of domestic populations, and transforms the type of FDI available to a particular host economy (Chen and Khan 1997; Billington 1999). Moreover, economic growth has the potential to promote changes in a nation's industrial structure, aiding the development of industries better positioned to compete on a global stage (Wheeler and Mody 1992).[2]

Political Explanations

Although economic explanations have dominated the empirical literature on FDI, several recent empirical studies have begun to acknowledge the importance of political factors (cf., Wheeler and Mody 1992). Among potential political indicators, a number of recent studies have focused on the importance of government capacity. Adji, Ahn, Holsey, and Willett (1997) show that variants of relative political reach and political extraction have significant and substantive positive effects on FDI at the national level.

Feng (2003) found a statistically significant relationship between relative political capacity and the stock of FDI inflows in his exhaustive empirical study of political institutions. More recently, Coan and Kugler (2008) provide evidence to suggest the presence of an interactive relationship between open market policy environments and a nation's level of relative political capacity. Coan and Kugler's findings support the notion that governments attract FDI when they have the political capacity to realize their commitments to liberal economic policies.

Foreign Direct Investment in India

Until recently, India placed high levels of restrictions on the inflow of foreign capital and closely monitored the industries open to foreign investment. Although a number of protectionist policies remain in place, India enacted its first major financial reforms in the mid-1990s.

Recent studies indicate that these reforms had immediate, positive implications for India's level of economic development (cf., Bhaduri 2005). Moreover, a number of studies suggest that economic liberalization was central to the dramatic increase in FDI over the 1990s and into the 2000s (Shirai 2004). Prior to 1991, in order to gain government approval, foreign firms interested in investing in India were required to enter into a joint venture with a domestic firm. These early investments in the mid-1990s thus represented the creation of India's first wholly owned foreign subsidiaries.

While economic liberalization enhanced India's ability to attract foreign capital, the increase in FDI was distributed unevenly across Indian provinces. According to Bhalla (1998), early investment was concentrated primarily in southern India due to a higher level of perceived commitment to deregulation in southern provinces. As described in more detail below, much of India's FDI continues to flow to southern India in general and to the province of Maharashtra in particular. In summary, most analysts agree that India has benefited a great deal from economic liberalization, though most experts agree that the country still has a long way to go (Srivastava and Sen 2004).

Foreign Direct Investment in China

Foreign direct investment inflows can be traced as far back as the inception of the People's Republic of China. Indeed, during the 1950s and 1960s a relatively small level of foreign investment entered China from other socialist nations. For example, during the 1950s, joint ventures such as the Sino-Soviet Xinjiang Non-ferrous Metal Company, Sino-Polish Joint Stock Shipping Company, and the Sino-Czechoslovakian International Marine Transport Company were established. With the deterioration of Sino-Soviet relations in the 1960s, however, many of these joint ventures collapsed, although a few of the Eastern bloc nations such as Poland continued to invest in China (Wei and Liu 2001). Nevertheless, the magnitude of FDI inflows during this period was very small.

With the ending of the Cultural Revolution and the rise to power of Deng Xiaoping, China began to liberalize its economic policies and to open itself to the West. The economic reforms that materialized after 1979 had substantial impacts on the magnitude of foreign investment inflows. FDI no longer was constrained to the "socialist world." Rather, the new political leadership understood that if economic prosperity was to be achieved, capital, technology, and managerial experience was required—all of which could be attained through foreign direct investment (Wei and Liu 2001).

Although reforms began in the early 1980s, considerable institutional inertia remained that opposed perceived dependence on foreign sources of investment. It was not until the 1990s that the Chinese government sent serious signals to the outside world that China was truly committed to market-oriented policies, and as a result FDI increased dramatically (Wei and Liu 2001; OECD 2002).

The ability of India and China to maximize their investment potential in the future will depend in large part on a continued political commitment to maintaining the open market policies crucial to securing a profitable international investment environment. Moreover, maintaining adequate levels of government capacity will be crucial to sustained economic reform in the face of domestic opposition. With these potential challenges in mind, the remainder of this study turns to analyzing the empirical relationship between economic factors, political capacity, and the flow of FDI.

THEORY AND HYPOTHESES

How does politics impact a government's ability to attract foreign investment? As demonstrated above, there is a burgeoning empirical literature on the relationship between political capacity and FDI. This study seeks to extend these past works by examining the empirical relationship between foreign investment and political capacity at the subnational level. There exist many conceptualizations of government capacity in the academic literature; however, the approach utilized in this study centers on the influential work on relative political capacity carried out by Kenneth Organski and extended in Arbetman and Kugler (1997).

Following Organski, Arbetman, and Kugler, we define political capacity as a government's ability to carry out a given set of policy objectives in the face of groups with competing political priorities. Regarding foreign investment, high levels of political capacity imply a government's ability to carry out market-friendly economic policies despite the possibility of political opposition.

The ability of governments to extract resources from domestic populations is at the heart of our conception of political capacity. As outlined in Arbetman-Rabinowitz and Johnson (2007),

Governments all require resources in order to enact policies. Taxation represents willingness on the part of the population (or enforcement ability on the part of the government) to transfer resources from private individuals to the government. This resources transfer is the bridge between politics and money; taxation demonstrates an endorsement or at least acceptance of the government by the population. (4)

Governments with a high level of extractive capacity are in a better position to pursue their political objectives. In the context of FDI, high levels of political capacity imply that governments have the capability to provide the physical infrastructure and political institutions and mobilize the human resources necessary to ensure a profitable investment environment. This discussion suggests the following proposition relating political capacity and FDI:

> *Proposition 1: There is a positive relationship between provincial political capacity and the attraction of FDI.*

Empirical researchers must be careful, however, not to oversimplify the relationship between extractive political capacity and FDI. Overtaxation is likely to hinder business development, as local governments walk the fine line between developmental and predatory economic policies. Moreover, some have argued that the potential for predation is particularly acute in socialist democratic India.[3] This argument suggests that positing a monotonically increasing relationship between political capacity and FDI may be inconsistent with empirical realities in Indian provinces. In order to examine the possibility of nonlinearities in political capacity, we examine the following corollary:

> *Corollary 1: There is an inverted U-shape relationship between provincial political capacity and the attraction of FDI.*

To our knowledge, this is one of the first studies to examine the empirical relationship between political capacity and FDI in India and China at the subnational level. The remainder of this study outlines the data and methods used to test the above propositions, provides a description of the empirical results, and concludes by discussing the relevance of the results for subnational economic development in India and China.

DATA

Dependent Variable: FDI

In order to examine the empirical relationship between FDI and government capacity in India and China, we examine provincial-level data over the period 2000 to 2005.[4] The dependent variable in the analyses below for India is level of "approved" foreign direct investment provinces.[5] For India, approved FDI is available from the Indian Ministry of Commerce and Industry and is measured as a crore of rupees.[6] Figure 9.1 displays the geographic distribution of the average level of FDI and Political Capacity across Indian provinces over the six-year period under study.

As shown in the right map of figure 9.1, the province with the darkest shade, Maharashtra, serves as a major center for India's foreign investment. This finding is not surprising given that Maharashtra also serves as the center of India's industry and commerce. Figure 9.1 indicates that the average level of FDI falls precipitously as one moves north from Maharashtra into the largely agricultural states of Madhya Pradesh and Bihar. Overall, it appears that provinces located around Maharashtra with access to coastal sea ports tend to attract greater foreign investment—though the spatial relationship appears weak at best.

China has a clearer data collection when it comes to FDI, and because of this factor FDI is not "approved" as in India but actual FDI in U.S. dollars. This data has been compiled by the China Data Center at the University of Michigan and the National Bureau of Statistics of China. The clarity of data and the standardization of its measurements allow for a greater degree of understanding on how and where FDI moves within the country.

As the bottom map in figure 9.2 shows, FDI in China, over the past five years, is located primarily on the coastal provinces and then has started to move toward the interior.

The provinces of Guangdong and Jiangsu are of particular interest as both had many of the first economic reforms. These free economic zones then

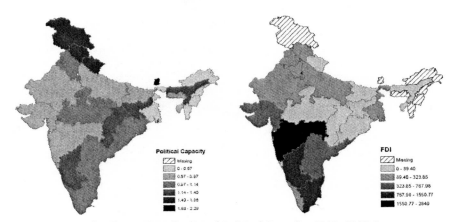

Figure 9.1.   Indian State FDI Inflows and Political Capacity, 2000–2005 Average

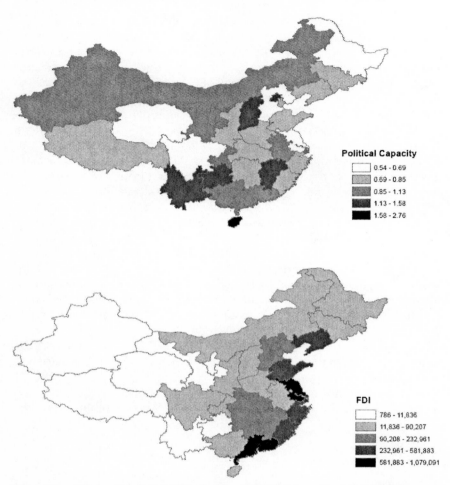

Figure 9.2. **Chinese Provincial FDI Inflows and Political Capacity, 2000–2005 Average**

led to large investments in physical capital such as new container ports, transportation networks, and other massive construction projects within the cities. Notice that this isn't due to the conditions on the ground. Policy created the first avenues for FDI, and as you can see from the figure, FDI has started to move toward the other noncoastal regions of China.

Key Independent Variable: Political Capacity

Political capacity is approximated by the measure of relative political extraction (RPE) first explored by Arbetman and Kugler in 1997 and now outlined in detail in this volume. At the national level, RPE has been used to explain a wide range of economic and political phenomena, from economic growth (Leblang 1997) to civil conflict (Johnson 2007), and more recently FDI (Coan and Kugler 2008). The measure is constructed using a series of multiple regression models to predict the expected levels of government extraction and compares the expected levels to actual levels of extraction.

More important for this chapter is that several recent studies have extended the concept to the provincial level, modifying the empirical specification to incorporate subnational dynamics (Johnson 2007).[7] The measure is constructed such that higher values indicate greater levels of provincial political capacity. For India, the average *RPE* level is 1.04—i.e., the expected level of capacity—and the standard deviation is .46. In China the mean provincial political capacity level is 1.04 while the standard deviation is .52.

The left map in figure 9.1 displays the average level of *RPE* across Indian provinces over the six-year period under study. As shown in the figure, there is a good deal of spatial dependence associated with political capacity. *RPE* is relatively high in the southern provinces of Tamil Nadu and Karnataka, close to the expected level in provinces located in the middle of the country, and low in the largely agricultural regions of Uttar Pradesh and Bihar. It is also important to note that even after controlling for federal transfers, the conflict-torn northern region in and around Kashmir maintains high levels of extraction.

The upper map in figure 9.2 offers a geographic representation of the average level of *RPE* in China for the sample period. Provincial-level political capacity seems to exhibit less spatial dependence compared to that of India. Some descriptive patterns are evident nevertheless. Major metropolitan centers such as Beijing and Shanghai perform above their predicted level of extraction, while the western provinces of Qinghai and Sichuan have low levels of political capacity. Heilongjiang, which borders Russia, along with the coastal provinces of Hebei and Jiangsu also seem to be underperforming on average for the period studied. In contrast, aside from the aforementioned metropolitan areas, the highest-performing provincial governments seem to be located in the southern part of China.

Economic Control Variables

In order to ensure proper specification of the regression equations presented below, a number of control variables were introduced. While the economics literature suggests a wide range of potential correlates, Chakrabarti's (2001) "global sensitivity analysis" at the national level demonstrates that only measures of market size show a robust relationship with FDI.

To control for the potential effects of market size, we include two measures: the natural logarithm of population and a province's level of economic output, which is measured as GDP. In addition to measures of market size, we incorporate real GDP growth given the prevalence of empirical studies that include the measure. Both GDP and economic growth are lagged in order to mitigate problems associated with endogeneity.

MODEL SPECIFICATION AND RESULTS

Given that the dependent variable used in this analysis is continuous, we utilize standard ordinary least squares (OLS) estimates to arrive at our statistical results. Before specifying the statistical model, however, it is important to address a variety of statistical issues associated with our data set, including issues related to pooling observations across time and space. Problems associated with unequal variance across pooled observations may affect the validity of statistical results (Sayers 1989). To address this issue, we analyzed a series of models that included two-way fixed effects to control for differences across distinct regions and time.[8,9] Previous empirical studies on FDI have discussed the problem of first order autocorrelation when estimating investment inflows across units and time. To account for this, we estimate our fixed-effects models with robust standard errors clustered by province (Arellano 1987; Rogers 1993). With these econometric considerations in mind, we constructed the model found here.[10]

The empirical results for this statistical model, including the nonstandardized regression coefficients and robust standard errors, are presented in tables 9.1 and 9.2 for India and China, respectively. Three alternative specifications are provided: (1) the "Base Model" tests the nonlinear political capacity hypothesis without other controls by including *RPE* and *RPE*[2]; (2) the "Base + Population Control" incorporates the effects of population size; and (3) the final model introduces the key economic variables described above. Each model includes both region and time fixed effects.

India Empirical Results

Turning first to the Base Model results for India displayed in table 9.1, although the *RPE* and *RPE*[2] parameters are statistically insignificant, they display the correct theoretical signs—positive and negative, respectively. Further, the base model explains approximately 19 percent of the variation of provincial FDI inflows in India. The political capacity measures become

Table 9.1.   FDI Analysis, India (2000–2005)

	Base Model	Base + Population Control	Full Model
RPE	886.0	− 58.97	3616.1***
	(1594.8)	(1461.0)	(1066.3)
RPE²	− 430.6	73.71	− 1052.2**
	(722.0)	(712.9)	(407.2)
ln(Population)		192.4***	− 551.7***
		(62.51)	(97.29)
Growth$_{t-1}$			699.9
			(1038.9)
GDP$_{t-1}$			0.000252***
			(0.0000223)
Region FE	Yes	Yes	Yes
Year FE	Yes	Yes	Yes
Observations	101	100	90
R²	0.193	0.246	0.620

Standard errors in parentheses
Note: Two-way Fixed Effects Results; Coefficient (Standard Error); Standard errors clustered by State
* $p<0.10$, ** $p<0.05$, *** $p<0.01$

statistically significant once the economic controls are included in the fully augmented model.

The empirical results provide strong support for the proposition that there is an inverted U-shape relationship between political capacity and the accumulation of foreign capital in the Indian context. Regarding the economic controls, both the natural logarithm of population and the lagged market size indicator have a positive and statistically significant relationship with provincial FDI inflows, although curiously population is in the opposite direction (negative) once the economic indicators are included. It should be noted that the explained variance of the Full Model is quite large ($R^2 = 0.62$), indicating that the model fits well with observations of FDI in India over the period studied.

In order to provide a more meaningful interpretation of the empirical results, it is useful to outline the substantive implications associated with increasing *RPC* across Indian provinces. The curvilinear shape of the political capacity effect suggests that there is a critical point at which additional capacity begins to imply diminishing returns for foreign investment. Maximizing the Full Model with respect to *RPE* demonstrates that political

Table 9.2.   FDI Analysis, China (2000–2005)

	Base Model	Base + Population Control	Full Model
RPE	−130550.6	−82451.2	176870.3*
	(219253.7)	(230914.8)	(87721.2)
RPE²	8852.9	9521.1	−37409.8
	(54692.2)	(58562.1)	(22300.1)
ln(Population)	—	86801.1*	−114301.0***
		(49366.8)	(23406.3)
Growth$_{t-1}$	—	—	−223774.0
			(204851.4)
GDP$_{t-1}$	—	—	98.74***
			(8.140)
Region FE	Yes	Yes	Yes
Year FE	Yes	Yes	Yes
Observations	186	186	186
R²	0.050	0.119	0.834

Standard errors in parentheses
Note: Two-way Fixed Effects Results; Coefficient (Standard Error); Standard errors clustered by Province
* $p<0.10$, ** $p<0.05$, *** $p<0.01$

capacity must reach a level of 1.72 before it begins to diminish a province's ability to attract FDI.

This result suggests that Indian provinces can extract a good deal more than expected based on economic characteristics alone before deterring foreign investors. A survey of the changes in predicted values of FDI inflows for specific Indian states as political capacity approaches the aforementioned inflection point gives us a sense of the substantive role that government capacity plays in investment flows. Beginning with the province of Maharashtra—i.e., India's major industrial hub—the Full Model suggests that an increase from the province's 2005 level of *RPE* (0.96) to the optimal level of extraction (1.72) leads to an expected 610 crore increase in approved FDI or an approximate 22 percent increase in accumulated capital.

Moving to the southern tip of India, these data suggest that if the province of Tamil Nadu increased *RPE* from its 2005 level (1.21) to the optimal level, the province would experience a 30.7 percent increase in FDI. Moreover, given the nonlinear nature of the Full Model, the effects are particularly pronounced for provinces with low levels of political capacity. For instance, a similar move for the eastern province of West Bengal—i.e., from its 2005 level of .61 to the optimal value—implies an expected shift from a net inflow of 390.12 crore to one of 1,692 crore. These results are quite strong and suggest that capacity is not only statistically but also substantively significant in the Indian context.

China Empirical Results

The results of the estimation of FDI inflows in China are presented in table 9.2. Turning to the Base Model, the political capacity indicators are statistically insignificant at the traditional levels. The variance of the dependent variable that is explained by political capacity alone is 5 percent. Once the economic controls are accounted for, however, the U-shaped relationship takes form and *RPE* becomes significant at the 10 percent error level. It should be noted that RPE^2 is marginally significant (p-value = 0.141).

The lagged provincial GDP indicator has a strong statistically significant positive effect on FDI inflows. The lagged provincial growth rate is insignificant across all specifications. Similar to the Indian case, we find that once the economic controls are included in the specification, population once again exhibits a significant negative direction. Lastly, regarding model fit, the Full Model explains a significantly large share of the variation of inward FDI flows at the provincial level in China ($R^2 = 0.834$).

CONCLUSIONS AND POLICY IMPLICATIONS

The analysis above provides additional empirical support for the proposition that political capacity impacts the accumulation of foreign capital. Consistent with a number of recent studies on the politics of FDI (Adji et al. 1997; Feng 2003; Coan and Kugler 2008), this chapter demonstrates the utility of taking a political-economic approach to understanding FDI flows. Furthermore, this chapter also extends political explanations centering on government capacity to the subnational level, suggesting that RPC helps to explain intra- as well as international variation in FDI flows. Specifically, our core findings include:

- The econometric results suggest that the relationship between government capacity and FDI is both statistically and substantively significant.
- Investment within India is more open, as would be expected. Within China we have less of a clear view of investment flows due to the central government's historical restrictions. As these restrictions decline, investors will start to evaluate provinces in competition with each

other. This will mean that the measurements of political efficiency will be very valuable. Investors will want to know where they can get the best return on the renminbi. This trend already is observable as China seeks to open up the western provinces as it has the east.

In addition to extending the academic literature, these findings have a number of important policy implications. First, the Political Economy Model could be used to identify areas that will benefit considerably from small changes to political efficiency. As demonstrated above, we would anticipate nontrivial increases in FDI in a province such as West Bengal, with its population center in Calcutta, for India, but also equally large increases in FDI in the Central Regions of China in provinces such as Shanxi and Jiangxi.

This information may prove useful to policy makers interested in facilitating Indian and China economic development but could be more important to investors who are increasingly allowed to invest in interior provinces due to economic liberalization. These limitations have profound importance as economic polarization increases within both countries. This problem of inequality is one of the primary questions for the future of each country, and it will be in the provinces that the policies are enacted to either deal with the issue or help to exacerbate it.

The predictive capabilities of our political-economic model are not fully developed, but already they provide a nuanced view on the dynamics of FDI in India and within China. This will increase over time as we add new elements to the model. As a first step, this chapter provides evidence of the relationship between politics and FDI flows, while also demonstrating the utility of taking a subnational approach to understanding the dynamics of capital accumulation.

NOTES

1. We are extremely grateful to Siddharth Swaminathan and the TransResearch Consortium for providing us with provincial-level estimates of relative political capacity. Without his and their generosity this study would not have been possible.

2. For a complete overview of the whole range of economic variables thought to influence FDI and the empirical robustness of each measure, see Chakrabarti (2001).

3. Sauvik Chakraverti, "Predatory State—The Black Hole of Social Science," *Times of India*, September 22, 1999.

4. Problems associated with missing data are common in empirical studies of FDI and these problems are particularly acute at the subnational level. Consistent with national-level studies on the correlates of FDI, close to 50 percent of the possible observations are omitted in the analysis below due to missing data and list-wise

deletion. In India, as in other developing nations, missing data tends to be highly correlated with the size and development status of the province. Moreover, according to a series of logistic regression models, missing FDI data is highly correlated with low levels of political capacity. Thus, while our sample may be biased toward more developed provinces, these biases likely make it harder, not easier to confirm our hypotheses. Provinces with lower levels of development and low RPC are likely the provinces also failing to accumulate foreign capital.

5. A potential limitation of this measure is that the FDI is "approved" but not actually spent. However, given the hypotheses above, our concern is primarily with where foreign investors choose to invest—i.e., FDI is the dependent variable in the analyses below. This measure would be less appropriate for scholars interested in using FDI as a explanatory variable.

6. A crore is equivalent to ten million.

7. Extending the measure of RPC to the provincial level requires a number of modifications to the core specification presented in Arbetman and Kugler (1997). Scholars must pay special attentic ꞁ to the structure of a nation's tax system, the level of government primarily responsible for tax collection, and the potential confounding influence of intergovernment transfers. For an overview of modeling political capacity at the subnational level, see Arbetman and Johnson (2007) or Johnson (2007, appendix II).

8. While the Indian population is diverse, historical analysis suggests that the country may be reasonably broken up into four distinct regions. These four regions include:

1. Northern Region: This region consists of the states of Uttaranchal, Haryana, Punjab, Himachal Pradesh, Uttar Pradesh, Jammu, and Kashmir. These provinces are located at the foothills of the Himalayan mountains and were the area of the great Moghal migrations of the tenth and twelfth centuries and the heart of their later empire.

2. Southern Region: This region consists of the states of Tamil Nadu, Goa, Karnataka, Kerala, and Andhra Pradesh. Historically this region was the battleground of the European colonial wars with the Portuguese, British, and French all having local allies and armies.

3. Eastern Region: This region consists of the states of Sikkim, West Bengal, Tripura, Meghalaya, Mizoram, Manipur, Arunachal Pradesh, Chattisgarh, Manipur, Orissa, Assam, Bihar, Jharkhand, and Nagaland. These provinces have the largest variance in language and culture in India, with Bihar often being associated with Northern Indian groups, Sikkim being an isolated Buddhist Kingdom in the vein of Bhutan, and lastly Mizoram, Nagaland, and Manipur having connections to Southeast Asia.

4. Western Region: This consists of Maharashtra, Gujarat, Rajasthan, and Madhya Pradesh. This is the industrial heartland of the country with the majority of its chemical, petrochemical, textiles, steel, and other heavy industries.

9. We aggregate Chinese provinces into three general groups:

1. Western Region: This region consists of the provinces of Chongqing, Gansu, Guizhou, Ningxia, Qinghai, Shaanxi, Sichuan, Tibet, Xinjiang,

and Yunnan. This region has had a great deal of conflict with ethnic and racial tensions increasing in Tibet and the surrounding provinces as well as in Xiangiang with the local Uighurs. It is also in this region that the central government has mandated increasing the population with forced or incentivized population movements and settlements.

2. Central Region: This region consists of the provinces of Anhui, Heilongjiang, Henan, Hubei, Hunan, Inner Mongolia, Jiangxi, Jilin, and Shaanxi. The region stretches from the center of the country up toward Mongolia and into the ex-Manchurian provinces. It is also the primary source location for coal mines.

3. Eastern Region: This region consists of the provinces of Bejing, Fujian, Guangdong, Hainan, Hebei, Jiangsu, Liaoning, Shandong, Shanghai, Tianjin, and Zhejiang. This was the region with the original economic reforms and, as it is primarily coastal, has also had the largest proportion of trade and increased investment both from the domestic arena and international.

10. $FDI_{it} = \beta_0 + \beta_1 RPE_{it} + \beta_2 RPE^2 + \alpha C_{it} + \gamma FE_R + \lambda FE_T + \delta_{it}$ (1)

Where *FDI* represents the stock of foreign direct investment inflows; *RPE* represents relative political capacity; RPE^2 adjusts the model for possible nonlinearities in political capacity; *C* is a vector of control variables; FE_R represents regional fixed effects; FE_T represents time fixed effects; and e represents the stochastic error term. The subscripts in (1) denote country *i* in time *t* and thus incorporate the model's panel structure.

REFERENCES

Adji, S. S., Y. S. Ahn, C. M. Holsey, and T. D. Willett. 1997. "Political Capacity and Capital Flows." M. Arbetman and J. Kugler, eds., *Political Capacity and Economic Behavior*. Boulder, CO: Westview Press.

Arbetman, M., and J. Kugler. 1997. *Political Capacity and Economic Behavior*. Boulder, CO: Westview Press.

Arbetman-Rabinowitz, M., and K. Johnson. 2007. "Relative Political Capacity: Empirical and Theoretical Underpinnings." Paper presented at Claremont Graduate University, Claremont, CA, October 2007.

Arellano, M. 1987. "Computing Robust Standard Errors for Within-Group Estimators." *Oxford Bulletin of Economics and Statistics* 49: 431–34.

Banga, R. 2003. "Impact of Government Policies and Investment Agreements on FDI Inflows." Indian Council for Research on International Economic Relations, New Delhi Working Papers 116, Indian Council for Research on International Economic Relations, New Delhi, India.

Bhaduri, S. N. 2005. "Investment, Financial Constraints and Financial Liberalization: Some Stylized Facts from a Developing Economy, India." *Journal of Asian Economics* 16: 704–18.

Bhalla, A. S. 1998. *Globalization, Growth, and Marginalization*. London: Macmillan.

Billington, N. 1999. "The Location of Foreign Direct Investment: An Empirical Analysis." *Applied Economics* 31: 65–76.

Borensztien, E., J. De Gregorio, and J-W. Lee. 1998. "How Does Foreign Direct Investment Affect Growth?" *Journal of International Economics* 45: 115–35.

Bravo-Ortega, C., and J. De Gregorio. 2005. "The Relative Richness of the Poor? Natural Resources, Human Capital, and Economic Growth." Policy Research Working Papers no. WPS 3484, The World Bank.

Chakrabarti, A. 2001. "The Determinants of Foreign Direct Investment: Sensitivity Analyses of Cross-Country Regressions." *Kyklos* 54 (1): 89–113.

Chen, Z., and M. S. Khan. 1997. "Patterns of Capital Flows to Emerging Markets: A Theoretical Perspective." IMF Working Paper WP/97/13.

Coan, T., and T. Kugler. 2008. "The Politics of Foreign Direct Investment: An Interactive Framework." *International Interactions* 34 (4): 402–22.

De Soto, H. 1989. *The Other Path: The Invisible Revolution in the Third World.* New York: Harper & Row.

———. 2000. *The Mystery of Capital: Why Capitalism Triumphs in the West and Fails Everywhere Else.* New York: Basic Books.

Dunning, J. H. 1981. *International Production and the Multinational Enterprise.* Boston: Allen and Unwin.

Feng, Y. 2003. *Democracy, Governance, and Economic Performance: Theory and Evidence.* Cambridge: The MIT Press.

Johnson, Kristin. 2007. "Sub National Capabilities and Internal Conflict." PhD diss., Claremont Graduate University, Claremont, CA.

Kaufmann, D., A. Kraay, and M. Mastruzzi. 2003. "Governance Matters III: Governance Indicators for 1996–2000." Policy Research Working Paper 4654, The World Bank.

———. 2008. "Governance Matters VII: Governance Indicators for 1996–2007." Policy Research Working Paper 3106, The World Bank.

Leblang, David. 1997. "Political Capacity and Economic Growth." Marina Arbetman and Jacek Kugler, eds., *Political Capacity and Economic Behavior.* Boulder, CO: Westview Press.

Mansfield, E., and A. Romeo. 1980. "Technology Transfer to Overseas Subsidiary by US-Based Firms." *Quarterly Journal of Economics* 95 (4): 737–50.

Organisation for Economic Co-operation and Development. 2002. *Foreign Direct Investment in China: Challenges and Prospects for Regional Development.* Paris: OECD Publications.

Rogers, W. H. 1993. "Regression Standard Errors in Clustered Samples." *Stata Technical Bulletin* 13: 19–23.

Sayers, Lois W. 1989. *Pooled Times Series Analysis.* Newberry Park, CA: Sage Publications.

Schneider, F., and B. Frey. 1985. "Economic and Political Determinants of Foreign Direct Investment." *World Development* 13: 161–75.

Shirai, S. 2004. "Assesing the Impact of Financial and Capital Reforms on Firms' Corporate Financing Patterns in India." *South Asia Economic Journal* 5 (2): 189–208.

Srivastava, S., and R. Sen. 2004. "Competing for Global FDI: Opportunities and Challenges for the Indian Economy." *South Asia Economic Journal* 5: 233–60.

Wei, S. 2000. "How Taxing Is Corruption on International Investors?" *The Review of Economics and Statistics* 82 (1): 1–11.

Wei, Yingqi, and Xiaming Liu. 2001. *Foreign Direct Investment in China: Determinants and Impact*. Northampton, MA: Edward Elgar Publishing.

Wheeler, D., and A. Mody. 1992. "International Investment Location Decisions." *Journal of International Economics* 33 (1–2): 57–76.

The World Bank. 2005. *World Development Report 2005: A Better Investment Climate for Everyone*. Washington, DC: The World Bank Publications.

———. 2007. *Doing Business in 2007*. Washington, DC: The World Bank Publications.

———. 2010. Data retrieved March 2, 2010, from World Development Indicators Online (WDI) database.

10

Indian Performance, Religion, and Economic Growth

Yi Feng and Saumik Paul

CONTEXT

The objective of this chapter is to examine the effects of ethnic and religious conflict and government capacity on growth rates across states in India. In the past, the domestic conflict between the Hindu and Muslim populations has dominated the politics of the nation. In this chapter, on the one hand, we argue that ethnic and religious violence and conflict in India do have a negative impact on its economy; on the other, we explore the impact of government capacity at the state level to moderate violence and achieve economic growth.

We hypothesize that relative parity of Islamic and Hindu populations in a state has a negative impact on growth and that government capacity holds a positive effect on growth and a negative one on riots. These hypotheses were tested in the context of empirical studies on economic growth in seventeen large states in India over the period of 1980 through 2000.

Our findings demonstrate that the states where the Hindu and Muslim populations tend to be close in numbers are likely to have intense conflict and experience low economic growth. We also find that government capacity increases growth while uncontrolled by religious parity, suggesting a complex relationship between religion and government capacity.

The second section presents some highlights of ethnic and religious riots in India. The third section outlines the differential economic growth rates in India while the fourth section discusses the central thesis delineating the effects of ethno-religious interactions and government capacity on growth. This is followed with a presentation of the analytical model and data specification. Our findings flow from that including the statistical evidence of convergence in growth and the significance of cultural factors, specifically religious conflicts, to explain growth disparity along with other economic characteristics in India. Lastly, we provide certain appropriate policy conclusions.

BACKDROP: RIOTS IN INDIA

India was born in the wrath of destructive communal violence of the partition of the undivided region between India and Pakistan. Evidence abounds of violence all over India since its independence in 1947. Kashmir, the bordering northern state between India and Pakistan, has been reduced to armed occupation resulting in the suppression of normal civic life for the past four decades. Assam, a bordering state in northeast India, has been a witness to conflict and violence between different ethnic minorities for greater autonomy since the 1970s. Terrorist activities, rather than communal riots, are prominent in these two states.

Violence between different levels and sects of castes has also rendered the state of Bihar a battlefield since the mid-1980s. The 1990 tragic incidents of Ram Janmabhumi, the birthplace of Lord Rama in the Hindu mythology and home of the Babri Masjid, holy mosque for Muslims, turned India into bloodshed.[1] Hundreds of people were killed and thousands wounded in this destructive, violent communal riot. In the state of Gujarat, more than one thousand Muslims died in March 2002, following the incident in which some Muslims reportedly set fire to a train carrying Hindu nationalists, killing more than fifty people.[2]

Figure 10.1 shows the number of riots reported in the seventeen major states of India in the years 1980, 1990, and 2000, including all different causes, though communal riots overall dominate the statistics. In states such as Bihar, Andhra Pradesh, and Assam, the number of reported cases of riot increased in 1990; in other states such as Kerala, Karnataka, and Maharashtra, riots peaked in 2000. In West Bengal and Uttar Pradesh the number of reported riots decreased over time.

Varshney (2003) cites the absence of civic ties between the members of the two communities as the cause of riots. He further discusses the associational and routine forms of engagement that dampen riots if directed in positive ways. He concludes that urban areas are more likely to have riots than rural areas, supporting the findings in Nandy et al. (1995) that almost 90 percent of the riots are reported as originating in cities.[3]

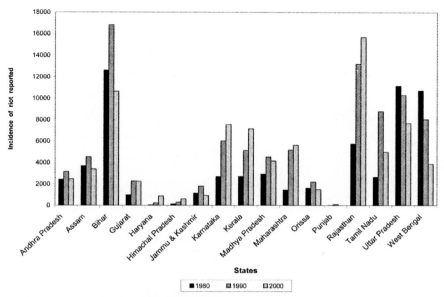

Figure 10.1.   Incidence of Riots Reported in Indian States, 1980, 1990, and 2000.
Source: Crime statistics, Statistical Abstracts of India.

Reported incidents of riots at the state levels reveal that some of the states are comparatively riot prone. The states of Bihar and Uttar Pradesh in northern India; West Bengal in eastern India; Rajasthan and Maharastra in the west; and Karnataka and Tamilnadu in the south are the most conflicted areas. States of Bihar, Uttar Pradesh, Rajasthan, and West Bengal experienced more than eight thousand incidents of riots reported every year in the period 1980–2000.[4]

In every democracy there is a necessary tension between majority rule and minority rights. In India, diverse ethnicities, religions, and languages further compound this tension. Explaining riots in India is as complex as its political and social system. Numerous studies on the causative factors explaining riots in India exist; some relying on the systematic political manipulation behind violence (Wilkinson 2004), some stressing the lack of associative factors across conflicting groups (Varshney 2003).

There is no ambiguity among them regarding the pernicious effect of riots on society. However, little work has been done so far to study the systemic effects of ethnic and religious conflict on the economy across the Indian states, except some case studies on a few areas where incidence of riots is high (e.g., Brass 2003). This study empirically links conflict, riots, and religion to economic growth within Indian states.

INTELLECTUAL ENVIRONMENT:
ECONOMIC GROWTH IN INDIA

In this chapter, we examine seventeen major Indian states in India during the period of 1980 through 2000. These states account for almost 98 percent of the total population and more than 90 percent of the physical area. The overall disparity in both interstate growth of gross state domestic product (GSDP) and per capita gross state domestic product (PCGSDP) has increased during the 1990s, compared to the 1980s and the 1970s.

The 1980s was the period when the horizontal inequality across the states was low compared to the later periods, while the early 1990s witnessed the most pronounced magnitude of disparity. The less-developed states such as Bihar, Orissa, Uttar Pradesh, and Madhya Pradesh were recorded below the all-India average during the most recent period of 1993–1994 and 1998–1999. In the last half of the 1990s the gap between the less-developed and developed states narrowed. Table 10.1 provides the standard deviation of growth rates and the coefficient of variation of growth disparity across the Indian states.

According to the neoclassical growth model, the per capita incomes of economies continuously converge toward their steady state level, resulting in a reduction in income inequality among these economies over time. This proposition has been extensively tested in the growth literature using both cross-country data as well as data from regions within a single economy. In this context, a number of studies have been conducted to examine the convergence hypothesis against the data on the Indian states.

One of the earlier and influential works on growth in India is by Cashin and Sahay (1996), who test convergence among Indian states over the period of 1961 through 1991. Their result suggests that absolute convergence was observed during that period due to initially poor states catching up with richer states in India. The study by Cashin and Sahay (1996) indi-

Table 10.1.   Disparity among States/Union Territories

Period	Measure of Disparity in Growth (Standard Deviation)		Relative measure of disparity in growth between per capita income and NSDP (Covariance)
	NSDP	Per Capita NSDP	
1970–1971 to 1979–1980	2.22	1.81	3.67
1980–1981 to 1990–1991	1.71	1.02	0.71
1993–1994 to 1998–1999	3.13	2.40	5.23

Source: Central Statistical Organization, *Planning Commission of India Development Trend Report and Tenth Plan Supplementary*

cates that the value of this measure of dispersion increases from 0.292 in 1961 to 0.333 in 1991, indicating sigma divergence.

Also looking at the convergence issues in India, Nagaraj et al. (1998) test for conditional convergence, instead of absolute convergence, by including independent variables, such as the share of agriculture in the output, apart from the initial values of per capita output. Their results support the conditional convergence hypothesis for the states of the Indian economy. Nagaraj et al. (1998) use the coefficient of variation of the real per capita state domestic product across states to confirm that inequalities have indeed risen over the period of 1960 through 1994. The estimated dispersion shows a steady rise from 0.22 in 1965–1966 to 0.39 in 1994–1995.

Continuing this tradition, Rao, Shand, and Kalirajan (1999) compute the standard deviation of per capita state domestic product (PCSDP) across states from the mid-1960s to the mid-1990s. Ahluwalia (2001) investigates the trends in interstate inequality for the pre-reform period (the 1980s) and the post-reform period (the 1990s), by constructing a population weighted Gini coefficient based on per capita gross state domestic product (PCG-SDP). His study reveals that coefficient of variation remained stable until 1985–1986, after which it rose to 0.17 during the closing years of the 1980s. During the 1990s, the coefficient climbed steeply, reflecting worsening interstate inequality, reaching 0.23 in 1998–1999.

In general, there are mixed evidence and findings in the research on the convergence hypothesis across states in India. As mentioned earlier, in the early 1990s, a sharp divergence took place among the economies in India, leading to the increase of the gap of wealth between rich and poor states. Eventually the latter half of the 1990s experienced a convergence, reducing the wealth gap of the states significantly. However, economic principles alone cannot interpret all the fluctuations in economic performance in India. In the next section, we turn to political and cultural dimensions to find some additional answers for the variance of growth trajectories across countries.

ETHNO-RELIGIOUS CONFLICT AND ECONOMIC GROWTH

The literature in the past couple of decades shows that economic growth is significantly affected by various social and political factors along with economic conditions. These vast arrays of social and political factors vary from country to country, region to region, accounting for growth disparities over decades. In some regions (for instance, Latin America), political instability is a harbinger of poor economic performance (Feng 1997, 2005), whereas in other regions, ethnic conflict (Alesina et al. 1999) and lack of trust (Zak and Knack, 2001) result in dismal economic growth.

La Porta et al. (1997) find countries with more dominant hierarchical religions have shown overall poor economic performance. A study by Barro and McCleary (2003) finds that religiosity reduces overall economic growth, although religious beliefs are positively related to education. A recent study by Noland (2005) demonstrates that Islam promotes growth on both cross-country and within-country regressions.

Unlike other studies on economic growth of India or other countries, we focus on proclivity toward religious conflict as an explanation of lack of economic performance. Particularly, we emphasize the demographic structure as a proxy of interactions of religious communities.

All religions may have their positive contributions to civilizations and economic growth. For instance, the Confucian South Korea, Christian Botswana, and Muslim Tunisia all registered rapid economic growth. Meanwhile, Buddhism is consonant with peace and harmony in Thailand, where it is a dominant religion (95 percent of the population), but does not ameliorate conflict in Sri Lanka where it (69 percent) shared the population with Hindus (15 percent), Christians (8 percent), and Muslims (8 percent).

India has long been a land of multiple religions, and conflicts between them have shaped the nation geographically, culturally, and economically. Geographical and cultural effects of religions are evident, but their economic consequences are difficult to trace. In India the term *communal* largely refers to interactions between the Hindus and Muslims.

Each year several hundred incidents of communal violence and riots are officially reported, and their number and intensity have considerably grown in recent years. Muslims today are India's largest religious minority, accounting for almost 13 percent of the total population. Among other religious groups, the Sikhs, some of whom in 1947 sought an independent Sikhistan, are concentrated in the northern state of Punjab and constitute less than 2 percent of India's total population. The other religious practitioners such as Christians, Buddhists, Jains, Parsees, and Jews further add to India's religious diversity, but their comparatively small populations only accentuate the overwhelming proportion of the Hindus.

Figure 10.2 shows population share of each religion in seventeen major states of India in 2001. Except in Assam, Jammu and Kashmir, Kerala, Punjab, and West Bengal, the Hindu population comprises more than three-quarters of the total population in the large states in India. In Jammu and Kashmir, Muslims are the majority whereas in Punjab, Sikhs constitute around 60 percent of the total population. Kerala has the highest Christian population share, and Maharashtra has the highest concentration of Buddhists.

While different religions may have certain doctrines in favor of economic

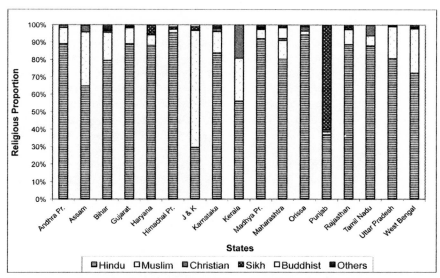

Figure 10.2. **State-wise Percentage of Religions in India, 2001. Source: Census of India, religion data, www.censusindia.net/results/religion_main.html**

growth through work ethics, we emphasize the pernicious effects of religious conflict on economic growth. Historically, the Hindu and Muslim populations in India have been involved in conflict. We argue that when the proportions of Hindu and Muslim populations are relatively close, conflict between the two populations will happen frequently, causing social violence and economic uncertainty, thus reducing economic growth. In this sense, it is not really individual religions that matter; it is the interactions between the opposing religious populations that matter.

When Hindu-Muslim populations approach parity, the possibility of riots substantially increases. The frequency of riots and other forms of violence should be very high in the states where the ratio of Hindu to Muslim populations approaches one. Economic growth will be retarded as the result of political instability, which both directly interrupts the productive process, as labor is involved in the acts of violence, and indirectly deters capital from being invested as the consequence of economic uncertainty.

MODEL AND DATA SPECIFICATION

For the analytical purpose, we apply Barro and Sala-i-Martin's (1995) framework to understand the growth process of Indian states. This framework relates growth process with the notion of classical convergence to explain the differences in levels and growth rates of income across different states. This empirical approach applies to seventeen major states in India for the period of 1980 to 2000. The dependent variable in our study is the growth rates of real per capita net state domestic product (NSDP) over four subperiods: 1980–1985, 1985–1990, 1990–1995, and 1995–2000.

We have several theoretical variables. One is government capacity at the state level in India. We adopt the operation and data compiled for this book and will not elaborate here, as it has been specifically discussed in the previous chapter.

Another central theoretical variable is a joint measure of the sizes of the Muslim and Hindu populations in a state. This variable, INTER, is calculated as the product of Hindu and Muslim population shares, weighted by population, in each state for the four periods starting from 1980 to 2000.

The construct of this variable reflects two considerations. The closer the two religious groups in terms of population, the higher is the value for the variable. Hypothetically, the strongest degree of hostilities will ensue when interactions are the most frequent and the most concentrated between two opposing faith communities. We expect that the variable INTER has a negative impact on growth. In addition, we include the number of riots divided by the population in a state as a confirmatory variable to our central thesis. The control variables include the initial level of per capita net state domestic product (PCNSDP), literacy rate, productive capital, and religion population shares in a state.[5]

Our study uses the data published by the Central Statistical Organization in the volumes of Statistical Abstract of India from 1980 to 2000 in the crime data section. This organization collects and compiles data from the National Crime Records Bureau, the Ministry of Home Affairs, and the police authorities of the state governments. According to the Ministry of Home Affairs, an incident of riot is defined as the gathering of five or more people in creating social disturbances.[6]

The Home Ministry of India data available on riot include communal riots between Hindus and Muslims as well as riots from other causes like agrarian disputes or caste conflicts within the Hindu religion. We recognize the lack of accuracy in the data source. The number of riots, however, is only a confirmatory variable to our central thesis, considering that incidents of riots from sources other than communal are significantly fewer in number than Hindu-Muslim riots.

As mentioned earlier, the neoclassical model of growth argues that a nation's growth rate tends to be negatively related to its level of development (Solow 1956; Barro 1991). The main reason for this phenomenon in neoclassical growth models is diminishing returns to reproducible capital. In contrast, human capital plays a critical role in endogenous growth models, which hold that knowledge-driven growth can lead to a constant—or even increasing—rate of return. In Romer's work for instance, human capital is the major input to research and development, which innovates technologies necessary for continued growth (Romer 1990). Therefore, states with larger initial human capital stocks are more likely to create new products and will grow faster than other countries. Empirical evidence has revealed a positive relationship between education and growth.[7] We expect that the literacy rate of a state is positively related to economic growth.

Investment has long been considered the engine of growth. According to Kormendi and Meguire and Levine and Renelt, investment share of GDP has a significant and positive effect on growth (Kormendi and Meguire 1985; Levine and Renelt 1992). Some studies of the relationship between growth and capital investment in developing countries have borne out the positive influence of capital formation on growth (Robinson 1971; Tyler 1981; Levy 1988). In our study, we use the share of investment as the ratio between productive capital and net state domestic product. It is expected that productive capital has a positive impact on growth. All the three control variables take the values of the initial year for the five-year period to reduce the endogeneity problem.

FINDINGS

Table 10.2 presents descriptive statistics of all the variables used in this chapter. We have a panel of sixty-eight observations for the periods 1980–1985, 1985–1990, 1990–1995, and 1995–2000 on per capita net state domestic product, investment, literacy rate, number of riots over population, and the religious population share in each state. The standard deviation of investment is found to be very high, indicating the growing disparity of investment across states. The same applies to the number of riots. The average population share for Hindus is in the neighborhood of 80 percent across the states, for Muslims about 13 percent, for Christians around 2 percent, for Sikhs 5 percent, and for Buddhists roughly 0.5 percent across the states under study. The RPE is averaged toward one, which is by design, with a range of 0.6 to 1.7.

Table 10.3 presents correlations among the variables. RPE is positively correlated with Growth and negatively correlated with Interaction and Riots, though the associations are moderate. The signs are consistent with theoretical arguments. Government capacity may reduce riots and vice versa, and it may also be weakened by relatively equal population sizes of divergent religious faiths. At the same time, higher government capacity may lead to higher growth and the reversed causality may hold too.

Table 10.2.   Descriptive Statistics

Variable	Observations	Average	Standard Deviation	Minimum Value	Maximum Value
NSDP per capita (in Indian Rs)	68	1955.10	3701.130	917	4177
Investment share of NSDP	68	0.407	0.194	0.053	0.980
RPE	68	1.016	.238	.606	1.70
Literacy	68	51.669	15.586	24.4	90.85
Riot per capita	68	0.0001	7.95E-05	2.62E-07	0.0004
INTER	68	0.080	0.066	0.002	0.207
Hindu Share	68	0.793	0.218	0.236	0.969
Muslim Share	68	0.127	0.161	0.006	0.678
Christian Share	68	0.023	0.047	0.0004	0.208
Sikh Share	68	0.049	0.172	5.69E-06	0.740
Buddhist Share	68	0.006	0.015	3.52E-06	0.065

Table 10.4 reports regression results of the three models. Our central hypothesis finds strong support. *INTER* is highly statistically significant. The higher the value of the multiplicative term between Muslims and Hindus adjusted for population, the lower the growth rate for the state. Similarly, *RIOT* has a negative and significant impact on growth as well. The estimated relations between economic growth and riots and between growth and religious interaction respectively are statistically significant at 99 percent confidence level. Finally, we also find that government capacity increases growth while uncontrolled by the religious parity, suggesting a complex relationship between religion and government capacity.

All models also show growth convergence across the states during the period of 1980 through 2000. By contrast, investment levels are detrimental to economic growth. Literacy rates expectedly enhance the growth rate.

Table 10.3.   Correlation Analysis

	Investment share of NSDP	Literacy	Per capita Riot	Interaction	Per capita NSDP	RPC
Investment share of NSDP	1					
Literacy	0.0703	1				
Per capita Riot	−0.3199	−0.1021	1			
Interaction	−0.4772	−0.0837	0.5255	1		
Per capita NSDP	0.0981	0.5004	−0.4484	−0.3012	1	
RPE	−0.0799	0.3588	−0.2572	−0.3164	0.3784	1

Table 10.4. Regression Analysis, Dependent Variable: NSDP

	3.1	3.2	3.3	3.4	3.5	3.6
NSDP per capita	−0.091*** (0.030)	−0.088*** (0.033)	−0.092*** (0.031)	−0.094*** (0.030)	−0.092*** (0.031)	−0.094*** (0.030)
Investment share of NSDP	−0.379*** (0.089)	−0.282*** (0.075)	−0.381** (0.091)	−0.346*** (0.098)	−0.248*** (0.101)	−0.347*** (0.101)
Literacy	0.003** (0.001)	0.003* (0.002)	0.003** (0.001)	0.003* (0.002)	0.003 (0.002)	0.003* (0.002)
INTER	−0.884*** (0.268)		−0.847*** (0.291)	−0.746** (0.332)		−0.730** (0.339)
Riot per capita		−350.418** (161.949)	−65.634 (170.132)		−230.338 (181.876)	−33.458 (170.464)
RPC				0.088 (0.068)	0.146** (0.056)	0.087 (0.070)
Constant	1.332*** (0.210)	1.238*** (0.206)	1.346*** (0.211)	1.257*** (0.225)	1.128*** (0.206)	1.265*** (0.230)
Observations	68	68	68	68	68	68
R-squared	0.35	0.239	0.351	0.369	0.295	0.369

*p<.05, **p<.01, ***p<.001

In a cross-country setting, the investment share of GDP is one of the most powerful indicators of economic growth in the world. However, in the states of India, the investment share does not seem matter a great deal. Our statistical results indicate that investment may not have been well utilized in India and has therefore not achieved its intended objective of increasing the wealth of the society. What really determines the growth rate of the economy in the Indian states seems to be the relationships among religious groups, particularly between the Hindus and Muslims.

Table 10.5 demonstrates the relationship between the number of riots over population and religious shares of state population. Again, consistent with our argument, *INTER* has a positive and strong impact on *RIOT*. The estimated slope coefficient of interactions shows a very strong positive relation with riots at 99.9 percent confidence level. The correlation between riots and interactions is fairly strong, standing at around 0.50. In other words, interactions between Hindus and Muslims lead to an increase in the

Table 10.5. Regression Analysis, Dependent Variable: Riot per Capita

	(4.1) Riot per Capita	(4.2) Riot per Capita	(4.3) Riot per Capita	(4.4) Riot per Capita
INTER	0.0006*** (0.0001)	0.0004 (0.0002)	0.001*** 0.000	
Hindu Share		−0.0017 (0.0014)		−0.001 (0.002)
Muslim Share		−0.0017 (0.0014)		−0.001 (0.002)
Christian Share		−0.0015 (0.0014)		−0.001 (0.002)
Sikh Share		−0.0018 (0.0014)		−0.001 (0.002)
Buddhist Share		−0.0025 (0.0014)		−0.002 (0.002)
RPC			0 (0.000)	0 (0.000)
Constant	0.0001*** (0.0000)	0.0018 (0.0014)		0.001 (0.002)
R^2	0.28	0.35	0.285	0.339
Observations	68	68	68	68

*p<.05, **p<.01, ***p<.001

likelihood of riots. Also consistent with our theory is that religious groups, by themselves, do not cause riots; none of the religious population share is statistically significant. Government capacity is found to have little if no impact on conflict in our context.

CONCLUSIONS

We find empirical evidence confirming the narrowing of regional growth disparities in India, which supports both the convergence hypothesis of the neoclassical growth models (Solow 1956) and the general findings of cross-country analyses (e.g., Barro 1991, Feng 2005).

More importantly, the data strongly corroborate our argument that religion itself does not influence economic growth; rather, it is the interactions between opposing religious communities that switch investment incentives away from optimality and/or lead to political violence that reduces economic growth. Government capacity directly influences growth, but in this case does not appear to reduce conflict in the Indian context.

NOTES

1. See Nandy et al. (1995) for an elaborate description of the Ramjanmabhumi and Babri Masjid incidents.

2. See Wilkinson (2004) for a detailed description of the communal violence in Gujarat. Essays by Nandy et al. (1995) and Puniyani (2003) portray the pernicious and brutal effect of these riots over decades in India.

3. Nandy et al. 1995, 15.

4. In very recent years (2001–2002) Gujarat experienced the most destructive violence and riots and has become one of the riot prone states. The table shows data only until 2000.

5. The source of data is Central Statistical Organization, *Planning Commission of India Development Trend Report and Tenth Plan Supplementary,* and Premi (2004).

6. There are a number of problems with the reliability of this data published by the Home Ministry among the scholars. First, the Home Ministry data is available only from 1954. Second, it collects only state- and national-level data, where often riots are based on city or smaller region (Varshney 2003). Finally, the Home Ministry data shows the number of cases that have been filed with police as a criminal case of riot. There may be some discrepancies between actual figures of riots and the number of riot cases filed in the police department. But these discrepancies exist in various private sources also, which are mostly collected from different media sources since the state has significant power in controlling both means.

7. For the theoretical argument, see Lucas (1988); Romer (1986, 1990); and Young (1992). For empirical works, see Levine and Renelt (1992); Barro (1991); and Young (1992).

REFERENCES

Ahluwalia, M. S. 2001. "State Level Performance under Economic Reforms in India." *Economic and Political Weekly*, May 6.

Alesina A., R. Baqir, and William Easterly. 1999. "Public Goods and Ethnic Divisions." *Quarterly Journal of Economics* 114 (4): 1243–84.

Austin, Dennis. 1995. *Democracy and Violence in India and Sri Lanka*. New York: Council on Foreign Relations Press.

Barro, Robert J. 1991. "Economic Growth in a Cross-section of Countries." *Quarterly Journal of Economics* 106: 408–43.

———. 1997. *Determinants of Economic Growth: A Cross-Country Empirical Study*. Cambridge: MIT Press.

Barro Robert J., and Rachel M. McCleary. 2003. "Religion and Economic Growth across Countries." *American Sociological Review* 68: 760–81.

Barro, Robert J., and Xavier Sala-i-Martin. 1995. *Economic Growth*. New York: McGraw-Hill

Brass, Paul. 2003. *The Production of Hindu-Muslim Violence in Contemporary India*. Washington, DC: University of Washington Press.

Cashin, P., and R Sahay. 1996. "International Migration, Center-State Grants, and Economic Growth in the States of India." International Monetary Fund staff papers 43.

Central Statistical Organization. *Planning Commission of India Development Trend Report and Tenth Plan Supplementary*. New Delhi: Department of Statistics, Ministry of Planning, India.

Feng, Yi. 1997. "Democracy, Political Instability and Economic Growth." *British Journal of Political Science* 27: 391–18.

———. 2005. *Democracy, Governance, and Economic Performance: Theory, Data Analysis, and Case Studies*. Cambridge: MIT Press.

Kormendi, Roger C., and Phillip G. Meguire. 1985. "Macroeconomic Determinants of Growth: Cross-Country Evidence." *Journal of Monetary Economics* 16: 141–63.

La Porta, R., F. Lopez-de-Silanes, A. Shleifer, and R. W. Vishney. 1997. "Trust in Large Organizations." *American Economic Review* 87 (2): 333–38.

Levine, Ross, and David Renelt. 1992. "A Sensitivity Analysis of Cross-Country Growth Regressions." *American Economic Review* 82: 942–63.

Levy, Victor. 1988. "Aid and Growth in Sub-Saharan Africa: The Recent Experience." *European Economic Review* 32: 1777–95.

Lucas, Robert E. 1988. "On the Mechanics of Economic Development." *Journal of Monetary Economics* 22: 3–42.

Nagaraj, R., A. Varoudakis, and M. Veganzones. 1998. "Long Run Growth Trends and Convergence across Indian States." OECD Development Center Technical Paper 131.

Nandy, Ashis, Shikha Trivedy, Shail Mayaram, and Achyut Yagnik. 1995. *Creating a Nationality: The Ramjanmabhumi Movement and the Fear of the Self*. Delhi: Oxford University Press.

Noland, Marcus. 2005. "Religion and Economic Performance." *World Development* 33 (8): 1215–32.

Premi, Mahendra. 2004. "Religion in India: A Demographic Perspective." *Economic and Political Weekly*, September 25.

Puniyani, Ram. 2003. *Communal Politics: Facts versus Myths*. New Delhi: Sage Publications India.

Ramsey, Frank P. 1928. "A Mathematical Theory of Savings." *Economic Journal* 38: 543–59.

Rao, G., R. T. Shand, and K. P. Kalirajan. 1999. "Convergence of Incomes across Indian States: A Divergent View." *Economic and Political Weekly* 17 (13).

Robinson, Sherman. 1971. "Sources of Growth in Less Developed Countries: A Cross Section Study." *Quarterly Journal of Economics* 55: 391–408.

Romer, Paul M. 1986. "Increasing Returns and Long-Run Growth." *Journal of Political Economy* 94: 1002–1037.

———. 1990. "Endogenous Technological Change." *Journal of Political Economy* 98: S71–S102.

Solow, Robert M. 1956. "A Contribution to the Theory of Economic Growth." *Quarterly Journal of Economics* 34: 65–94.

Tyler, William G. 1981. "Growth and Export Expansion in Developing Countries: Some Empirical Evidence." *Journal of Developmental Economics* 9: 121–30.

Varshney, Ashutosh. 2003. *Ethnic Conflict and Civic Life: Hindus and Muslims in India*. New Haven, CT: Yale University Press.

Wilkinson, Steven. 2002. "Putting Gujarat in Perspective." *Economic and Political Weekly*, April 27.

———. 2004. *Votes and Violence: Electoral Competition and Ethnic Riots in India*. Cambridge Studies in Comparative Politics Series. New York: Cambridge University Press.

Young, Alwyn. 1992. "A Tale of Two Cities: Factor Accumulation and Technical Change in Hong Kong and Singapore." Oliver J. Blanchard and Stanley Fischer, eds., *NBER Macroeconomics Annual*, 13–54. Cambridge: MIT Press.

Zak, Paul J., and Stephen Knack. 2001. "Trust and Growth." *The Economic Journal* 111: 295–321.

11

The Politics of Births in India

Evidence from the States

Siddharth Swaminathan and John Thomas

CONTEXT

This chapter investigates the impact of political development on demographic change. We first present estimates of relative political extraction as a measure of political development for the twenty-eight Indian states for the period 1981–2005. Using this measure of political performance of the Indian states, we test a political model of demographic change and explain variation in subnational birth rates in the fifteen largest states for the period 1981–2001.

We find that the extractive ability of states conditional on per capita income has a significant negative effect on birth rates. The effect of relative political extraction on births is greatest in the poor and middle-income states. As the income level in a state increases, the impact of political extraction diminishes.

The analysis further reveals the differential effects of relative political extraction in lowering births in rural and urban areas. Political extraction plays a significant role in reducing urban births but only a limited role in lowering rural births. The results suggest that the most efficient among the Indian states will likely experience gains despite economic constraints, reap the benefits of a demographic dividend, and provide the motor for economic growth in the twenty-first century.

The key question explored in this chapter is the impact of relative poli-

Table 11.1.   Average Crude Birth Rates (1981–2001) by Income Quartile

	Poorest 25% Less than Rs. 5,184	Second Quartile Less than Rs. 6,399	Third Quartile Less than Rs. 8,874	Richest 25% Less than Rs. 15,257
Crude Birth Rate	33.76	29.51	27.75	24.83

tical extraction on birth rates across the Indian states. Why have some relatively poor states performed more effectively in lowering birth rates compared to their richer counterparts? After controlling for the well-documented effects of socioeconomic factors, does political capacity of the state government have any impact in lowering births?

These questions are motivated by the observation that states such as Andhra Pradesh, Karnataka, Kerala, and Tamil Nadu at average income levels between Rupees (Rs.) 7,000 and 8,500 have recorded birth rates below the relatively richer states of Gujarat, Haryana, Maharashtra, and Punjab with average income levels above Rs. 9,500. While, on average, poorer states in India report higher birth rates and the richer states lower values, the variation across states within India is considerable. Consider tables 11.1 and 11.2.

The poorest income quartile, consisting of observations from the states of Bihar, Orissa, and UP (with mean SDP/Capita levels below approxi-

Table 11.2.   Average Crude Birth Rates (1981–2001) by State

State	CBR	SDP/Cap
Andhra Pradesh	26.2 (3.8)	6685.7 (1605.1)
Assam	30.8 (2.9)	5412.8 (359.9)
Bihar	34.1 (3.3)	3868.1 (298.3)
Gujarat	29.0 (3.3)	9503.1 (2560.2)
Haryana	32.1 (3.6)	10332.0 (2045.9)
Karnataka	26.1 (2.8)	7304.8 (2057.6)
Kerala	20.1 (2.9)	7228.0 (2728.0)
Madhya Pradesh	34.9 (2.8)	6058.1 (981.8)
Maharashtra	26.2 (3.3)	10362.1 (2864.5)
Orissa	29.0 (3.2)	4690.6 (595.4)
Punjab	26.4 (3.1)	11619.0 (2084.4)
Rajasthan	34.6 (2.8)	6244.0 (1546.1)
Tamil Nadu	22.2 (3.3)	8240.7 (2434.9)
Uttar Pradesh	35.8 (2.3)	5006.8 (553.4)
West Bengal	26.4 (1.4)	6511.0 (1552.7)
ALL SAMPLE	28.9 (5.5)	7271.1 (2808.7)

mately Rs. 5,184), are characterized by high average CBR ranging from 25 to 34 births per 1,000 population. The richest quartile, mainly composed of Gujarat, Haryana, Maharashtra, and Punjab (with mean SDP level greater than approximately Rs. 9,000), exhibit relatively lower average CBR ranging from 15 to 25. The middle-income states, Assam, MP, Rajasthan, and WB (in the second quartile) and AP, Karnataka, Kerala, and TN (in the third quartile), exhibit considerable variation in average CBR ranging from 19 (Kerala) to 34 (MP).

These patterns are consistent given the expected negative relationship between income and fertility, yet the relatively poorer states of Kerala and Tamil Nadu (in 2001) have recorded crude birth rates of 17.3 and 19.1 births (per 1,000 population) respectively, compared to the richer states such as Gujarat and Haryana that report birth rates of 25 and 26.8. It is to answer this puzzle that we turn our attention to assessing the impact of politics on fertility change.

We first generate subnational estimates of relative political extraction, based on extant national level estimates, for twenty-eight states in India for the period 1981–2005.[1] Relative political extraction is used as an indicator of political capacity to empirically evaluate, at a subnational level, specific theoretical expectations generated by a political model of demographic change. Specifically, we assess the effect of relative political extraction on birth rates in the fifteen largest Indian states over the time period 1981–2001.

Consistent with expectations, relative political extraction conditional on per capita income levels has a significant negative effect on birth rates. However, this effect gets weaker as the income level in a state increases, suggesting that political development has limited effects on fertility behavior and that these effects are greatest in the poor and middle-income states. At comparable income levels, states with higher extractive capacity on average register lower birth rates. The analysis also reveals the differential effects of relative political extraction on rural and urban birth rates. The conditional effect of political extraction on urban births is significant, but weak for rural births. Our results raise significant policy questions regarding government action in lowering rural births in India.

This chapter is structured as follows. The first section examines the intellectual environment that supports our analysis. This is followed by an outline of the theoretical expectations that link political extraction, and political performance in general, with birth rates at a subnational level. Then we present empirical tests of the above expectations and discuss the results in the context of the Indian experience. The last section provides conclusions.

INTELLECTUAL ENVIRONMENT

Political capacity speaks to the effectiveness of political systems in the tasks they set out to perform. Do government elites have the tools to effectively implement a chosen national agenda in the face of competing demands? How successful are political systems in collecting, pooling, and allocating human and material resources toward national goals? Political capacity is defined as the ability of a government to mobilize available human resources (political reach) within its society and collect material resources (political extraction) to implement national goals. Political reach and political extraction are the components that drive the scale and scope of government activities within society, resulting in the "massive expansion and transformation of the political system" (Organski and Kugler 1980, 7).

Our measure of relative political extraction is based on the method outlined in Arbetman and Kugler (1997). Relative political extraction is measured as the taxable capacity of a state government.[2] The amount of tax revenue extracted by a state government depends on (a) the economic resources available from which to extract and (b) the political effort exerted by the same government in collecting those resources.

Relative political extraction for a given state is estimated as the ratio of actual state tax ratio to predicted state tax ratio after controlling for the economic resources. The deviation from the expected performance is an indicator of the political effort exerted by a state government in collecting material resources. A state government that is extracting revenues at higher than expected levels given its level of development is considered capable relative to one that is extracting at lower than expected levels at a similar level of development. As Arbetman and Kugler (1997, 20) observe, this measure of political capacity does not directly measure its political components but the "shadow of politics."

The empirical model used to estimate relative political extraction is located here.[3]

Tables 11.3a and 11.3b present the estimation results for nonspecial category and special category states.

Consistent with the literature, we find that higher levels of agricultural output (*Agri*) result in lowered state tax ratios for nonspecial states. A 1 percent increase in the value of output from agriculture results in a 0.07 to 0.09 percent decrease in the expected tax ratio in the nonspecial category states. In the case of special category states, the coefficient on *Agri* is positive in model 1B (0.006) but negative in Models 2B (-0.012) and 3B (-0.006). However, the coefficient is not significantly different from zero in all three models.

Similarly, consistent with expectations we find that higher levels of per capita domestic product result in higher state tax ratios. The coefficient is

Table 11.3a. Political Extraction Regressions (Non-Special Category States), Dependent Variable: STR

	Model 1A	Model 2A	Model 3A	Model 4A	Model 5A	Model 6A
Agri/SDP	−0.08***	−0.07***	−0.09***			
	(0.007)	(0.007)	(0.006)	—	—	—
SDPCap				0.02***	0.02***	0.02***
	—	—	—	(0.001)	(0.002)	(0.001)
Min/SDP			0.23***			−0.14***
	—	—	(0.04)	—	—	(0.03)
Transfers/SDP		−0.51***	−0.02		0.006	0.26
	—	(0.13)	(0.16)	—	(0.13)	(0.15)
Time	0.00003	−0.00002	−0.0001	−0.0001	−0.0001	−0.0001
	(0.0001)	(0.0001)	(0.0001)	(0.0001)	(0.0001)	(0.0001)
Constant	0.10***	0.10***	0.11***	−0.14***	−0.14***	−0.14***
	(0.003)	(0.003)	(0.008)	(0.01)	(0.01)	(0.01)
N	379	379	379	379	379	379
R²	0.26	0.27	0.37	0.33	0.33	0.36
F	77.73	58.45	68.50	92.23	61.59	64.10
RMSE	0.015	0.015	0.014	0.015	0.015	0.014

Robust standard errors in parentheses. *** $p < 0.01$; ** $p < 0.05$; * $p < 0.10$

stable across all models and is statistically significant for the nonspecial category states. A 1 percent increase in per capita state domestic product results in a 0.02 percent increase in expected state tax ratio for the nonspecial category states. For the special category states, the coefficient on per capita income is positive across all the models but is not statistically significant.

For the nonspecial category states, the coefficient on the value of output from mining (*Min*) has a negative sign. A 1 percent increase in *Min* results in a 0.23 percent decrease on the expected tax ratio (Model 3A). The value of the coefficient drops to -0.14 in Model 6A. The coefficient is statistically significant in both models.[4] In the case of the special category, the coefficient on mining is positive and statistically significant. A 1 percent increase in *Min* results in a 0.12 percent increase on the expected tax ratio in both Models 3B and 6B.

Discretionary transfers (*Transfer*) from the federal to the state level are expected to lower state tax ratios (Jha, Mohanty, Chatterjee, and Chitkara 1999). Yet, the results indicate that the effect of transfers varies from model to model. For instance, the coefficient is negative in Models 2A and 3A and

Table 11.3B. Political Extraction Regressions (Special Category States), Dependent Variable: STR

	Model 1B	Model 2B	Model 3B	Model 4B	Model 5B	Model 6B
Agri/SDP	0.006	−0.012	−0.006			
	(0.024)	(0.026)	(0.026)	—	—	—
SDPCap				0.00004	0.008	0.009
	—	—	—	(0.006)	(0.006)	(0.005)
Min/SDP			0.124**			0.12**
	—	—	(0.046)	—	—	(0.04)
Transfers/SDP		−0.25***	−0.20**		−0.34***	−0.29***
	—	(0.07)	(0.082)	—	(0.09)	(0.09)
Time	0.0005	0.0003	0.0003	0.0006**	0.0004	0.0003
	(0.0002)	(0.0002)	(0.0002)	(0.0002)	(0.0002)	(0.0002)
Constant	0.024*	0.042***	0.036**	0.025	−0.03	−0.04
	(0.012)	(0.013)	(0.014)	(0.05)	(0.05)	(0.04)
N	244	244	244	219	219	219
R^2	0.03	0.09	0.10	0.05	0.15	0.17
F	3.21	8.17	13.69	5.64	12.62	17.21
RMSE	0.019	0.018	0.018	0.018	0.017	0.017

Robust standard errors in parentheses. *** $p < 0.01$; ** $p < 0.05$; * $p < 0.10$

the change in the magnitude of the coefficient is relatively large (from −0.51 to −0.02 respectively). The coefficient switches signs to positive when moving to Models 5A and 6A. The coefficient on transfers is consistently negative for the special category states. A 1 percent increase in *Transfer* received by a state results in a 0.20 percent decrease in the expected tax ratio.

Consider the variation in political effort expended by states across levels of per capita output in figure 11.1.[5] The poorest states tend to be the least capable states. The richest states exhibit the least relative variation and extract around expected levels. States constituting the second and third income quartiles once again indicate considerable variation. Across the middle quartiles, we find that states such as AP, Karnataka, Kerala, and TN are among the relatively capable states while others such as Assam, MP, Rajasthan, and WB are relatively less so. Thus, consistent with Arbetman and Kugler (1997), we see that the states at lower income levels reflect low capacity while the middle-income states have a wider range of political capacity. The rich states exhibit relatively stable patterns of extraction.

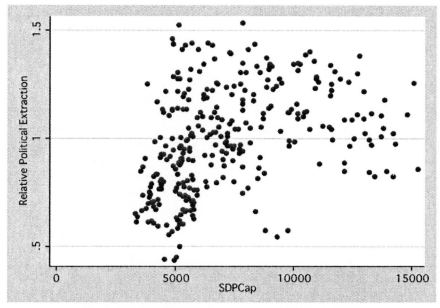

Figure 11.1. Relative Political Extraction Across Income Levels (1981–2001)

RELATIVE POLITICAL EXTRACTION AND BIRTHS: THEORETICAL EXPECTATIONS

Studies analyzing the impact of national political development on vital rates find that politically capable governments are able to reduce birth and death rates, with the greatest effects felt in developing nations (Arbetman and Kugler 1997; Feng, Kugler, and Zak 2000, 2002; Feng, Kugler, Swaminathan, and Zak 2008; Kugler, Organski, Johnson, and Cohen 1983; Organski, Kugler, Johnson, and Cohen 1984, Rouyer 1987).

Capable governments can induce reductions in fertility partly through family planning programs and other forms of direct interventions and indirectly through the effects of other governmental activities. Indirect effects arise from transformations of infrastructure, improvements in public health, and legislation that increases education and employment opportunities for women and restricts employment of child labor. Such governmental activities leading to the expansion of the state apparatus have the unintended effect of lowering vital rates. Thus, a relatively capable nation will have a stronger indirect negative effect on fertility than less capable ones.

Feng, Kugler, and Zak (2000) develop a dynamic general equilibrium model of fertility and economic development based on political capacity, political stability, and political freedom. Controlling for the expected effects of physical and human capital, politics critically affects fertility decisions that in turn determine the transmission of human capital from parents to children. Human capital provides the foundation for sustained increases in living standards as individuals with new ideas enter into the production processes.

Politics is identified as a primary cause of countries falling into a low-income poverty trap. An expectation of political instability increases the likelihood of a poverty trap because it affects income adversely and raises fertility, allowing human capital to decrease over generations and causing reductions in future output. More recently, Feng, Kugler, Swaminathan, and Zak (2008) provide strong empirical support for the hypothesized effects of political capacity, stability, and freedom on fertility and human capital, as well as economic development.

Studies have also extended this line of inquiry into specific nations such as China (Feng, Kugler, and Zak 2002) and India (Rouyer 1987). Rouyer specifies a path analysis model to identify the effects of political capacity and economic development on fertility in India. He finds that the ability of a national government to extract and distribute resources has a strong effect on fertility more so than economic development. Political capacity affects birth rates through both physical quality of life as well as family planning efforts.

National population and health policies since 1952 have emphasized a commitment to improving demographic and health outcomes in India (National Commission on Population 2000). While demographic and health goals are set by the federal government, the formulation and implementation of specific policies are responsibilities of state governments. Thus, state political extraction is expected to play a significant role in reducing births within that state.

Specifically, political extraction is expected to exert a downward effect on births. In addition, the effect of political extraction is conditional on levels of development. That is, political extraction is expected to play a stronger role in those states that are at lower levels of development relative to the wealthier states. As income levels increase, the effect of political extraction is expected to become weaker. Among the relatively poor states, states with higher political extraction are expected to register lower birth rates compared to the less capable ones. Within a level of development, a state with higher levels of political extraction is expected to register lower birth rates relative to a less extractive counterpart.

RELATIVE POLITICAL EXTRACTION AND BIRTHS: REGRESSIONS AND RESULTS

To investigate systematically the above theoretical expectations, specifically the conditional effect of relative political extraction on birth rates, we use cross-section time series data for the fifteen largest states in India from 1981 to 2001 (Appendix 11.2 provides summary statistics for the variables used in the birth rate regressions).[6] The estimation takes the form in this end-note.[7]

Level of economic development is measured using per capita state domestic product (SDPCap) in constant 1993–1994 rupees. Two particularly important control variables are used: female literacy levels and infant mortality rates. Female literacy rates are measured as the literate female population as a percent of the total population, and the data are taken from census reports. Infant mortality rate is the number of infant deaths per 1,000 live births, and the data are taken from the SRS bulletin various years.

We develop our empirical examination by estimating an autoregressive, interactive model located here.[8]

Table 11.4 (a, b, and c) presents the basic political-economic models that consider total, rural, and urban (adjusted) birth rates a result of political extraction, income, the interaction between political extraction and income, female literacy, and infant mortality. Consider Model 1 (Table 11.4a). All the variables in the model have expected signs.[9] A 10 percent increase in female literacy levels results in a 0.5 percent decrease in birth rates. While infant mortality rates have a positive effect on birth rates, the coefficient is not statistically significant. Finally, we see that per capita income has a negative effect on birth rates. The signs on the coefficients are consistent with extant results linking variation in fertility to socioeconomic changes.

The key parameter of interest here is β_{RS}, the conditional impact of relative political extraction on birth rates across development levels. This effect is estimated using a multiplicative interaction term given by ($RPE*SDP$-Cap). In models including an interaction term, the "unconditional" effects of the independent variables cannot be interpreted and tested for significance as they typically are in linear regression without interaction terms (Brambor, Clark, and Golder 2005; Braumoeller 2004; Jaccard, Turrisi, and Wan 1990).[10]

Table 11.5 reports the marginal impact of RPE across the range of per capita SDP on total, rural, and urban adjusted birth rates, and figures 11.2, 11.3, and 11.4 present the statistical significance of the marginal effects respectively.[11]

Table 11.5 indicates that RPE conditional on SDPCap has a negative effect on total births. As expected, this effect diminishes as income levels increase. In figure 11.2, RPE has a significant effect on total births only when SDP is less than approximately Rs. 6,124 (representing 47 percent of the observations in the sample). RPE does not have an impact on births at higher income levels. For the states falling below the above income level, a 10 percent increase in relative political extraction brings about a 0.6 to 0.3 percent decrease in total births.

Table 11.4a.   Total Birth Rates (Adjusted) Regressions

	Model 1 (PW-PCSE)
SDP/Capita *t-1*	− 0.12 (0.03)
RPE *t-1*	− 0.53 (0.26)
(RPE*SDP) *t-1*	0.05 (0.03)
FLIT *t-1*	− 0.05*** (0.01)
IMR *t-1*	0.01 (0.01)
ABR (Total) *t-1*	0.78*** (0.04)
Constant	1.95 (0.40)
Fixed Effects	Yes
Observations	300
Groups	15
R²	0.97
Wald χ²	35034.83
□	− 0.09

Panel corrected standard errors in parentheses. *** $p < 0.01$; ** $p < 0.05$; * $p < 0.10$

We find an identical negative effect of relative political extraction on rural and urban birth rates. The marginal effect of RPE decreases across increasing income levels. In the case of rural birth rates, the coefficient loses significance beyond an SDPCap level of approximately Rs. 5,650 as seen in figure 11.3 (about 40 percent of the observations). Within this income level, the marginal effect of RPE ranges from − 0.05 to − 0.03.

In the case of urban births, however, the marginal effect of RPE remains significant up to a higher income level of approximately Rs. 10,300 as seen in figure 11.4 (about 84 percent of the observations). The magnitude of the effect ranges between − 0.10 and − 0.06. These results confirm our expectations that urban births respond to an expansion of government activity more so than rural births. Models in table 11.4b and 11.4c also show that

Table 11.4b. Rural Birth Rates (Adjusted) Regressions

	Model 2 PW-PCSE
SDP/Capita *t-1*	− 0.15 (0.04)
RPE *t-1*	− 0.78 (0.28)
(RPE*SDP) *t-1*	0.08 (0.03)
FLIT *t-1*	− 0.05*** (0.01)
IMR *t-1*	0.01 (0.01)
ABR (RUR) *t-1*	0.79*** (0.04)
Constant	2.24 (0.48)
Fixed Effects	Yes
Observations	300
Groups	15
R²	0.97
Wald χ²	18526.57
□	− 0.10

Panel corrected standard errors in parentheses. *** $p < 0.01$; ** $p < 0.05$; * $p < 0.10$

female literacy rate has a negative and significant effect on both rural and urban births. A 10 percent increase in female literacy results in a 0.5 and 0.8 percent decrease in rural and urban birth rates respectively. Similarly, rural and urban infant mortality rates have the expected positive signs but are not statistically significant. SDPCap has a stable negative effect ranging from 0.12 to 0.15 across all levels of RPE for the three models, suggesting that a 10 percent increase in per capita state product results in a 1.2 to 1.5 percent decrease in births.

Our results are consistent with the expected effects of relative political extraction on birth rates as noted in national-level analyses. In the context of the states, we find that in the wealthier states, composed of Gujarat, Haryana, Maharashtra, and Punjab, political extraction has not played a sig-

Table 11.4c. Urban Birth Rates (Adjusted) Regressions

	Model 3 (PW-PCSE)
SDP/Capita t-1	−0.14 (0.05)
RPE t-1	−0.43 (0.37)
(RPE*SDP) t-1	0.03 (0.04)
FLIT t-1	−0.08*** (0.01)
IMR t-1	0.01 (0.01)
ABR (URB) t-1	0.74*** (0.04)
Constant	2.36 (0.48)
Fixed Effects	Yes
Observations	300
Groups	15
R^2	0.96
Wald χ^2	20511.31
□	−0.10

Panel corrected standard errors in parentheses. *** $p < 0.01$; ** $p < 0.05$; * $p < 0.10$

nificant role in reducing births and deaths. Wealth emerges as the key determinant in providing better health outcomes. We find that income and not political effects dominate in the richer states.

Within the set of middle- and low-income states, we see relatively large political effects with these effects getting weaker across income levels. In addition, politically capable states within this set have lower births and deaths relative to less-capable ones at comparable levels of income. The capable states of AP, Karnataka, Kerala, and TN have been the most successful in lowering birth and death rates. Within this group there are states such as Assam, MP, and Rajasthan that are relatively less-capable states reporting higher birth rates. The poorest states of Bihar and UP are also among the least capable and exhibit the highest birth rates in the country.

Table 11.5. Marginal Effect of PC on Total, Rural, and Urban Adjusted Birth Rates

SDP/Cap	ABR (Total)	ABR (Rural)	ABR (Urban)
3000	−0.06 (−0.01, −0.11)	−0.08 (−0.02, −0.13)	−0.10 (−0.03, −0.18)
4000	−0.05 (−0.01, −0.09)	−0.06 (−0.02, −0.10)	−0.10 (−0.03, −0.16)
5000	−0.04 (−0.008, −0.07)	−0.03 (−0.00002, −0.06)	−0.09 (−0.03, −0.14)
6000	−0.03 (−0.0005, −0.06)	—	0.08 (−0.03, −0.13)
7000	—	—	−0.07 (−0.02, −0.12)
8000	—	—	−0.07 (−0.02, −0.12)
9000	—	—	−0.06 (−0.02, −0.12)
10000	—	—	−0.06 (−0.0007, −0.12)

95% Confidence Intervals in parentheses

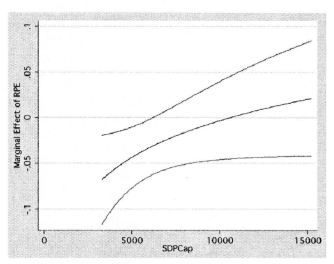

Figure 11.2. Marginal Effect of RPE on Total Births (Adjusted)

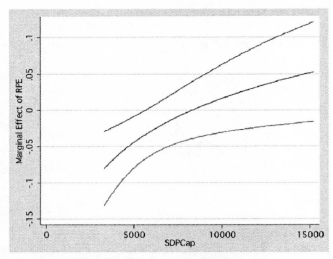

Figure 11.3.   Marginal Effect of RPE on Rural Births (Adjusted

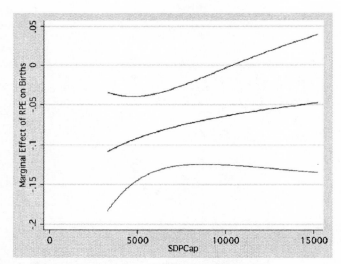

Figure 11.4.   Marginal Effect of RPE on Urban Births (Adjusted)

CONCLUSIONS

Why is political development unable to effect changes in fertility in rural regions relative to urban areas? What policy changes are required to bring about reductions in rural births? Is rapid urbanization of the countryside the path toward reducing fertility? This is of critical importance in India where 60 percent of the population is engaged in agricultural activities and is typically rural.

Our results are consistent with theoretical expectations. Governments find it easier to reduce death rates than birth rates. Providing populations with potable water, immunization, basic health care, and security brings about drastic reductions in infant and adult mortality rates and increases in life expectancy. Birth rates are less easy to manipulate through government actions.

Changes in household fertility decisions require not only availability of and access to contraceptive methods but changes in expected future earnings, long-held beliefs regarding children as "old age insurance," and a transformation from traditional to modern value systems relating to family size. As Feng, Kugler, and Zak (2002) note in the Chinese context, population control policies are less successful in rural areas due to weaker political mechanisms relative to urban areas.

Urbanization of the countryside and increases in female literacy appear to be the keys to lowering rural births. State governments also tend to be more successful with population-related policy in urban regions within states. States that successfully accomplish these ends are the ones likely to benefit from a demographic dividend and to provide the motor for economic growth in the twenty-first century.

NOTES

1. The states include: Andhra Pradesh (AP), Arunachal Pradesh, Assam, Bihar, Goa, Gujarat, Haryana, Himachal Pradesh, Jammu and Kashmir, Karnataka, Kerala, Madhya Pradesh (MP), Maharashtra, Manipur, Meghalaya, Mizoram, Nagaland, Orissa, Punjab, Rajasthan, Sikkim, Tamil Nadu (TN), Tripura, Uttar Pradesh (UP), West Bengal (WB), and the newly created states of Chattisgarh, Jharkand, and Uttarakhand.

2. Tax assignment between federal and state levels, outlined in the Seventh Schedule to the Indian Constitution, follows the principle of "separation," that is, the power to levy a tax belongs exclusively to the assigned level. Federal-level taxes include (nonagricultural) income and customs and excise duties. Sources of tax revenue for the state include tax on sales and purchase of goods, land revenue, agricultural income tax, state excise duties on liquor, stamp duty and registration fees, and motor vehicle tax. Sales tax constitutes approximately 65 percent of a state's own

tax revenue, while the others make up smaller shares. Despite the similarity of tax structures, the state tax ratio exhibits considerable variation across the states: from a high of 12 and 11 percent of state domestic product in Karnataka and Tamil Nadu respectively to a low of 4 percent in Uttar Pradesh among the nonspecial category states. In addition, a state's own tax revenue is substantially higher in the nonspecial category states relative to the special category states. For extensive discussions on Indian fiscal federalism see Rao and Singh 2006.

3. $STR_{it} = \alpha + \beta_k X_{kit} + \epsilon_{it}$ (1)

where STR_{it} (StateTaxRatio) = State's Own Tax Revenue (SOTR)/Nominal State Domestic Product for state i at time t^3 and X represents the economic bases for extraction including the value of output from agriculture (*Agri*), the value of output from mining (*Min*), and discretionary transfers from the federal to state governments (*Transfer*). Relative political extraction (RPE) is computed as:

$$RPE = STR/S\hat{T}R$$

where $S\hat{T}R$ is the predicted value obtained from (1).

Given its level of development, a state with an RPE index greater than one is considered to be extracting more than what can be expected, while a state with an index value less than one is considered to be performing at levels below expectation.

4. There is considerable debate on the role of mining in economic development. A World Bank study reviews this debate and concludes that mining may play a positive role in generating growth. With respect to extraction, the negative sign on mining is a departure from Arbetman and Kugler (1997), who report a positive coefficient on mining, suggesting that the presence of mining activity results in an increase in the tax ratio. Bahl and Tumennasan (2002), however, find that mining has a negative impact on subnational tax ratios in Indonesia. They suggest that mining may not be a significant source of revenue for governments as levels of productivity from manufacturing and other nonextractive, nonagriculture-based industries increase.

5. We use estimates from Model 2A in our subsequent analyses, which is restricted to the larger nonspecial category states. Summary statistics for estimates from all regressions are presented in appendix 11.1.

6. The states include all nonspecial category states (except Goa, Jharkhand, and Chattisgarh) and a special category state, Assam.

7. Birth Rate = $f(RPE, ED, P*E, X)$

Where *RPE* represents relative political extraction, *ED* is the level of economic development within a state, $P*E$ is the interaction between political extraction and level of economic development, and X a vector of other control variables.

The dependent variable in the estimation is the crude birth rate adjusted for age-sex composition. The crude birth rate measures the number of births/thousand population. Since crude birth rates are not strictly comparable across populations with dissimilar age-sex composition, they are adjusted using the following formula:

ABR (Adjusted Birth Rate) = $(CBR_{it}) * (PWP_{it}/PWSP_{it})$
PWP_{it}: Proportion of women ages 15–44 in state population
$PWSP_{it}$: Proportion of women ages 15–44 in standard population (All India)

8. $ABR_{it} = \alpha + \phi ABR_{it-1} + \beta_R RPE_{it-1} + \beta_S SDPCap_{it-1} + \beta_{RS}(RPE{*}SDPCap)_{it-1} + \gamma X_{it-1} + \epsilon_{it}$,

where α, ϕ, β_R, β_S, β_{RS}, γ are parameters to be estimated and ϵ is the random disturbance, for $i = 1, \ldots, N$ states and $t = 1, \ldots, T$ years. The above specification provides Prais-Winston estimates with panel corrected standard errors (PW-PCSE), where PW estimates are used but where standard errors are corrected for panel heteroskedasticity and contemporaneous correlation (Beck 2001; Beck and Katz 1995, 1996). All regressions include state fixed effects and one period lagged effects from the dependent variable.

9. The coefficient on the lagged value of ABR is statistically less than 1 for all models presented here. The Levin-Lin-Chu Pooled ADF test rejects the null hypothesis of a unit root process [Levinlin $t^* = -2.95$] (Levin, Lin, and Chu 2002).

10. The coefficients on RPE and SDPCap do not capture the average effects of political extraction and income on ABR. For instance, the coefficient on PC (-0.53 from model 1) is the effect on ABR of a 1 percent increase in RPE when SDPCap = 0. Similarly, the coefficient on SDPCap represents the percent change in ABR for a 1 percent increase in SDPCap when RPE = 0. We get no information from these coefficients when SDPCap≠0 (in the former) and when RPE≠0 (in the latter). Since the range of data in our sample does not include values of zero for either RPE or SDPCap, the unconditional effects of these variables and their statistical significance are not considered as meaningful.

11. The marginal effect of RPE conditional on SDPCap is given by $\partial ABR/\partial RPE = \beta_R + \beta_{RS}SDPCap$ and the standard error of RPE conditional on SDPCap is:

$$^s\beta_R + \beta_{RS}SDPCap = \sqrt{var(\beta_R) + var(\beta_S)SDPCap^2 + 2Cov(\beta_R\beta_S)SDPCap}$$

REFERENCES

Ahituv, A. 2001. "Be Fruitful or Multiply: On the Interplay between Fertility and Economic Development." *Journal of Population Economics* 14: 51–71.

Arbetman, Marina, and Jacek Kugler, eds. 1997. *Political Capacity and Economic Behavior*. Boulder, CO: Westview Press.

Bahl, R. and B. Tumennasan. 2002. "How Should Revenues from Natural Resources Be Shared in Indonesia?" Can Decentralization Help Rebuild Indonesia: A Conference Sponsored by the International Studies Program, Andrew Young School of Policy Studies, Georgia State University, Atlanta, Georgia.

Beck, N., and J. Katz. 1995. "What To Do (and Not To Do) with Time Series Cross-Section Data." *American Political Science Review* 89: 634–47.

———. 1996. "Nuisance vs. Substance: Specifying and Estimating Time-series-Cross-section Models." *Political Analysis* 6: 1–36.

Becker, G., K. Murphy, and R. Tamura. 1990. "Human Capital, Fertility, and Economic Growth." *Journal of Political Economy* 98: S12–S37.

Brambor, T., W. Clark, and M. Golder. 2005. "Understanding Interaction Models: Improving Empirical Analysis." *Political Analysis* 13: 1–20.

Braumoeller, B. 2004. "Hypothesis Testing and Multiplicative Interaction Terms." *International Organization* 58: 807–20.

Feng, Yi, Jacek Kugler, Siddharth Swaminathan, and Paul Zak. 2008. "Path to Prosperity: The Dynamics of Freedom and Economic Development." *International Interactions* 34 (4).

Feng, Yi, Jacek Kugler, and Paul Zak. 2000. "The Politics of Fertility and Economic Development." *International Studies Quarterly* 44: 667–93.

———. 2002. "Population Growth, Urbanization, and the Role of Government in China." *Urban Studies* 39 (12): 2329–43.

Jaccard, J., R. Turrisi, and C. K. Wan. 1990. *Interaction Effects in Multiple Regression*. Thousand Oaks, CA: Sage Publications.

Jha, R., M. S. Mohanty, S. Chatterjee, and P. Chitkara. 1999. "Tax Efficiency in Selected Indian States." *Empirical Economics* 24 (4): 641–654.

Kugler, J., A. Organski, J. Johnson, and Y. Cohen 1983. "Political Determinants of Population Dynamics." *Comparative Political Studies* 1 (16): 3–36.

Levin, A., C. F. Lin, and C. Chu. 2002. "Unit Root Test in Panel Data: Asymptotic and Finite Sample Properties." *Journal of Econometrics* 108: 1–25.

National Commission on Population. 2000. *National Population Policy*. Government of India: http://populationcommission.nic.in/npp.htm

Notestein, F. 1945. "Population, The Long View." T. W. Schultz, ed., *Food for the World*. Chicago: Chicago University Press.

Organski, A. F. K., and Jacek Kugler. 1980. *The War Ledger*. Chicago: University of Chicago Press.

Organski A. F. K., Jacek Kugler, Timothy Johnson, and Youssef Cohen. 1984. *Births Deaths, and Taxes: The Demographic and Political Transitions*. Chicago: University of Chicago Press.

Rao, M. G., and N. Singh. 2006. *The Political Economy of Federalism in India*. Oxford: Oxford University Press.

Rouyer, Alvin. 1987. "Political Capacity and the Decline of Fertility in India." *American Political Science Review* 81 (2).

Thompson, W. S. 1929. "Population." *American Journal of Sociology* 34: 959–75.

Appendix 11.1.   Relative Political Extraction Estimates (A: Non-Special Category States; B: Special Category States)

	RPE 1A	RPE 2A	RPE 3A	RPE 4A	RPE 5A	RPE 6A
ALL SAMPLE	0.99 (0.21)	0.99 (0.21)	0.99 (0.20)	0.99 (0.20)	0.99 (0.20)	0.99 (0.20)
Min – Max	0.42 – 1.45	0.41 – 1.49	0.53 – 1.61	0.50 – 1.58	0.50 – 1.58	0.55 – 1.56
	RPE 1B	RPE 2B	RPE 3B	RPE 4B	RPE 5B	RPE 6B
ALL SAMPLE	1.00 (0.57)	1.00 (0.60)	1.00 (0.59)	1.00 (0.55)	1.10 (1.71)	1.02 (0.69)
Min – Max	0.06 – 2.83	0.06 – 3.31	0.06 – 2.93	0.14 – 2.89	0.13 – 25.01	0.13 – 7.50

Appendix 11.2. Descriptive Statistics of Variables Included in Birth Rate Regressions across States

State	CBR	RPE	SDP/Cap	IMR	Literacy (F)
Andhra Pradesh	26.2 (3.8)	1.10 (0.17)	6685.7 (1605.1)	72.9 (7.6)	34.8 (8.3)
Assam	30.8 (2.9)	0.98 (0.10)	5412.8 (359.9)	87.2 (13.3)	43.2 (7.5)
Bihar	34.1 (3.3)	0.75 (0.10)	3868.1 (298.3)	83.1 (18.0)	23.7 (5.2)
Gujarat	29.0 (3.3)	1.04 (0.05)	9503.1 (2560.2)	80.0 (20.5)	48.4 (6.2)
Haryana	32.1 (3.6)	1.16 (0.10)	10332.0 (2045.9)	78.0 (12.0)	40.6 (9.1)
Karnataka	26.1 (2.8)	1.25 (0.07)	7304 .8 (2057.6)	66.8 (8.0)	44.5 (7.5)
Kerala	20.1 (2.9)	1.11 (0.09)	7228.0 (2728.0)	20.9 (8.0)	83.7 (4.0)
Madhya Pradesh	34.9 (2.8)	0.95 (0.06)	6058.1 (981.8)	109.9 (15.4)	31.2 (9.6)
Maharashtra	26.2 (3.3)	0.92 (0.07)	10362.1 (2864.5)	59.5 (10.8)	53.0 (8.2)
Orissa	29.0 (3.2)	0.81 (0.10)	4690.6 (595.4)	114.2 (14.6)	36.0 (7.9)
Punjab	26.4 (3.1)	1.18 (0.11)	11619.0 (2084.4)	60.6 (9.6)	50.8 (7.3)
Rajasthan	34.6 (2.8)	0.92 (0.07)	6244.0 (1546.1)	92.8 (12.7)	24.1 (9.3)
Tamil Nadu	22.2 (3.3)	1.08 (0.07)	8240.7 (2434.9)	65.3 (13.7)	51.7 (7.4)
Uttar Pradesh	35.8 (2.3)	0.76 (0.07)	5006.8 (553.4)	110.3 (27.2)	27.3 (7.9)
West Bengal	26.4 (1.4)	0.69 (0.09)	6511.0 (1552.7)	66.6 (12.3)	47.1 (7.4)
ALL SAMPLE	28.9 (5.5)	0.99 (0.19)	7271.1 (2808.7)	77.9 (27.2)	42.7 (16.4)

Appendix 11.3. Correlation Matrix of Variables Included in Birth Rate Regressions

	RPE	SDP/Capita	Literacy (F)	IMR	Birth Rates
RPE	1.0				
SDP/Capita	0.3409	1.0			
Literacy (F)	0.3087	0.5680	1.0		
IMR	− 0.3649	− 0.5440	− 0.8381	1.0	
Birth Rates	− 0.2829	− 0.5497	− 0.8628	0.8182	1.0

IV

LOCAL PERFORMANCE

12

Government Performance and U.S. Residential Building Energy Codes

Hal T. Nelson

CONTEXT

This chapter analyzes the relationship between government performance and building energy codes. Building energy codes are an ideal test of governmental effectiveness for several reasons. First, building energy codes are cost effective. The incremental costs of construction practices and energy-consuming equipment mandated by the energy codes are repaid over the relevant life of the equipment (and in many cases two to three years). From a governance perspective, their adoption therefore represents an increase in aggregate social welfare.

While code versions, or vintages, differ in their energy savings, the adoption of building energy codes in jurisdictions that are currently without codes can be considerable. For instance, the adoption of the most recent residential code in Wyoming is associated with energy savings of approximately 22 to 27 percent over current building practices. A study for Illinois estimated savings from energy code adoption from future commercial building construction over the next twenty years at approximately $1 billion (Cort and Belzer 2002).

These studies, and other like them, show the increases in net social welfare from the adoption of building energy codes.[1] Increases in net social welfare from building energy codes are likely as they mitigate behavioral and market failures that occur in energy services.[2] These failures occur because the builder of a residential or commercial building has an incentive to install the cheapest possible equipment, while the buyer, who is liable for the energy bills, would prefer more efficient equipment (Gillingham et al. 2009). A similar failure exists between building landlords and tenants (Murthishaw and Sayanthe 2006). Building energy codes provide a minimum acceptable level of performance, which mitigates these market and behavioral failures, but are politically contested because of their redistributive aspects between the above actors.

The welfare-enhancing aspects of government adoption of building energy codes are especially important given two critical aspects of building energy use. The first is irreversibility. The majority of the energy efficiency measures that building codes cover can be considered "lost opportunities" measures. Lost opportunities reflect the fact that if the measure is not installed within the window of opportunity, then savings from the measure are lost (NW Council 2005). Wall insulation in a new building is a potential lost opportunity, as would be the replacement of a worn-out refrigerator with a non-energy-efficient model. The investment in a more-efficient refrigerator can only occur during a specific period, during the purchase. In contrast, non-lost-opportunity measures are retrofit measures that can occur at any time. Buildings have extremely long lives of fifty or more years, so the energy efficiency of a building is going to contribute to state energy demand for many decades.

The second reason that building energy codes are an ideal test of governmental effectiveness is that they represent one of the most important policy mechanisms that a state can implement to reduce energy consumption. Building codes and appliance standards, which affect energy consumption through design and/or construction, are the largest sources of reductions in the Department of Energy's weatherization program evaluations (Schweitzer et al. 2003).

As one of the most powerful policy "levers" that a jurisdiction can pull, the impact of construction practices, including building energy codes, is reflected in energy demand. Buildings use more than 40 percent of all primary energy in the country. In 2004/2005 residential buildings accounted for almost 22 percent and commercial buildings represented the balance of 18 percent of primary energy use. Total energy use in buildings in the United States has increased by 40 percent from 1985 to 2006 (U.S. DOE, 2008b) and has been driven by new building construction.

For the residential sector, per household, delivered energy consumption has been falling steadily for decades, and in 2006 it was 23 percent below its 1980 level (U.S. DOE, 2008b, table 2.1.4). Energy consumption per household has declined in spite of larger homes being built as well as an increase in penetration of energy-intensive appliances such as air conditioning. Building energy consumption would have been much higher were it not for the adoption of building energy codes and appliance standards by federal, state, and local governments.

INTELLECTUAL ENVIRONMENT: STATE
BUILDING ENERGY CODE ADOPTION

Building energy codes are a subset of a larger group of building codes that include fire and plumbing, occupant safety, urban planning, and other codes. Jurisdictions adopt building codes because they are explicit about what actions and equipment are acceptable and thus are enforceable by the relevant agencies. Building codes adopt standards developed by experts in a certain area. For example, commercial energy codes reference standards developed by the American Society of Heating, Refrigerating, and Air-conditioning Engineers, Inc. (ASHRAE).

In recent years, residential energy codes are adopted by the International Energy Conservation Code (IECC), which is developed by the International Code Council. The IECC released its first code in 1998. The IECC has revised its code every three years since the year 2000 and has plans to revise it again in 2012 (International Code Council 2008). Revisions typically result in each new energy code being more strict, resulting in additional energy efficiency gains.

The Energy Policy Act (EPACT) of 1992 required the Department of Energy to rule on whether each new energy code version offers energy efficiency improvements over the previous version and this evaluation is published in the Federal Register. This ruling then provides guidance to states, counties, or municipalities that want to adopt the most recent energy code. However, compliance is optional under EPACT. With respect to residential building codes, EPACT 1992 says that "each State *may* [italics added], to the extent consistent with otherwise applicable State law, revise the provisions of its residential building code regarding energy efficiency to meet or exceed CABO Model Energy Code, 1992, or may decline to make such revisions."

It was not until 2009 that the federal government took action to improve states' building energy codes. The American Recovery and Reinvestment Act of 2009 (ARRA) stipulated that for states to receive any of the $3.1B under the State Energy Program, they had to signal their "Intent to adopt" the most recent vintage residential and commercial codes, as well as plans for achieving high compliance with these codes within eight years. The effects of ARRA are outside the temporal sample for this analysis, in which states had wide autonomy to adopt, or not adopt, building energy codes.

THEORETICAL MODEL

Mandatory building energy codes are regulatory in nature because they use governmental authority to dictate the behavior of private actors regarding building practices and minimally acceptable equipment (for a review of regulatory research in the United States, see Gerber and Teske 2000). Developing a theoretical explanation of U.S. states' building energy code adoption requires the explication of the underlying rationale for why a state would or would not adopt these codes given the institutional and political-economy context within each state. As mentioned above, under EPACT (1992), energy code adoption is voluntary for states. While there is a veritable trove of information on state policy implementation under federalism, building energy code adoption is not a top-down process where states implement federal guidelines (see Ringquist 1993; Holland et al. 1996; Lester and Lombard 1998). It is expected that the factors that drive the adoption of building energy codes cross multiple theoretical lines.

Political Capacity

Having the resources to enact and enforce the building codes is perhaps the most critical aspect of state policy adoption. Not only do states need the "upstream" resources to assess the suitability of each complex energy code for their climate, but they also need resources for the "downstream" implementation element of building energy codes. The code process entails builders submitting building plans and blueprints for permitting prior to construction, as well as building code inspectors checking completed new buildings and major retrofits for compliance. Energy code adoption and compliance is complex and varies considerably between states, with the Northwest states typically exhibiting the highest compliance rates (Yang 2005). Within the Northwest region, the state with the highest compliance rates is California, which provides considerable technical support toward enforcement.

To facilitate compliance with its energy code, California provides training manuals, a code hotline, a newsletter, access to technical support staff, and energy efficiency training for compliance with its building codes. Public-private partnerships include California's building industry providing builder training. Training for code inspectors is also critical. As typical of recent surveys of builders, one item that has been identified is adequate training for code officials so they understand what they are enforcing (Building Codes Assistance Project 2009).

All these efforts cost money. The EPA (2008) notes, "In all cases, successful energy code programs require *sufficient budget and staff resources* [italics added] to involve stakeholders, support implementation, and evaluate progress." Building energy code enforcement funding typically comes from fees included in building permits. The costs of Seattle's energy code program have been estimated at .86 percent of the price of a new single family house, .29 percent of the cost of a new apartment building, and .22 percent of the cost of a new office building (Benningfield and Hogan 2003, 11).

Reluctance to impose these costs on the construction industry for code implementation results in the failure of legislative initiatives to adopt codes. In South Carolina, a bill (S.66), filed in 1994 to require all munici-palities and counties to adopt the most current building codes, passed the South Carolina State Senate in February 1996 and was sent to the Real Estate Subcommittee of the House Labor, Commerce and Industry Com-mittee, where it was rejected. Opposition was based on the need for local governments to raise taxes or fees to implement the codes (U.S. DOE 2008b).

Relative Political Capacity

This review of the costs associated with energy code adoption implies that the ability of a jurisdiction to fund the building energy code program is a prerequisite for successful code adoption. One possible way to measure the capacity of a state to implement directives is the relevant U.S. census category for state expenditures. Huang et al. (2007) found state environ-mental expenditures negatively predicted the adoption of state renewable energy quotas. This is not surprising as there are validity issues with this measure as it doesn't directly measure the energy and the environmental issues associated with energy, but rather costs of administering the natural resources within the state.

Western states with large public land holdings would therefore rank higher in expenditures, which is not necessarily an indicator of commit-ment to environmental protection or progressive energy policy. Further-more, absolute measures of spending do not capture the large fixed costs associated with service delivery, and thus overstate the relative spending of small states compared to large states.

A better measure of political capacity is one that controls for population and level of development. For the United States, the measure employed to measure governmental effectiveness is relative political extraction, labeled for convenience as RPC. Tax effort is measured from U.S. Census state and local government data and is calculated as:[3]

> **Total Own Source Revenue**
> Less Utility Revenue
> Less Social Security Contributions
> Less Liquor Store Revenue
> *Plus Liquor store net income*
> _____
> = **Tax Effort**

The tax effort measure calculated here is very similar to the U.S. Census measure General Own Source Revenue, employed by the Brookings Institu-tion's Tax Policy Center.[4] However, our RPC measure adds back in liquor store net income, which is a discretionary funding source for states with liquor stores. The additional revenue source (liquor store net income) is largest in New Hampshire at .16 percent of GSP, but doesn't affect the relative rankings of any of the states by tax effort between the Brookings formulation and the RPC formulation. The Census government surveys were not administered in years 2001 and 2003, so the data for these years is interpolated from the year prior and following.

The calculation of RPC is a three-step process based on the tax effort of the jurisdiction. The specific formulas and calculations are found here.[5]

The three-stage estimation process yields RPC values in figure 12.1, which shows the most current three-year average values. The low RPC states cluster in the Southwest and Southeast except for South Dakota, Connecticut, and New Hampshire. The high RPC states are largely coastal, with the exception of Michigan and West Virginia. Appendix 12.1 contains the relative political capacity values and rankings for the year 2006.

The information in figure 12.1 is relatively static and doesn't reflect any changes in political capacity over the sample period. Figure 12.2 indicates the change in relative political capacity over the time period. Over the 1977–2006 time period, there are some surprises in the change in RPC. Louisiana's and Oklahoma's RPC increased, but from initially low levels because these states are still in the bottom quartile distribution.

Conversely, New York experienced a major decline in RPC, but is still ranked in the top eight states in 2004–2006. These changes in relative rankings occurred over a period when absolute tax effort increased by 20

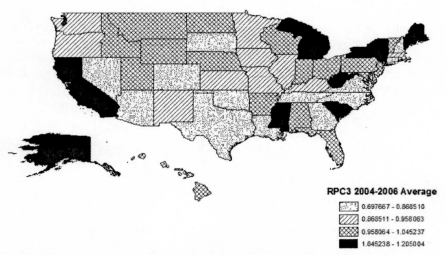

RPC3 2004-2006 Average
- 0.697667 - 0.868510
- 0.868511 - 0.958063
- 0.958064 - 1.045237
- 1.045238 - 1.205004

Figure 12.1.   Map of 2004–2006 Average Relative Political Capacity (Extraction)

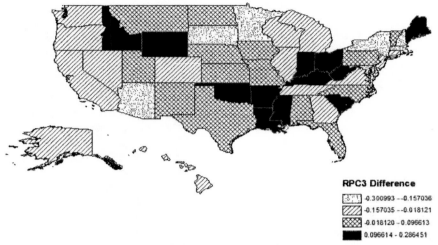

RPC3 Difference

▨	-0.300993 – -0.157036
▨	-0.157035 – -0.018121
▨	-0.018120 – 0.096613
■	0.096614 – 0.286451

Figure 12.2.   Map of Differences between 2004–2006 and 1977–1979 Average Relative Political Capacity (Extraction)

percent. The fifty-state three-year average tax effort was 11 percent in 1977–1979, which increased to 13.3 percent in 2004–2006.

The net contribution of the two RPC maps is to identify states with the necessary political capacity to update building codes.

Policy Diffusion and Spatial Variables

The above observation that low RPC states cluster in the Southeast and Southwest leads us next to consider spatial explanations for building code adoption. Geography is an important predictor of public policy, yet it is only sparsely included in empirical analyses. For this analysis, we code a state with a coastline as a 1 and interior states as a 0. We suspect that coastal states are more progressive in their energy and other public policies, even after controlling for demographic variables such as wealth and population density.

That policies can diffuse across jurisdictions has been an integral part of the policy literature for decades because of interstate cooperation or competition (Walker 1969; Berry and Berry 1990; Vogel 1995; Shipan and Volden 2006). Building energy codes in a jurisdiction could be influenced by the adoption of these codes in neighboring jurisdictions who might be competing to attract local commercial businesses or residents who are cost sensitive to a building's initial cost.[6] If this is the case, then we would see a "race to the bottom" in building energy codes where lax building energy code adoption in one state predicts slow updating of energy codes in a neighboring state.

Conversely, a race to the top in building construction practices might be driven by states adopting neighboring states' codes or from the diffusion of building practices by interstate construction firms. Concurrent state energy code adoption might also be facilitated by policy networks of code officials and policy makers interested in building codes in neighboring states. The measure of policy diffusion used in this analysis is the simple average of the annual vintage of contiguous states' building energy codes.

State Ideology

The values of elites and citizens in a jurisdiction also determine the policies that are promulgated regarding energy and the environment. Studies that have found liberal institutional control lead to pro-environmental outcomes include Hays, Elser, and Hays (1996). Ka and Teske (2002) find that liberal legislative ideology is a significant predictor of higher residential energy prices. One lawmaker might view energy codes as a needless intrusion of government into the construction market.

A lawmaker on the other side of the aisle might view energy codes as a way to save citizens money and at the same time reduce air and water pollution and greenhouse gas emissions. These are much more than "mental models"; rather they are embedded value systems relating to the proper role of government in society. State ideology comes from Berry et al. (1998). Brace et al. (2005) note that of the common measures of state ideology, the Berry et al. measure assessing elite ideology is preferred over voter ideology measures (537). Because of potential construct validity issues with measures of ideology, a robustness check was performed with presidential voting records.

Level of Economic Development and Human Capital

Wealth has been posited to partially determine a jurisdiction to environmental protection (Grossman and Krueger 1995). A jurisdiction might adopt regulations or implement an environmental regime because it can afford to pay for its implementation (Lester and Lombard 1990; Feiock and West 1993; Meyer and Koniskey 2007). In this argument, more wealthy states prefer better building codes because the adoption of building energy codes requires incremental capital expenditures to finance energy-efficient equipment instead of baseline equipment.

These costs can be financed either through existing mortgages or other construction finance. Even in cases where the energy-efficient equipment might have some cash incentive or tax rebate associated with it, the builder must finance the equipment up front and carry the cost until the time the rebate or incentive is returned from the relevant organization. Economic development is measured as the log of per capita GSP from the Bureau of Economic Analysis (2009). As a robustness measure we also test for the effects of educational attainment. Secondary school graduation rates from the U.S. Census (2000) are used as an indicator for educational attainment.

Property Rights

Property rights arguments posit that environmental policies will result from overconsumption of common pool resources and perceptions of scarcity. Lubell et al. (2005) categorizes increased population pressure and urbanization as property rights indicators. Population growth reflects demands for new residential and commercial buildings. Jurisdictions with declining populations might have surplus of low efficiency existing buildings whose owners would not like to have competition from new energy efficient building stock. States with faster population growth could prefer more recent and aggressive building energy codes. Lagged population growth in Meyer and Koniskey (2007) was a significant predictor of local environmental institutions. Similarly, states with higher population density should also prefer more recent building energy codes.

Economic Need

Another reason for states to adopt energy codes is their economic needs. One source of economic need is the climate of the state, where states with more extreme weather might prefer more efficient buildings. States that have a greater number of days that require space heating and cooling could also be more likely to adopt building energy codes. Residents in a cold, interior state like North Dakota spend a greater share of their income on heating than residents in mild, coastal states. Payback periods of energy-efficient measures decrease as energy expenditures increase. States typically will perform building simulations based on local building stock types and climate conditions in order to determine whether or not the adoption of a model energy code will save the consumers in a state money. The state climate data comes from NOAA (2005) and is population weighted.

The other element of economic need is energy costs. States with higher energy costs would also be expected to adopt building energy codes. The incremental costs of high efficiency building code measures are more cost effective for building owners and operators. The measure of energy price is the average natural gas price from U.S. DOE State Energy Data (2010).

Interest Group Strength

Legislators and agencies overseeing the adoption and updating of build-ing energy codes are subject to lobbying by organized interest groups. The importance of land-based elites dominating local politics to expand local economies with the goal of accumulating wealth was portrayed as a "growth machine" by Molotch (1976). The construction industry is able to tie itself to local economic development outcomes, increasing the power and legitimacy of its policy preferences. The construction industry is well organized and financed and has been found to have significant influence on land use decisions by local governments (Lubell et al. 2005). U.S. Bureau of Economic Analysis (2009) data for construction industry output as a per-cent of total private industry output is used as the measure of the growth machine in each state.

RESEARCH DESIGN

This research uses panel data of building energy code adoption in the lower forty-right states from 1977 to 2006. Alaska and Hawaii do not have cli-mate data so they are excluded from the analysis. The dependent variable in each state-year is whether or not a state adopted a new vintage of residential building energy codes, indicated with 0 or 1. The energy code adoption must be *mandatory and statewide* for the state to receive a code of 1 for a code update. This excludes states that have significant jurisdictions with mandatory codes, such as major metropolitan regions.

The logic behind this coding is twofold. First, for a state to maximize its social welfare from cost-effective building energy codes, energy codes need to be implemented across the entire state. Therefore, statewide implemen-tation potentially represents mobilization of political capacity in order to maximize welfare in the state. The other rationale for coding energy code efforts statewide is that this is how the data is reported, and available resources did not allow county or municipal data collection efforts. Appen-dix 12.2 contains a description of the building energy code data sources.

The following tables summarize the code data for the years 1977–2006. Table 12.1 indicates that among the fifty U.S. states, the mean number of energy code adoptions was 3.5. On average, each state updated its building

Table 12.1. Summary Statistics on Cumulative Number of Residential Building Energy Code Adoptions/Updates by 2006

Variable	Obs	Mean	Std. Dev.	Min	Max
Updates	50	3.56	4.05	0	14

codes slightly more that once a decade. However, there is a lot of variation in the data which has a range of 0 to 14 updates, with a standard deviation of 4.

Much of the variation in the data is due to the 38 percent of states who have not adopted residential building codes over the sample period, along with the few states who are serial adopters such as California and Florida. Table 12.2 shows the distribution of the dependent variable of energy code adoption.

The large coastal states of California and Florida lead the sample in the number of code adoptions over the period. Other large states like Texas and New York have been much less active in updating residential energy codes.

METHODS

Developing explanations and predictions for residential building code adoption requires estimation techniques beyond binary (logit or probit)

Table 12.2. Strata of Residential Building Energy Code Adoptions from 1977–2006

Number of Code Updates	Frequency	Percent	Cumulative	States
0	19	38	38	AL, AK, AZ, CO, ID, IL, KS, LA, ME, MS, MO, NV, ND, OH, OK, SD, TN, WV, WY
1	1	2	40	TX
2	4	8	48	HI, MI, PA, VT
3	6	12	60	AR, DE, IN, NE, NH, NY
4	5	10	70	MD, MA, NC, SC, WI
5	1	2	72	MN
6	5	10	82	CT, IA, KY, NJ, NM
7	2	4	86	GA, MT
9	1	2	88	RI
10	2	4	92	UT, VA
12	1	2	94	OR
13	1	2	96	WA
14	2	4	100	CA, FL
Total	50	100	50	

time series models. Event history analysis of repeated events is the appropriate estimation technique for state policy adoption and is favored over logit or probit analyses (Jones and Branton 2005). Logit and probit models employ a distributional assumption that predicts that risk of state policy adoption is invariant to time. This is due to the log-odds, exponentiated linear prediction, which implies that the hazard rate is the same for all time periods. The hazard rate is the conditional probability of the event occurring in the next year. This analysis uses a Cox proportional hazard duration model that generates a hazard rate, or risk of a jurisdiction adopting a policy at a given time, that is time variant.

The hazard rate (h) at time t in the Cox model for the jth subject is defined as:

$$h(t|x_j) = h_o(t)e (x_j, \beta_x) \qquad \text{(Eq. 1)}$$

where the x = predictor values, and regression coefficients β_x are estimated from the data (Cleves et al. 2008).

There is an additional advantage to using duration models for state policy adoption. The Cox proportional hazards (PH) duration model doesn't specify the functional form of the baseline hazard rate. The hazard rate is estimated from the data itself, which is preferred when there is no a priori theoretical reason for specifying the baseline hazard rate. As Box-Steffensmeier and Jones (2004) note, there are "few instances . . . where one would prefer a parametric duration model" (p66). When theorizing about the adoption of residential building energy codes, there is no prior research or strong theory to guide the selection of distributional assumptions. Thus, the Cox model is employed. Furthermore, Cox models are more appropriate when a researcher is interested in the effects of the covariates, as opposed to the effects of time, when a Weibull parametric model might be more appropriate.

Explicating the factors that influence states to adopt residential building energy codes requires that the analysis include repeat events, in this case multiple code adoptions. Table 12.2 above indicates that 60 percent of states have updated their residential building energy codes two or more times. In risk analysis terms, each of the states that adopted new vintage building energy codes had a new risk set following each adoption. The duration time resets after each code adoption event. This is known as conditional gap time and utilizes all the failures (code adoptions) in the data set. The Cox PH models tested here employ robust standard errors clustered by state. This reduces concerns about heteroskedasticity and nonindependence of cases.[7] Robust standard errors clustered by states allow for serial time or spatial dependence by dividing the data into the state clusters and then computes standard errors across the clusters. Robust standard errors are higher than nonrobust errors, resulting in lower p-values for the same sample.

In addition, model 1 was run in OLS and tested for multicollinearity between variables using the variance inflation factor test. None of the covariates, or the global model, showed VIF scores higher than 3, well below the 7–10 considered to be problematic. Table 12.3 identifies the correlation between variables in the model. Table 12.4 presents the summary statistics for the model.

RESULTS

Table 12.5 shows results for the models used in the analysis. All three models have omnibus tests of pseudo-Log likelihood ratios that indicate Prob > chi2 = 0.0000. This indicates that the coefficients of the models' covariates in aggregate are significantly different from zero.

The Cox model allows us to estimate the shape of the baseline hazard rate over time. To do this, covariates in the model were centered to estimate the baseline hazard rate. This rescales the covariates so that the baseline rates are calculated at meaningful levels (covariate means) because the baseline hazard rate is the time-only rate when all covariates are zero. Figure 12.3 shows that the hazard rate increases each year that a state is in the risk set, up to about eleven years. If a state has been at risk for failure (code adoption) for that long without experiencing a code adoption, then the hazard rate decreases through the balance of analysis time.

The proportional hazards (PH) assumption in the Cox model was also evaluated using the Therneau and Grambsch test of the Schoenfeld residuals. A proportional hazards test was performed (not shown) that showed the proportional hazards assumption held for all the individual covariates in the trimmed model. However, the overall (global) model rejects the PH assumption that hazards are proportional for both groups (adopters and nonadopters) over the analysis time. The global test implies that the slope coefficient for the effects of time is not equal to zero for both groups. Given that the assumption held for all covariates in the model, and the baseline hazard rate is not the primary concern of this analysis, the global violation of the PH assumption is a minor concern.[8]

Given this baseline hazard estimation, how do the variables in the theoretical model perform? The values reported in table 12.5 are the covariate regression coefficients, as opposed to hazard ratios. The regression coefficients are more easily interpretable than hazard (odds) ratios, but where hazard ratios are important they are discussed in the text. If a coefficient in table 12.5 for a covariate is greater than zero, it indicates an increasing haz-

Table 12.3. Correlation Matrix

	Climate	Coastal State	GSP/Capita	Pop. Density	Pop. Growth	Republican Presidential Vote	Government Ideology	Contiguous Energy Code	Natural Gas Price	Construction /GSP	High School Graduates	Political Capacity
Climate	1.00											
Coastal State	-0.50	1.00										
GSP/Capita	0.06	0.23	1.00									
Population Density	-0.31	0.55	0.31	1.00								
Population Growth	-0.29	0.06	0.19	-0.21	1.00							
Republican Presidential Vote	-0.01	-0.27	-0.20	-0.52	0.21	1.00						
Government Ideology	-0.07	0.27	0.15	0.38	-0.12	-0.49	1.00					
Contiguous Energy Codes	0.05	0.29	0.30	0.35	-0.01	-0.38	0.28	1.00				
Natural Gas Price	-0.23	0.60	0.16	0.54	0.03	-0.33	0.28	0.46	1.00			
Construction/GSP	-0.03	-0.06	0.08	-0.31	0.68	0.26	-0.13	-0.02	-0.01	1.00		
High School Graduates	0.57	-0.23	0.37	-0.29	0.17	0.13	0.09	0.01	0.08	0.22	1.00	
Relative Political Capacity	0.22	0.01	-0.28	0.04	-0.27	-0.20	0.18	0.00	0.10	-0.19	0.26	1.00

Table 12.4. Summary Statistics

Variable	Obs	Mean	Std. Dev.	Min	Max
Climate	1440	6025.31	1202.28	3372.00	8583.00
Coastal State	1500	0.46	0.50	0.00	1.00
Log of GSP/Capita	1500	9.98	0.48	8.78	11.15
Population Density	1500	4.31	1.42	−0.25	7.06
(Log of 000 pop/mile^2)					
Population Growth	1500	0.01	0.01	−0.06	0.10
Republican Presidential Vote %	1500	49.99	9.54	27.00	74.50
Government Ideology	1500	49.35	23.63	0.00	97.92
Contiguous Energy Codes	1440	1979.97	6.76	1972.00	2001.67
Natural Gas Price	1500	6.73	3.38	0.00	33.70
Construction/GSP	1500	0.05	0.01	0.03	0.18
High School Graduates	1500	76.50	8.91	48.72	93.00
Relative Political Capacity	1500	1.00	0.15	0.49	2.50

ard ratio for that covariate as it increases. If the covariate is less than zero, its hazard ratio is decreasing as that covariate increases.

The Cox event history model show several surprises for the theoretical justifications for cost-effective energy code adoption, including the economic need results. There is not a strong relationship between a state's climate extremes and the hazard ratio for a state to adopt a new vintage code in the following year. It would appear that the higher number of days that require heating and cooling are not, or are slightly negatively, correlated with more efficient building regulations. In models 1 and 3, the negative relationship between climate and building code adoption is not significant, but in model 2 it is significant at the 90 percent level.

This lack of a strong connection between climate and energy codes is valid, even controlling for coastlines that moderate a state's population weighted climate. Coastal states are more temperate, yet are more likely to adopt new code vintages. Since the coastal variable is binary and significant in both models, it is worth examining the impact of geography on residential energy code adoption. The hazard ratio in model 1 for coastal $= \exp(.93) = 2.5$, indicating that a coastal state has more than two times the odds of adopting residential building codes in the next year as a noncoastal state.

In terms of the price argument for energy codes, the models in table 12.5 indicate higher natural gas prices are not associated with more recent vintage energy codes in the residential sector. That building code adoption is not associated with higher energy prices is troublesome, especially when combined with the counterintuitive climate results that show a weak negative relationship between heating and cooling needs and code adoption.

Table 12.5. Cox Model Regression Coefficients

Variables	1	2	3
Akiake Information Criterion (AIC)	1038.9	1023.9	1027.2
Climate	−0.00	−0.00*	−0.00
	(0.00)	(0.00)	(0.00)
Coastal State	0.93**	0.78**	0.83**
	(0.41)	(0.37)	(0.37)
Log of GSP/Capita	0.58		
	(0.41)		
Population Density	0.09	0.16	0.01
	(0.13)	(0.12)	(0.14)
Population Growth	39.64**	32.41**	23.34*
	(15.73)	(13.54)	(13.57)
Republican Presidential Vote	−0.02	−0.02	−0.03
	(0.02)	(0.02)	(0.02)
Government Ideology	0.00	0.00	0.00
	(0.00)	(0.00)	(0.00)
Contiguous Energy Codes	−0.05**	−0.06***	−0.06**
	(0.02)	(0.02)	(0.03)
Natural Gas Price	−0.03	−0.02	0.02
	(0.08)	(0.06)	(0.07)
Construction/GSP	−7.68	−10.95	−11.13
	(14.49)	(14.23)	(14.39)
Relative Political Capacity	2.94***	2.31**	
	(0.94)	(0.91)	
High School Graduates		0.07***	0.08***
		(0.03)	(0.03)
Tax Effort/GSP			−32.54
			(23.55)
Number of Subjects	48	48	48
Observations	1235	1235	1235

Robust standard errors below regression coefficients
*** p<0.01, ** p<0.05, * p<0.1

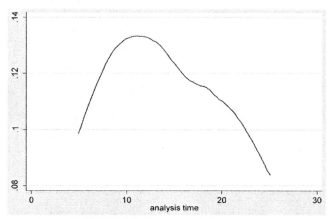

Figure 12.3.   Smoothed Hazard Estimate for Trimmed Model (For Interior States with Covariates Held at Their Means)

The evidence presented here clearly indicates that benefit-cost analyses are not driving state building energy code adoption, and that other factors are at play.

Let us now turn to the property rights arguments for planning and environmental protection. These theories find mixed support in table 12.5. Population density does not predict more recent residential building energy codes. To the extent that energy codes reflect environmental protection, the evidence presented here hints that urbanization as sprawl apparently doesn't enhance perceptions of common pool resource scarcity and threat. Scarcity would make a jurisdiction more likely to regulate the residential development that is interfacing with natural areas, but there is no sign of such regulation in this policy domain.

However, in all the models, there is evidence that population growth affects code adoption. Population growth, as a result of in-migration or high fertility rates, does increase the odds of code adoption in the models. Considering that population growth manifests itself as more residential building construction, regulators in fast-growing states are apparently mindful of lost opportunity measures that occur during new residential construction. Population growth in this policy domain can be thought of as a severity variable and does find support as in other studies of state outputs (Bacot and Dawes 1997).

There is some support for increased wealth driving code adoption. Model 1 shows no statistically significant relationship between per capita GSP and code adoption. However, in model 2, the percent of high school graduates in the state was used as a proxy for per capita income. Each increase in high school graduation rate predicts a .07 higher hazard rate, as exp(.07) = 1.07, for states adopting new code vintages. Educational attainment has been found to predict state adoption of renewable portfolio standards (Huang et al. 2007).

The economic importance of the construction industry does not conform to theoretical expectations in table 12.5. The interest group strength indicator of state construction sector activity as a percent of state GSP is not a significant predictor of building energy code adoption. The growth machine (Molotch 1976) appears to be sputtering.

The diffusion indicator shows a potential race to the bottom for residential building energy codes in all models. This result runs counter to evidence of the relationship between large states that lead code adoption and some smaller neighboring states. Oregon has adopted much of its building energy codes from California, which indicates a race to the top, not to the bottom. There is no clear reason for a race to the bottom in residential building codes. States with no codes would have lower construction costs, and thus lower resale values, but buyers would face higher operating costs that would more than offset the lower initial costs. The negative coefficient estimated here needs further analysis to be fully understood.

Figure 12.4 shows a map of the spatial distribution of the energy code updates, which can potentially further our understanding of spatial aspects of the data generating process. Clearly, the coastal vs. interior variable is capturing the majority of the spatial dynamics of code adoption. The race to the bottom measure employed here is a simple average of the vintage of contiguous states and thus doesn't account for the effects of leaders like California and Florida (nor laggards like Texas and New York). Future spatial econometrics research can help parse out this intriguing result.

Figure 12.4.   Summary Statistics of Mandatory Statewide Energy Codes 1977–2006

There is no evidence that political ideology in a state drives (or hinders) residential building code adoption. The Berry et al. (1998) measure of citizen and institutional ideology was not significant in any model specification. The simpler measure of the percent of voters voting for the Republican candidate in the previous presidential election also shows no significance in the models. In sum, a state's motivation to adopt residential energy codes is not due to the ideology of elites in the state, nor from the ideology represented by presidential voting records. Perhaps there are other, better measures of political ideology, but the two tested here show no relationship to building energy codes.

Finally, political capacity explanations meet mixed support. The legislative professionalism measure predicts no significant relationship between more recent residential codes in states with more professional legislatures. We find no support for Perry (1981) and Ka and Teske (2002) and others who have found that legislative professionalism positively predicts energy outcomes.

However, RPC is strongly significant in model 2, indicating a state's relative tax effort is a powerful predictor of energy code adoption. The hazard ratio for the RPC covariate $= \exp(2.31) = 10.06$. This indicates that a one unit increase in RPC is associated with a tenfold increase in the odds of adoption of a new vintage energy code in the following year. As the standard deviation of RPC in the data is only .15, a one unit increase in RPC represents more than a six standard deviation increase and thus is not practical, but it shows the large effect size of the RPC covariate.

THEORETICAL IMPLICATIONS FOR GOVERNMENTAL EFFECTIVENESS RESEARCH

One of the most powerful and consistent explanatory variables in the above models is the measure of relative political extraction. Unlike RPC, other measures of government "wealth" do not predict residential energy code adoption.[9] Model 3 drops RPC and uses a state's total state and local tax effort as a percent of GSP to predict code adoption. This measure is negative and not significant. The Akaike Information Criteria (AIC) is a measure of the goodness of fit of a model that is used for model selection as it accounts for the tradeoff between complexity and accuracy of models.

The model with the lowest AIC measure is considered the best model. Model 2 with RPC is clearly superior to model 3 with the nonsignificant tax effort/GSP measure. Relative political capacity is a superior measure of governmental effectiveness because it controls for population, economic structure, and wealth. Small states have higher fixed costs and thus have higher revenues/GSP than do large states. Furthermore, resource extractive states like Alaska and Wyoming have higher tax revenues than nonextractive states, and this needs to be controlled for in calculating capacity.[10]

To further examine the effects of political capacity, the cases were dichotomized into groups where states with an RPC value below the mean RPC value of one in any year were coded as a zero, and states with an RPC value of one or greater were coded as a one. Figure 12.5 shows the hazard rates for these two groups for interior states with covariates held at their means. The hazard rate for the low RPC group reaches its maximum at 9 percent while the high RPC group's maximum hazard rate is almost double that at 17 percent. Furthermore, the peak hazard rate occurs in the high RPC group at nine analysis years, while the low RPC group's hazard rate doesn't peak until sixteen years into the analysis time.

This simple empirical specification shows support for the theoretical link between governmental effectiveness and relative political capacity. Effective governments update their cost-effective building energy codes more frequently than do ineffective governments.

CONCLUSIONS

The evidence presented here is notable for its lack of support for many convincing and popular explanations for state policy adoption. Neither energy costs in a state, its climate, nor its wealth predict residential energy code adoption. Traditional benefit-cost analyses are not driving state building energy code adoption. The two measures of political ideology are not predictors of the government providing effective and efficient building energy

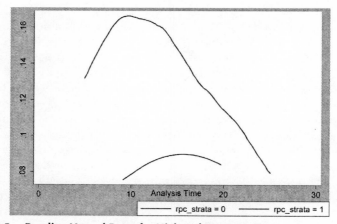

Figure 12.5. Baseline Hazard Rates for High and Low RPC States

codes. Furthermore, theories ⸤f regulatory capture do not get any support in this policy domain.

Only geography, political capacity, and population growth positively predict energy code adaption. Of these, only political capacity is readily manipulable for stakeholders in states that are interested in improving net social outcomes by adopting building energy codes. Increasing the relative resources in a state is a necessary condition to implementing good government.

While this is the first analysis of the political economy and governance aspects of building energy code adoption, hopefully these results can inform future policy interventions as building codes are currently at the forefront of federal energy policy. The American Recovery and Reinvestment Act of 2009 Sec 410 (32) requires that any state that applies for $3.1 billion in energy grant funds from the U.S. government must have intentions to adopt the recent building energy code vintage. Also, the American Clean Energy and Security Act of 2009 passed by the U.S. House develops a new national energy code and mandates that states comply. The assumption is that all states will be able to do so. The analysis presented here indicates differing levels of capacity among U.S. states, regardless of whether federal action is a mandate or an incentive. Those that can, will. Those that cannot, will not.

NOTES

1. For a list of the energy, economic, and environmental studies of state building code adoption, see the Technical Assistance Reports done by PNNL at www .energycodes.gov/implement/tech_assist_reports.stm.

2. Reductions in energy use also mitigate the environmental externalities associated with energy production and consumption such as global warming, chronic morbidity and mortality, soil and water pollution, and others. For a short exposé of the externalities associated with coal, see Natural Resources Defense Council (2009), "Coal is Dirty and Dangerous," www.nrdc.org/energy/coalnotclean.asp. Thus, building energy codes could also be considered governance structures to address physical externalities as described in Abbott and Snidal (2001).

3. www.census.gov/govs/www/state.html.

4. www.taxpolicycenter.org/.

5. Generate ordinary least squares estimates using the following functional specification:

$$TaxEffortGSP_{i,t} = \gamma_0 + \gamma_1 Year_{i,t} + \gamma_2 GSPcapita_{i,t} + \gamma_3 MiningGSP_{i,t} \qquad \text{Eq. (1)}$$
$$+ \gamma_4 Oil\&GasGSP_{i,t} + \gamma_5 Agt/GSP_{i,t} + \gamma_6 Population_{i,t} + e_{it}$$

Where
Year = data field year

GSPcapita = current per capita Gross State Product (GSP) in chain weighted 2005 dollars

Mining/GSP = Percentage share of mining output divided by GSP

Oil&Gas/GSP = Percentage share of oil and gas output divided by GSP

Ag/GSP = Percentage share of mining output divided by GSP

Pop = natural log of current year state population

2. The predicted values for Tax Effort/GSP are obtained from Eq. (1). The model explains 25% of the variance in the dependent variable (not reported).

3. A measure of political capacity is calculated from the following ratio:

$$\text{Political Capacity}_{it} = \frac{STR_{it}}{\hat{STR}_{it}} \qquad\qquad \text{Eq. (2)}$$

where TR_{it} is the observed value for tax effort and $\hat{TR}_{it}$ represents the fitted value from Equation 2.

6. This assumes that operating and maintenance costs are less salient to buyers and renters of residential and commercial building than amortization of initial costs. Efficient buildings have lower operating costs that offset their higher initial cost.

7. The units of analysis (states) show no clear theoretical reason to employ variance corrected or frailty models that estimate baseline hazard rates based on stratifications in the data. Since there is no intervention being tested (such as the efficacy of a drug in clinical studies) or attribute of the units (male or female in clinical studies), there isn't a compelling case to use a stratified model. In this analysis, robust standard errors clustered by state, as well as the use of conditional gap time, help account for potential unit-level heterogeneity and serial dependence in observations.

8. There are assurances that the model is correctly specified as a linktest was performed. A linktest tests that the squared coefficient of the covariates is not statistically significant, or put more simply that a model of squared predictors isn't preferable to the standard (unsquared) model.

9. A measure of relative political reach for American states was tested as a predictor of energy code adoption as well (not reported). It was nonsignificant, as was its interaction with relative political extraction.

10. There is no reason that a measure of fiscal health as popularized by Berry and Berry (1990), which is a measure of state expenditures less revenues, would be any better at predicting energy code adoptions than absolute tax effort.

REFERENCES

Abbott, K. W., and D. Snidal. 2001. "International 'Standards' and International Governance." *Journal of European Public Policy* 8 (3): 345–70.

Aldo, A.W., and W. Polasub. 2009. "The Political Economy of State-Level Adoption of Natural Resource Damage Programs." *Journal of Regulatory Economics* 35: 312–30.

Anthony, J. 2004. "Do State Growth Management Regulations Reduce Sprawl?" *Urban Affairs Review* 39 (3): 376–97.

Bacot, A. H., and R. A. Dawes. 1997. "State Expenditures and Policy Outcomes in Environmental Program Management." *Policy Studies Journal* 25 (Fall): 355–70.

Bamberger, R. 2003. *Automobile and Light Truck Fuel Economy: The CAFE Standards.* Washington, DC: Congressional Research Service. www.ncseonline.org/NLE/CRSreports/03Jul/IB90122.pdf.

Benningfield, Lynn, and John Hogan. 2003. *Building Energy Code Enforcement A Look at California and Seattle.* Prepared for the Natural Resources Defense Council, November 7, 2003. www.imt.org/files/FileUpload/files/PDF/BuidlingCodeEnforcementInTheUnitedStates.pdf.

Berry, W. D., and F. S. Berry. 1990. "State Lottery Adoptions as Policy Innovations: An Event History Analysis." *American Political Science Review* 84 (2): 322–30.

Berry, William D., Evan J. Ringquist, Richard C. Fording, and Russell L. Hanson. 1998. "Measuring Citizen and Government Ideology in the American States, 1960–93." *American Journal of Political Science* 42 (1): 327–48. Updated through 2006 at: arc.irss.unc.edu/dvn/dv/iqss/faces/study/StudyPage.xhtml?studyId=42425&tab=files.

Box-Steffensmeier, J., and B. S. Jones. 2004. *Event History Modeling: A Guide for Social Scientists.* New York: Cambridge University Press.

Brace, P., K. Arceneaux, M. Johnson, and S. Gulbig. 2005. "Does State Political Ideology Change over Time?" *Political Research Quarterly* 7 (4): 529–40.

Building Codes Assistance Project. 2008. *Residential Building Energy Codes—Enforcement and Compliance Study.* Prepared for the North American Insulation Manufacturers Association. bcap-energy.org/files/Residential_Survey_Report_Oct08.pdf.

———. 2009. *A Survey of Advanced Residential Building Techniques and Technologies and Their Impacts on Energy Codes.* EF%20Advanced%20Residential%20Building%20Survey.pdf.

Bureau of Economic Analysis. 2009. GDP by State. www.bea.gov/iTable/iTable.cfm?ReqID=70&step=1&isuri=1&acrdn=1. Accessed July 12, 2010.

Cleves, M., R. Guitierrez, W. Gould, and Y. Marchenko. 2008. *An Introduction to Survival Analysis Using Stata,* 2nd ed. College Station, TX: Stata Press.

Cort, K. A., and D. B. Belzer. 2002. *Statewide Savings Projections from the Adoption of a Commercial Building Energy Code in Illinois.* www.energycodes.gov/publications/techassist/illinois_statewide …savings.pdf .

Feiock, R. C., and J. P. West. 1993. "Testing Competing Explanations for Policy Adoption: Municipal Solid Waste Recycling Programs." *Policy Research Quarterly* 46 (2): 399–419.

Fiorina, M., and R. Noll. 1978. "Voters, Bureaus, and Legislators." *Journal of Public Economics* 9 (April): 239–54.

Gerber, B. J., and P. Teske. 2000. "Regulatory Policymaking in the American States: A Review of Theories and Evidence." *Political Research Quarterly* 53 (4): 849–86.

Gillingham, H., R. Newell, and K. Palmer. 2009. *Energy Efficiency Economics and Policy.* RFF Discussion Paper 09–13. www.rff.org/RFF/Documents/RFF-DP-09–13.pdf.

Grossman, G., and A. Krueger. 1995. "Economic Growth and the Environment." *Quarterly Journal of Economics* 3: 53–77.

Hays, S. P., M. Elser, and C. F. Hays. 1996. "Environmental Commitment among the States: Integrating Alternative Approaches to State Environmental Policy." *Publius* 26 (2): 41–58.

Holland, K. M., F. L. Morton, and B. Galligan. 1996. *Federalism and the Environment: Environmental Policymaking in Australia, Canada, and the United States.* Westport, CT: Greenwood Press.

Huang, Ming-Yuan, et al. 2007. "Is the Choice of Renewable Portfolio Standards Random?" *Energy Policy* 35: 5571–75.

Infoplease Encyclopedia. 2008. *US Elections.* www.infoplease.com/ipa/A0764586.html. Accessed August 8, 2008.

International Code Council. 2008. *Typical Code Development Cycle.* Washington, DC: International Code Council. Available at www.iccsafe.org/cs/codes/pdf/CodeDev-typical.pdf.

Jones, B. S., and R. P. Branton. 2005. "Beyond Logit and Probit: Cox Duration Models of Single, Repeating, and Competing Events for State Policy Adoption." *State Politics and Policy Quarterly* 5 (4): 420–43.

Ka, S., and P. Teske. 2002. "Ideology and Professionalism: Electricity Regulation and Deregulation over Time in the American States." *American Politics Research* 30 (3): 323–43.

Lazarus, Richard J. 1991. "The Tragedy of Distrust in the Implementation of Federal Environmental Law." *Law and Contemporary Problems* 54 (4): 311–74.

Leblang, D. 1997. "Political Capacity and Economic Growth." Marina Arbetman and Jacek Kugler, eds., *Political Capacity and Economic Behavior.* Boulder, CO: Westview Press.

Lester, J. P., and E. N. Lombard. 1990. "The Comparative Analysis of State Environmental Policy." *Natural Resources Journal* 30: 301–20.

———. 1998. "Environmental Regulation and State-Local Relations." R. L. Hanson, ed., *Governing Partners: State-Local Relations in the United States*, 139–60. Boulder, CO: Westview Press.

Lubell, M., R. C. Feiock, and E. Rameriz. 2005. "Political Institutions and Conservation by Local Governments." *Urban Affairs Review* 40: 706–729.

Meyer, S. M., and D. M. Koniskey. 2007. "Adopting Local Environmental Institutions." *Political Research Quarterly* 60 (1): 3–16.

Miller, G., and T. Moe. 1983. "Bureaucrats, Legislators, and the Size of Government." *American Political Science Review* 77 (June): 297–322.

Molotch, H. L. 1976. "The City as a Growth Machine: Toward a Political Economy of Place." *American Journal of Sociology* 86: 1387–1400.

Mooney, C. Z. 1994. "Measuring U.S. State Legislative Professionalism: An Evaluation of Five Indices." *State and Local Government Review* 26 (2): 70–78.

Murthishaw, S., and J. Sayanthe. 2006. *Quantifying the Effect of the Principal-Agent Problem on US Residential Energy Use.* LBNL paper #59773.

National Oceanic and Atmospheric Administration (NOAA). 2005. *Historical Climatology Series 5–1 Monthly State, Regional, and National Heating Degree Days Weighted by Population (Includes Aerially Weighted Temperature and Precipitation).* lwf.ncdc.noaa.gov/oa/documentlibrary/hcs/hdd.200507–200607.pdf; lwf.ncdc.noaa.gov/oa/documentlibrary/hcs/cdd.200501–200607.pdf.

NW Council. 2005. *Achievable Savings: A Retrospective Look at the Northwest Power and Conservation Council's Conservation Planning Assumptions.* Council document 2007–13. Portland, OR: Northwest Power and Conservation Council.

Perry, C. 1981. "Energy Conservation Policy in the American States: An Attempt at Explanation." *Social Science Quarterly* 6 (2): 540–54.

Potoski, M. 2001. "Clear Air Federalism: Do States Race to the Bottom?" *Public Administration Review* 61 (3): 335–42.

Ringquist, E. J. 1993. *Environmental Protection at the State Level: Politics and Progress in Controlling Pollution.* Armonk, NY: ME Sharpe.

Sapat, A. 2004. "Devolution and Innovation: The Adoption of State Environmental Policy Innovations by Administrative Agencies." *Public Administration Review* 64 (2): 141–51.

Scheberle, D. 2004. *Federalism and Environmental Policy*, 2nd ed. Washington, DC: Georgetown University Press.

Schweitzer, Martin, et al. 2003, January. *Estimating Energy and Cost Savings and Emissions Reductions for the State Energy Program Based on Enumeration Indicators Data* .weatherization.ornl.gov/pdfs/ORNL_CON-487.pdf.

Shipan, C. R., and C. Volden. 2006. "Bottom-Up Federalism: The Diffusion of Antismoking Policies from US Cities to States." *American Journal of Political Science* 50 (4): 825–43.

Sierra Club. 2009. Excel file sent by David Perry of the Sierra Club. October 2.

Squire, P. 2007. "Measuring State Legislative Professionalism: The Squire Index Revisited." *State Politics and Policy Quarterly* 7 (2).

Stoker, R. P. 1991. *Reluctant Partners: Implementing Federal Policy.* Pittsburgh: Pittsburgh University Press.

Swaminathan, S., and J. Thomas. 2007. "Saving the Next Generation: Political Capacity and Infant Mortality Decline in India's States." *International Interactions* 33: 217–42.

Tavares, Antonio Fernando F. 2001. "State Constraints and Local Environmental Programs: Solid Waste Management Policy Instrument Choice." Working Paper presented at the Midwest Political Science Association meeting in Chicago, April 19–21, 2001.

Travis, Rick, John C. Morris, and Elizabeth D. Morris. 2004. "State Implementation of Federal Environmental Policy: Explaining Leveraging in the Clean Water State Revolving Fund." *The Policy Studies Journal* 32 (3).

U.S. Census. 2000. *PHC-T-41. A Half-Century of Learning: Historical Statistics on Educational Attainment in the United States, 1940 to 2000.* www.census.gov/population/www/socdemo/education/introphct41.html.

U.S. Department of Commerce. 2006. *National Oceanic and Atmospheric Administration Series 5–1 Monthly State, Regional, and National Heating Degree Days.* Asheville, NC: National Climatic Data Center.

U.S. Department of Energy (DOE). 2005. *Residential Energy Consumption Survey Home Energy Uses and Costs.* Washington, DC: Energy Information Agency. www.eia.doe.gov/emeu/recs/contents.html.

U.S. Department of Energy (DOE). 2008a. *Current and Historical Monthly Retail Sales, Revenues, and Average Retail Price by State and by Sector (Form EIA-826).* Washington, DC: Energy Information Agency. www.eia.doe.gov/cneaf/electricity/epa/epat7p4.html.

U.S. Department of Energy (DOE). 2008b. *2008 Buildings Energy Data Book.* Table 2.1.1. Washington, DC: U.S. Energy Efficiency and Renewable Energy Office. buildingsdatabook.eere.energy.gov/?id = view_book.

U.S. Department of Energy (DOE). 2009a. *Baseline Studies.* Washington, DC: Efficiency and Renewable Energy Office. www.energycodes.gov/implement/baseline_studies.stm. Accessed August 28, 2009.

U.S. Department of Energy (DOE). 2009b. *South Carolina Additional State Info.* Washington, DC: U.S. Energy Efficiency and Renewable Energy Office. www.energycodes.gov/implement/state_codes/state_stat_more.p hp?state_AB = SC. Accessed August 28, 2009.

U.S. Department of Energy (DOE). 2009c. *Status of State Energy Codes.* Washington, DC: Office of Energy Efficiency and Renewable Energy. www.energycodes.gov/implement/state_codes/index.stm. Accessed October 12, 2009.

U.S. Department of Energy (DOE). 2009d. *Oregon Additional State Info.* Washington, DC: U.S. Energy Efficiency and Renewable Energy Office. www.energycodes.gov/implement/state_codes/state_stat_more.p hp?state_AB = OR. Accessed October 16, 2009.

U.S. Department of Energy (DOE) (2010). *State Energy Data. Annual Average Residential Natural Gas Price.* www.eia.doe.gov/emeu/states/_seds.html. Accessed May 25, 2010.

U.S. EPA. 2008. *Building Codes for Energy Efficiency.* www.epa.gov/cleanenergy/documents/buildingcodesfactsheet.pdf.

Vogel, D. 1995. *Trading Up: Consumer and Environmental Regulation in a Global Economy.* Cambridge, MA: Harvard University Press.

Walker, J. 1969. "The Diffusion of Innovation among the American States." *American Political Science Review* 63 (3): 880–99.

World Resources Institute. 2008. *Climate Analysis Indicators Tool.* cait.wri.org/cait-us.php?page = graphstate. Accessed July 15, 2008.

Yang, B. 2005. *Residential Energy Code Evaluations: Review and Future Directions.* bcap.energy.org/files/BCAP_RESIDENTIAL_ENERGY_CODE_EVALUA TION_STUDY …June2005.pdf.

Appendix 12.1.   2006 Relative Political Extraction

State	RPC	Rank
Alabama	1.00	23
Alaska	1.12	6
Arizona	0.86	41
Arkansas	1.01	21
California	1.09	9
Colorado	0.85	43
Connecticut	0.87	40
Delaware	0.71	50
Florida	1.06	11
Georgia	0.88	38
Hawaii	1.03	14
Idaho	1.02	17
Illinois	0.91	35
Indiana	1.17	4
Iowa	0.96	32
Kansas	0.96	31
Kentucky	0.97	28
Louisiana	0.77	48
Maine	1.23	1
Maryland	0.98	25
Massachusetts	0.93	34
Michigan	1.08	10
Minnesota	0.97	30
Mississippi	1.11	8
Missouri	0.90	36
Montana	1.04	13
Nebraska	0.98	26
Nevada	0.84	46
New Hampshire	0.84	45
New Jersey	1.02	18
New Mexico	1.02	16
New York	1.2	22
North Carolina	0.86	42
North Dakota	1.00	22
Ohio	1.05	12
Oklahoma	0.87	39
Oregon	0.97	29
Pennsylvania	1.02	15
Rhode Island	1.01	20
South Carolina	1.11	7
South Dakota	0.79	47
Tennessee	0.85	44
Texas	0.75	49
Utah	0.97	27
Vermont	1.15	5
Virginia	0.88	37
Washington	0.94	33
West Virginia	1.19	3
Wisconsin	1.02	19
Wyoming	0.99	24

Appendix 12.2. Building Codes Data

The residential building energy codes data come from a variety of sources, as there is no one-stop shopping for historical building energy codes. Our primary data source was a web-based survey administered to state building energy code experts in each of the fifty states. The survey response rate was 32 percent, and we received e-mails with historical building code data from another eleven state representatives, for a total response rate of 54 percent.

For states that did not respond to our determined requests for information, we consulted three secondary sources. The first was various editions of the *Directory of State Building Codes and Regulations* (see below). The next source of information for states was data provided by the Building Codes Assistance Project (2008) historical files (Dewein 2008). Finally, any remaining data needs were estimated from the U.S. DOE (2009c) website.

States that have mandatory statewide building energy codes on the books but do not provide any compliance and enforcement resources are coded as a 0. States like Idaho, Tennessee, and West Virginia fall into this category, where code enforcement is voluntary for local jurisdictions. Coding a state as a 0 for a lack of enforcement distinguishes our data from the U.S. Department of Energy code maps (2009c), which code states as having mandatory statewide codes and don't account for enforcement.

BUILDING CODES DIRECTORY REFERENCES

Bethel, Marla. 1985, April. *Directory of State Building Codes and Regulations, Third Edition*. Herndon, VA: National Conference of States on Building Codes and Standards.

Dewein, M. 2008. E-mail communication with code maps, July 1.

Directory of State Building Codes and Regulations, State Directory. 1994. Herndon, VA: National Conference of States on Building Codes and Standards.

McIntyre, Marla. 1987, May. *Directory of State Building Codes and Regulations. Fourth Edition*. Herndon, VA: National Conference of States on Building Codes and Standards.

———. 1989, July. *Directory of State Building Codes and Regulations*. Herndon, VA: National Conference of States on Building Codes and Standards.

———. 1991, May. *Directory of State Building Codes and Regulations, State Commercial Codes*. Herndon, VA: National Conference of States on Building Codes and Standards.

13

Do Local Governments Matter?

Impact of U.S. Municipal-Level Relative Political Extraction Capacity on Crime Rate

Masami Nishishiba, Marina Arbetman Rabinowitz,
Mariah Kraner, and Matthew Jones

CONTEXT

Cities, towns, villages, parishes, boroughs, counties, and villages are examples of different types of local government in the United States. Among their main responsibilities is the delivery of essential services, such as public safety, community health, education, and infrastructure development (roads, drinking water, utilities). These services directly affect citizens in their everyday lives and make the community a better place to live. Livability also promotes economic development and helps the community attract industry, commerce, and a qualified workforce.

Local government also allows citizens access and direct participation in policies closest to their interests, without the burden of bureaucratic layers in higher levels of government (e.g., Stenberg 2007). Scholars and practitioners have been studying local government performance in the United States (e.g., Folz and Abdelrazek 2009; Ingraham and Government Performance Project 2007; Ingraham, Joyce, and Donahue 2003), and this knowledge may be applied to other countries for comparative perspective to help distinguish key elements that would assist in community development elsewhere.

The purpose of this study is to contribute to this endeavor by applying the concept of Relative Political Extraction, already tested at the subnational and national level, to the local level. This is an uncharted area, not only regarding the data collection but also the crossover application of the concept from comparative and international political economy application to the local level and public administration.

INTELLECTUAL ENVIRONMENT

One of the main objectives of this book is to provide an objective assessment of how to measure government performance across societies and within societies across time. The same concept of Relative Political Extraction applied to the national and subnational level should be useful to explore at the local level. Governments at the national and subnational levels have a higher probability of implementing their desired policies when the governments have higher levels of political capacity compared to other governments. As the level of granularity of decision making increases, the expectation is that the more able local government will be able to manage programs, implement their desired policies, and quickly adapt to changes in the economic and social environment and deliver reforms in a more successful way than other local governments that have less political capacity.

Wide differences in political orientation or levels of economic development are mitigated when the analysis is done within country; for example, although the differences between New York City and Mobile, Alabama, are wide, they are not as wide as the differences between Sweden and Zimbabwe. Furthermore, local governments have less flexibility than national governments because their scope of action is legally limited, although they still make decisions that may impact future economic growth of the region, foster emigrations of labor, or attract new businesses. In sum, the concept of political performance that incorporates the ability of governments to reach their population and to convince them to support policy objectives, extract resources to implement chosen policies, and allocate those resources to meet expectations that secure the long-term survival of the political elite needs to be developed at the local level to increase our understanding of relative success in the implementation of policies.

The measurement of politics constitutes a difficult task for researchers, and our current work is a massive enhancement of the earlier RPC project initiated by A. F. K. Organski and Jacek Kugler in the 1980s. Specifically we have acquired and applied all these efforts relying on the idea that capable governments are able to enact their social, political, and economic goals to the local level. Governments and elites make different decisions about resource allocation; some heavily invest in social programs while others act to facilitate economic growth or seek some other objective.

This level of analysis allows for regional and intrastate analysis, which permits researchers to choose the appropriate measure depending on theoretical interests. We will show that the same approach can be used at the local level to determine how well local governments reflect their political capacity. Adaptation of national-level models of political capacity to the subnational level and then to local districts or cities requires the measurement of the extractive capabilities of local or regional governments and/or the transfer of resources from the central government to local governments. The measure captures how local districts are performing based on their economic endowments. In other words, are local governments performing in terms of resource extraction at the anticipated level based on their economic endowments? Estimation of political capacity of a local district or city is relative to other regions, states, or provinces within that country. Our local capacity or performance formula is found here.[1]

Public authorities at any level of government who are in possession of material resources can pursue their objectives more easily since money is fungible, choosing, for instance, to provide utility services or privatize them. The array of decisions at the local level—the dependent variable—is very different in scope than at the federal level, but all governments require resources in order to enact policies. Therefore, due to the differing taxation structures, some small adjustments in the estimation are required on a case by case basis.

In sum, the fiscal pressure represents the population willingness or enforcement ability on the part of the government to transfer resources from private individuals to the government once the preferences for public or private delivery of services is controlled for. This does not impact the overall estimation as the scores are relative for a given country.

Empirical Challenges

From a theoretical point of view, to calculate RPE it is necessary to define the geographic limits that determine the system. At the national level the answer is simple: this concept applies to all the countries in the world. At the subnational level the country's borders determine what will be included. As the level of analysis becomes more granular, defining the sample becomes important because RPE is a relative measure; for example, excluding a district that is very efficient or very inefficient would determine a totally different mean capacity for that sample. By the same token, the fact that it is a relative measure means that the position in the scale of RPE would be accurate. The reality is that it is not possible to gather data on all cities or districts of a country, and this is one of the limitations of data collection at the local level.

Another issue that needs attention is the definition of geographic borders of cities or districts. Often, in developed countries nearby cities expand in concentric circles as the population increases, resulting in de facto mergers of cities that in some cases maintain the responsibility of service distribution and tax collection but not in all. Again the decision becomes the researcher's responsibility to determine the unit of analysis.

Two other concerns need to be mentioned. From a data collection standpoint, special attention should be paid to the different accounting systems and to what is included in each budget line in the different cities. The structure of tax systems is also an important component in determining the appropriate model for the estimation of subnational political capacity. In some districts, local governments collect taxes and retain the revenues; in others taxation is centralized with all receipts relinquished to the central government. For this paper we based our analysis on the funds flow of different cities (data source: Municipal Analysis Services Inc.), which accounts for realized transactions as opposed to budget lines.

Finally, the structure of local governments in developed countries differs widely regarding the provision of utilities. In many cases water, electric services, or even transit services are offered by private enterprises in the same way that some fee-based services such as airports may show a level of revenue that needs to be adjusted by the expenses in the same category so that that city does not show a higher level of income than their counterparts that do not offer fee-based services.

RPE Local Level Model

The RPE model was calculated for seventy-two U.S. cities for the period 1990–2003 (with data for 1990, 1993, 1997, 1999, 2000, and 2003). Our formula and results are found here.[2]

The results are consistent with RPE calculations at the provincial and national level. The structure shows that the more revenues in the form of transfers from local and state sources, the higher the total revenue. In the same way, the higher the level of wealth of the city, the more probabilities of a larger fiscal base for that area. The control for airport income to the city is put in place to level the field of cities that do not have that income (note: the correlation between expenditures and income on airports is very high and on average the difference is less than 6 percent).

Empirically, the concept of RPE answers the question of what accounts for the difference in revenues once the economic structure has been accounted for. The assumption is that the difference between actual and predicted values of revenues reflects the political power the authorities exercise to stretch the fiscal base of the population. Therefore in relative terms, those cities with higher RPEs are the ones with more political capacity.

Impact of Municipal Political Capacity on Crime Rate

In this chapter we examine effect of the municipal-level RPE on crime rate. Crime rate was selected as a social indicator that describes the conditions of a municipality. Social indicators are the statistical data that provide information about the trend of the health and well-being of the population in a given government jurisdiction (Aristigueta, Cooksy, and Nelson 2001; Land 1983). We have chosen to use crime rate for this study, not only because it is a social indicator frequently used to assess the well-being of a community (e.g. Land and Felson 1976) but also because it is especially relevant to the political capacity of the municipal government in the United States. For almost all of the municipal governments in the United States, public safety is one of the core services they provide. Consequently, the police department typically consumes a significant proportion of the municipal government budget (Donahue and Miller 2006).

One of the puzzling and intriguing aspects of crime is that it has a high variance across time and space (Glaeser, Sacerdote, and Scheinkman 1996). It fluctuates over the course of the years, and there's a vast difference in its occurrence from place to place. According to the Bureau of Justice Statistics (2010),[3] the U.S.-wide total violent crime rate calculated based on adjusted violent victimization rates (i.e., number of victimizations per 1,000 population age twelve or older) declined from 51.7 percent in 1979 to 32.1 percent in 1999 and further declined to 16.9 percent in 2009.

When compared across the fifty states in the violent crime rate per 100,000 population in 2009, District of Columbia is the highest with 1,345.9, and Maine is the lowest with 119.8.[4] Social scientists have long been trying to identify the factors that contribute to the variance in crime. Some factors that are identified as the source of the variance in crime include: shift in demographics, especially in age, gender, and race (Levitt, 1998, 2004); economic conditions (Arvanites and Defina, 2006; Levitt 2004; Raphael and Winter-Ebmer 2001); legal arrangements (Joyce 2004; Levitt 2004); police operation (Kennedy 2009; Levitt 2004; Wilson and Boland 1993); and community characteristics (Messner, Baumer, and Rosenfeld 2004; Parâe, Felson, and Ouimet 2007; Sampson and Groves 1989).

Many of the studies that examine the relationship between social and community factors on crime have their base in Clifford Shaw and Henry McKay's (1969 [1942]) social disorganization theory. It focuses on the effects of the places that create conditions that are favorable or unfavorable to crime. Social disorganization means the community or the place is disorganized and does not have the capacity to realize common goals and solve problems. The original theory posits that the "poverty, residential mobility, ethnic heterogeneity, and weak social networks decrease a neighborhood's capacity to control the behavior of people in public, and hence increase the likelihood of crime" (Kubrin and Weitzer 2003, 2).

More recently, those who have developed on the social disorganization theory started to examine the impact of social ties and social network and how people exercise informal social control (Peterson, Krivo, and Harris 2000; Sampson and Groves 1989). Interestingly, not much has been done to examine the impact of the formal public institution's impact on social disorganization. In other words, as Kubrin and Weitzer (2003) point out, systematic examination of the impact of the formal governmental authorities in maintaining order and enforcing regulatory codes has been missing in this line of research.

This chapter examines the effect of municipal RPE on crime rate, filling this gap. We hypothesize that governments with higher level of political capacity will be able to exert formal control to maintain the social order in the community and will be able to implement policies that are conducive to less crime. To test this proposition, the model at this endnote was utilized.[5]

CONCEPTS AND MEASUREMENTS

Crime Per Capita: (1) CrimePC

The violent crime rate was constructed using the Uniform Crime Rate data from the Department of Justice (Uniform Crime Report for 1990, 1993, 1997, 1999, 2000, and 2003). The twelve-month total crime incidences were calculated by aggregating the reported number of crimes from the following four categories: murder, forcible rape, robbery, and aggravated assault. Crime Per Capita was calculated by dividing the total crime incidences with population (see appendix for more details).

Political Capacity of the Local Government: (1) RPE

As explained in the previous section, formal institutional strength sends a clear message to the population about the consequences of crime and will be able to maintain a social order that prevents crime. Furthermore, at the local level when the community lacks "social altruism," or "the willingness of communities to commit scarce resources to the aid and comfort of their members" (Chamlin and Cochran 1997, 204), that is distinct from what the state provides, a powerful government that may be willing to exercise coercion to get the job done becomes important. The expectation is that the higher the capacity of the municipal government, the lower the level of crime in that city.

Police Administrative Structure: (1) Police Employees (2) Police expenditures per capita (3) Professionalization

The internal organization of the different police departments has a direct effect on crime control (e.g., Kennedy 2009; Wilson and Boland 1978). One of these factors is the number of police employees. As is the case in any area of public life, shortage of personnel is often quoted as the reason why an institution cannot get the work done. In this case we control for number of police employees per 100,000 (*Police Employees*) to account for staff availability.

By the same token, monetary resources available should have a positive effect on the fight against crime; therefore, *Police Expenditures per capita* should be negatively correlated with crime. Our model describes a relationship where the more trained police officers are, the more effective they should be at deterring crime. We measure professionalization as the ratio of sworn officers/total number of police employees (*Professionalization*). Some would also say that the degree of professionalization is an indicator of "aggressive patrol strategy" (Wilson and Boland 1978), but generalizing, it measures the police departments as well as the municipalities' commitment to reduce crime (see appendix 13.1 for sources).

Local Economic Environment: (1) Income per Capita

The relationship between the community's socioeconomic conditions and the incidence of crime was recognized by the ecological theories at the University of Chicago as early as the 1940s (e.g., Shaw and McKay, 1969 [1942]). The motivation for crime is often born in the perception that the economic situation of the individual is unfair. Theories such as relative deprivation point out that when the expected trajectory of economic well-being differs from the actual situation, then the individual is more prone to react against the system. Furthermore, as this gap increases with the process of urbanization and the consequent social disorganization, then crime rates are expected to increase. Chamlin and Cochran (1997) write, "Traditional Marxist theories and anomie theories suggest that blocked opportunities produce frustration and thereby motivate the disadvantaged to engage in crime to satisfy their material needs" (211). To account for the average level of poverty as well as employment opportunities of the area, we include *Income per Capita* in our model (see appendix 13.1 for sources).

Other Controls: (1) Year (2) Region (3) South

The geographical location is used as a control in most of the empirical literature on crime. In general, the South of the United States has always provided less financial resources to fight crime and social disruptions, although most studies that highlight the South as more prone to violence point to racial issues as the cause (Blau and Blau 1982; Chamlin and Cochran 1997). A categorical variable (1–6) representing six different geographical areas of the United States is used to test for differences within regions of the United States. A further test using a dummy variable (0–1) will be performed to test the South–Non-South hypothesis.

Time series on crime data indicates a declining trend from the height in the 1970s and 1980s—when, for instance, the homicides per 100,000 in the United States were on average 9/10—to the 2000s when homicides averaged around 6 (Levitt 2004). To account for this declining trend we use year as a control (1990, 1993, 1997, 1999, 2000, and 2003).

Estimation and Results

The robust regression analysis is the most appropriate analysis given our data. Least squares regression models estimates would not have accounted for the outliers due to structural differences between large size cities data compared to medium size; for example, San Diego, California, compared to Mesa, Arizona. Robust estimation can account for possible heteroskedasticity as well as the presence of outliers. In this analysis, the error term may not be constant because the variance of crime/police resources is bigger in larger cities. In larger urban areas the variance in the distribution of fiscal resources is more a function of whether the cities have discretionary authority in making decisions on their resource allocation, and also their preferences on where to invest. Furthermore, the presence of outliers would render least squares estimation inefficient and biased, dragging the beta coefficients toward the boundaries of the regression lines.

Tests to explore the extent of multicollinearity were also performed. The correlation matrix shows that the only correlations that exceed .48 are police expenditure (.75) and police employees and RPE (.63). These results are not surprising. The solution is in this case to remove police expenditures as a predictor after re-estimating the equations with and without the variable and observing stability in the coefficients. The results show almost no variation in standard errors and produce similar findings (R^2 increases by 1 percent). The rest of the correlation matrix coefficients show no evidence of multicollinearity.

We also examined the variance inflation factors (VIF) scores to further check for evidence of collinearity. A VIF test shows that there is no multicollinearity between the independent variables. In the most conservative estimations a value below 5 indicates no multicollinearity, although values under 10 are considered acceptable.[6] In our case, the only value close to 5 is police expenditures, which as stated before will not be included as an independent variable.

Based on these tests, we consider that estimating the model with robust standard errors is the most reliable method for our time analysis. The results of our model show:

The results are consistent with our theoretical expectations: the political capacity of the local government, the police administrative structure, the local economic environment, time trend, and region have an impact on the level of crime per capita in this sample of seventy-two U.S. cities.

The level of crime has gone through a declining trend during the fourteen-year period of our sample: 1990–2003. The variable *year* is significant and shows that on average crime has been declining at a rate of .06 percent per year ($\beta = -.057$).

The literature points out that the geographic regions in the United States are different enough to be necessary to control for those differences. The southern states, given racial issues as well as lower income levels, are more prone to crime and are typically being controlled in the model (Blau and Blau 1982; Chamlin and Cochran 1997). When the model was run with a dummy *South*, the general results remain stable and *South* is not significant (table not included). Instead we run the model using regions as a control variable (with six regions identified as categorical variable); we find that the average Crime per capita differs statistically among the different regions of the United States (*region* is significant at the .05 level).

Looking at the average levels of crime in our sample, we can see that it is not the South that has the highest per capita crime but the Southeast and the Northeast. It is possible that since 1990 when our sample data starts, the crime trend has changed and the southern states are not so different from the rest of the country.

Table 13.1.   The Effects of Relative Political Capacity (RPE Local) on Crime

Variable	β Coeff.	Robust Std. Error	t	P>|t|
Year	−.058	.0076788	−7.49	0.000
Region	−.045	.0207752	−2.18	0.030
IncomePC	−.0001	6.29e−07	−2.19	0.029
RPE	−.245	.0482524	−5.08	0.000
Professionalization	−.671	.2494709	−2.69	0.007
Police Employees	.003	.0003688	8.39	0.000
Constant	116.06	15.30338	0.000	0.000

Number of obs = 365
$F(6, 358) = 25.60$
Prob > F = 0.0000
R-squared = 0.4086

Table 13.2.   Average Crime per Capita per Region in 72 U.S. Cities 1990–2003

Region	Variable Value	Average Per capita Crime
Northeast	1	1.684798
Southeast	2	1.718996
Midwest	3	1.285471
South	4	1.198467
Northwest	5	1.078046
South/Southwest	6	1.001888

The reasons generally cited in the literature for the decline in crime over the past thirty years are: drop in the crack epidemics, legalization of abortion, increases in the number of police, and rising prison population (Levitt 2004). The last two explanations are especially relevant to our hypothesis. In his study, Levitt (2004) finds that the elasticity of crime with respect to the number of police is -.30. In line with Levitt's results, our theoretical expectation was that the higher the number of police employees, the lower the level of crime.

Contrary to our theoretical expectation, our results show a perverse relationship: the higher the number of police employees, the higher the crime per capita. It is important to note that previous research results are also mixed. Some research has shown positive relationship between the number of police employees and crime rate; some has shown negative relationship; and some has shown no relationship (Levitt 2004). The reason cited why we see higher crime rate with higher police force is that the models are run as simultaneously determined. In other words, an increase in police force today will not have instantaneous effects on the reduction of crime. So our result using a simultaneously determined model might be correctly capturing what is happening with regard to the crime rate and the number of police employees when observed as a snapshot.

Some note that it is not the number of police employees that will deter crime but the degree of professionalization of the police force. The variable *Profess* shows exactly this. Our result shows that the higher the level of professionalization of the police force, the lower the crime per capita ($\beta = -.67$). One percent increase in the sworn officers relative to the total police force renders a decline of over half a percent in the level of per capita crime. We also tested the proposition that the rising prison population would be a deterrent to crime under the assumption that higher expenditures would indicate higher allocations to prisons. Our results (not included) show that the expenditures variable when run with police employees is not significant, but granted, the level of multicollinearity between the two variables is very high (.75). As expected, the administrative structure of the police departments makes a difference in controlling crime.

A lot of controversy has surrounded the effect of poverty on crime. Blau and Blau (1982), in an article about the cost of inequality, posited that poverty should influence crime but found that it is not poverty but inequality that is the main explanatory variable. Often, a high level of inequality also reflects poverty. In our model, to reflect the local economic environment, we used Income per Capita as a control. We find that the lower the income, the higher the level of crime; although the coefficient is very small ($\beta =$ -1.38e-06) it is statistically significant. Less crime is found in richer areas but it is not the main determinant.

Finally, the political capacity of the local government has a strong influence on the level of per capita crime. As expected, governments that are more capable will be able to implement their desired policies and achieve their goals. Political capacity works independently but also reinforces the other results. A police department that works under an effective local government will also be able to be more efficient. The RPE coefficient ($\beta = -.245$) shows that for every 1 percent increase in the level of local government capacity, the crime per capita will diminish .25 percent. This result begs the policy question of how local governments can be empowered and if more decentralization might be conducive to achieving higher levels of political capacity.

CONCLUSIONS

Local government directly affects the lives of citizens and the character of a community. This study makes three important contributions to the study of government performance. First, it adds a dimension to understanding government performance by applying the concept of Relative Political Extraction to the local level. As other chapters in this book illustrate, the model has previously been used only in the context of national and provincial governments. In this study, we succeeded in measuring political capacity at the local level, with a sample of seventy-two U.S. cities from 1990 to 2003.

Second, we built upon previous models of crime as a social indicator of community well-being and added RPE as a predictor of the crime rate. Crime containment is an important policy objective of local government. With a simple model, we found that political capacity in local government is a strong determinant of crime containment.

Third, we highlighted additional factors that predict crime, related to region and the administrative structure of the police department. Our model tested and confirmed that cities in the South did not have the highest crime rates, as often supposed; in overall comparison, cities in the East had higher crime rates. Locally, police departments with a higher degree of professionalization were associated with lower crime rates. This study provides important suggestions for crime containment: local governments need to be able to make investment decisions and allocate resources to the police force. Political capacity is an independent predictor that reinforces this allocation of resources and reduction of crime.

This study demonstrated one area where the Relative Political Extraction model can be applied to local government to produce an empirical measure of performance. The results encourage further applications to available data sources to assess key factors for effective government in the local policy environment.

We now have an empirical measure at the local level that would indicate how capable a local government is, relative to others, of implementing their desired policies. A challenging task is now ahead of us: to explore and apply this indicator to other policy areas.

NOTES

1. Basic RPE equation (see also chapter 1)

$Y_{it} = a + \beta\ X_{it} + V_r$
Y_{it} = Adjusted tax revenue for city i at time t
X_{it} = Vector of variables that determine potential tax collection
V = White noise disturbance

2. $\dfrac{Revenue}{income} = \alpha + \beta_1(time) + \beta_2(Local\ Funds\ Revenue) + \beta_3\ (State\ Funds\ Revenue) + \beta_4\ (Fee\ Base\ Service\ income) + \beta_5\ (Wealth) + e$

Given the data in the Government Funds Flow, the RPE Local equation is as follows (see appendix 13.1 for sources and description of the variables):

Local RPE OLS Regression
Revenue/Income = 2.06 − .0001 Time + 1.97 Local Aid-Revenue + 1.37 State Aid Revenue + (.056) (.006) (.000) (.000)
1.24 Airport Income + 6.74-08 Home Value
(.001) (.001)
Number of Obs = 438
$F(\ 5,\ 432) = 47.28$
Prob $>$ F = 0.0000
Adj R-squared = 0.3462

Where:

$$RPE\ (Local) = \frac{Actual\ Revenue/Income}{Predicted\ Revenue/Income}$$

3. bjs.ojp.usdoj.gov/content/glance/tables/viortrdtab.cfm.

4. www.ucrdatatool.gov/Search/Crime/State/RunCrimeOneYearofData.cfm.

5. Crime per Capita$_{ct}$ = Political Capacity of the Local Government + Police Administrative Structure + Local Economic Environment + Error

In more detail:

Crime per Capita$_{ct}$ = a + β_1 Year$_{pt}$ + β_2 Region$_{ct}$ + β_3 RPE$_{ct}$ + β_4 Professionalization-$_{ct}$ + β_5 Police Employees$_{ct}$ + β_6 Income per Capita$_{ct}$ + Error

where:

t = year

c = city 1 . . . 75

a = Constant

β_1 . . . β_6 = Coefficients

year$_{pt}$ = 1990–1993–1997–1999–2000 & 2003

Region$_{ct}$ = Region of USA (1 = NE; 2 = SE; 3 = Mid-W; 4 = S; 5 = NW & 6 = W/SW)

RPE$_{pt}$ = Relative political extraction of a city (see previous section)

Profess$_{ct}$ = 1- (Total number of Non-sworn officers/Total Number of Police Employees)

Police Employees$_{ct}$ = Police Employees per 100 K population

Income per capita$_{ct}$ = Income per person in current US$.

6. See table 13.3

Table 13.3. Variance Inflation Factor Scores

Variable	VIF 1	VIF
policeexp_pc	4.60	0.217570
policeemploy	3.65	0.273785
RPE5	2.15	0.465999
region	1.78	0.562841
year	1.26	0.794985
incomepc	1.23	0.811848
profess	1.21	0.825040
Mean VIF	2.27	

REFERENCES

Aristigueta, M. P., L. J. Cooksy, and C. W. Nelson. 2001. "The Role of Social Indicators in Developing a Managing for Results System." *Public Performance and Management Review* 24 (3): 254–69.

Arvanites, T. M., and R. H. Defina. 2006. "Business Cycles and Street Crime." *Criminology* 44 (1): 139–64.

Blau, J. R., and P. M. Blau. 1982. "The Cost of Inequality: Metropolitan Structure and Violent Crime." *American Sociological Review* 47 (1): 114–29.

Chamlin, M. B., and J. K. Cochran. 1997. "Social Altruism and Crime." *Criminology* 35 (2): 203–28.

Donahue, A. K., and J. M. Miller. 2006. "Experience, Attitudes, and Willingness to Pay for Public Safety." *The American Review of Public Administration* 36 (4): 395–418.

Folz, D. H., and R. Abdelrazek. 2009. "Professional Management and Service Levels in Small U.S. Communities." *The American Review of Public Administration* 39 (5): 553–69.

Glaeser, E. L., B. Sacerdote, B., and J. A. Scheinkman. 1996. "Crime and Social Interactions." *The Quarterly Journal of Economics* 111 (2): 507–48.

Ingraham, P. W., and Government Performance Project. 2007. *In Pursuit of Performance: Management Systems in State and Local Government.* Baltimore: Johns Hopkins University Press.

Ingraham, P. W., P. G. Joyce, and A. K. Donahue. 2003. *Government Performance: Why Management Matters.* Baltimore: Johns Hopkins University Press.

Joyce, T. 2004. "Did Legalized Abortion Lower Crime?" *The Journal of Human Resources* 39 (1): 1–28.

Kennedy, W. G. 2009. "The Impact of Police Agency Size on Crime Clearance Rates." PhD diss., University of North Carolina, Charlotte.

Kubrin, C. E., and R. Weitzer. 2003. "New Directions in Social Disorganization Theory." *Journal of Research in Crime and Delinquency* 40 (4): 374–402.

Land, K. C. 1983. "Social Indicators." *Annual Review of Sociology* 9: 1–26.

Land, K. C., and M. Felson. 1976. "A General Framework for Building Dynamic Macro Social Indicator Models: Including an Analysis of Changes in Crime Rates and Police Expenditures." *The American Journal of Sociology* 82 (3): 565–604.

Levitt, S. D. 1998. "Juvenile Crime and Punishment." *The Journal of Political Economy* 106 (6): 1156–85.

———. 2004. "Understanding Why Crime Fell in the 1990s: Four Factors That Explain the Decline and Six That Do Not." *The Journal of Economic Perspectives* 18 (1): 163–90.

Messner, S. F., E. P. Baumer, and R. Rosenfeld. 2004. "Dimensions of Social Capital and Rates of Criminal Homicide." *American Sociological Review* 69 (6): 882–903.

Parâe, P.-P., R. Felson, and M. Ouimet. 2007. "Community Variation in Crime Clearance: A Multilevel Analysis with Comments on Assessing Police Performance." *Journal of Quantitative Criminology* 23 (3): 243–58.

Peterson, R. D., L. J. Krivo, and M. A. Harris. 2000. "Disadvantage and Neighborhood Violent Crime: Do Local Institutions Matter?" *Journal of Research in Crime and Delinquency* 37 (1): 31–63.

Raphael, S., and R. Winter-Ebmer. 2001. "Identifying the Effect of Unemployment on Crime." *The Journal of Law and Economics* 44 (1): 259.

Sampson, R. J., and W. B. Groves. 1989. "Community Structure and Crime: Testing Social-Disorganization Theory." *American Journal of Sociology* 94 (4): 774–802.

Shaw, C. R., and H. D. McKay. 1969. *Juvenile Delinquency and Urban Areas: A Study of Rates of Delinquency in Relation to Differential Characteristics of Local Communities in American Cities.* Chicago: University of Chicago Press.

Statistics, Bureau of Justice. (2010). bjs.ojp.usdoj.gov/content/glance/tables/viortrdtab.cfm.

Stenberg, C. W. 2007. "Meeting the Challenge of Change." C. W. Stenberg, S. L. Austin. and International City/County Management Association, eds., *Managing Local Government Services: A Practical Guide*, 1–28. Washington, DC: ICMA Press.

Wilson, J. Q., and B. Boland. 1978. "The Effect of the Police on Crime." *Law and Society Review* 12 (3): 367–90.

———. 1993. *The Effect of the Police on Crime*. Washington, DC: Dept. of Justice, Law Enforcement Assistance Administration, National Institute of Law Enforcement and Criminal Justice.

Appendix 13.1.   Data Sources

In order to estimate RPE (Local), the following variables were used:

General Government Revenue, State Aid Revenue; Local-Aid Revenue and Airports-Fee Based Revenue: Source: Municipal Analysis Services, Inc., Austin, Texas, Greg Michels, President

Population: Source: Municipal Analysis Services, Inc., Austin, Texas, Greg Michels, President

MSA Per Capita Income: Source: Bureau of Economic Analysis website: www.bea.gov/regional/reis/-TableCA1-3-3.0 per capita personal income, All metropolitan areas, 1990, 1993, 1997, 1999, 2000, 2003

MSA Calculated Home Value: Source and Calculation: No single source calculates median home value for cities on a yearly basis; however, the decennial Census does include median home value. Base is city level 1990 median home value from American FactFinder: factfinder.census.gov/servlet/DTGeoSearchByListServlet?ds_name = DEC_1990_STF1_&_lang = en&_ts = 303238799391—Geographic type: Place—(select appropriate state and cities), next—Table: H023B (Median Value)

Using The Federal Housing Finance Agency's Housing Price Index Calculator to calculate the appreciation of the median home value from 1990 to each of the subsequent years. www.fhfa.gov/Default.aspx?Page = 86—appropriate MSA—Purchase Quarter: 1991 Quarter 1—Valuation Quarter: 4th Quarter of desired year (e.g., 1993 Quarter 4) Purchase Price: 1990 median value (from American FactFinder)

When multiple cities in our data set were grouped in the same MSA data, the city listed first in the MSA designation was used as a base. The cities in question are: Dallas-Fort Worth-Arlington, Phoenix-MesaGlendale, Los Angeles-Long Beach-Santa Ana, San Francisco-Oakland-(Fremont), Minneapolis-St Paul-(Bloomington). Adjustments to calculate the values of each of the cities and missing values from the previous sources were done using many sources: www.recenter.tamu.edu/1762.pdf; www.homeinsight.com; www.city-data.com; www.zillow.com; www.housingbubblebust.com; www.Payscale.com; www.quickfactcensus.com; www.citytowninfo.com; and several publications from each individual city. Other cities in this data set were in MSA groupings that did not result in missing data (e.g., Portland-Vancouver-Hillsboro).

Violent crime rate: constructed using the Uniform Crime Rate data from the Department of Justice published in the Uniform Crime Reports, *Crime in the United States*, Washington, DC: U.S. Department of Justice, Government Printing Office for the years 1990, 1993, 1997, 1999, 2000, and 2003. The twelve-month total includes an aggregate number from the following four categories: murder, forcible rape, robbery, and aggravated assault. Cities are not required to report this data to the Department of Justice, so that's why some of the data points are missing.

Professionalization: calculated by dividing the number of sworn officers by the number of police employees based on the LEMAS data. Data was obtained from U.S. Dept. of Justice, Bureau of Justice Statistics, *Law Enforcement Management and Administrative Statistics* (LEMAS), Washington, DC: U.S. Dept. of Commerce, Bureau of the Census (producer), 2006. Ann Arbor, MI: Inter-university Consortium for Political and Social Research (distributor), 2006-05-10. doi:10.3886/ICPSR04411

ACKNOWLEDGMENTS

This paper was supported in part by a grant from the Portland State University Office of Research and Strategic Partnerships. The authors thank Alexandra Bradspies for her research assistance and Greg Michels at Municipal Analysis Services, Inc. for his assistance in interpreting municipal financial data.

V

A NEW TOOL

14

The Contributions of
Political Performance

Jacek Kugler and Ronald L. Tammen

Political Performance is the intellectual cousin to Gross Domestic Product. They share a number of similarities. They can be used to systematically compare the economic and political performance of societies at one point in time or the growth path of societies over time. They each have predictive value when considering international conflict. Both can be disaggregated to the national, state, and local levels. The variance in each measure indicates political and economic inequality across and within nations.

But there are differences. Unlike Gross Domestic Product, Political Performance is not measured in explicit terms. Political performance captures the shadow of politics but does not measure the explicit value of outputs produced by politics.[1] Gross Domestic Product is measured in currency values while Political Performance is measured in relation to the performance of other societies. Finally, Political Performance can only be disaggregated to the local level while GDP variants can be used down to the individual level.

GDP comparisons aside, what is most important is the observation that Political Performance is the first objective measure of political institutions not contaminated either by economic performance or normative considerations. This gives the concept a certain math-like purity compared to value-laden concepts. And it provides users with an unusual versatility as demonstrated in this book. It can be used to assess political capabilities in the context of global systemic realignment, regional integration, or national economic growth. It is equally useful for thinking about conflict throughout its range from local terrorism to global war. The concept contributes to our understanding of demographic phenomena such as migration, fertility patterns, and infant mortality. And it has applications down to the local government level of analysis.

Unlike most indicators of politics, political performance does not overlap with wealth factors. The very poor and the most affluent nations can be politically capable or incapable. Affluent societies extract a high participation premium and for that reason show little variability across time or among similarly endowed societies. Ironically, the most developed societies are limited in their ability to dramatically expand political performance.

But less-developed societies have enormous political potential if they tap into the magic of political performance. The payoffs are enormous. The few that perform well above expectations can make major strides and can increase growth rates, generate prosperity, and increase military power if they so choose. These changes come about much quicker than the evolutionary rates in the more affluent societies. This tells us why the most dynamic societies, those undergoing fast growth rates, those whose societies seem "on the move," all demonstrate high political performance improvements. It some ways, political performance helps answer the two lingering questions people have when they visit China and India—how and why?

Political Performance is not an easy phenomenon to manipulate. The least developed societies, with the most serious challenges, have the most difficulty. When political performance is low, it is hard to reverse that condition. But the few that manage to escape from stagnation rapidly alter their standing. Like a long-distance runner approaching the top of a hill, a massive effort is required to reach the threshold that launches nations on a path to fast economic growth. But once achieved, these takeoff societies have enormous potential and they often amaze the world.

Having broken out of the poverty cycle, on the far side of the hill, economic growth accelerates, corruption declines, migrants no longer leave but return to their original country, concerns with low fertility replace worries about carrying capacity, longevity replaces infant mortality, educational achievement replaces illiteracy, stable growth replaces up and down cycling, attempts to join stable international arrangements replace a desire to change regional and international environments, the breeding grounds for terrorism are replaced by a thriving middle class, investment is seen as an opportunity not an unavoidable exploitation, resources are used as an advantage not a curse. The trajectory of India and China provides evidence of how both a democratic and a single-party regime transform failing societies into fast-growing entities that will soon share international leadership with the EU and the United States.

The components of political performance—extraction, reach, and allocation—answer some very fundamental questions. First, the "African Exception" challenges classical economic approaches as they fail to account for the lack of growth in many of the least developed African societies. We believe that this underspecification is linked to political performance.

Second, the recent emergence of the BRIC nations can be traced to changes in political performance. The economic potential of Brazil, for example, is in large measure due to the stability that the Lula government brought to that society, providing political cover for the dormant economic engine. The respecification of economic growth models provided here suggests that this path of inquiry can explain why some succeed and why some fail.[2]

Third, political performance helps account for the success and failure of governments in domestic or international conflicts. Political Performance increases the effectiveness of combatants and suggests the conditions under which civil war may emerge. Such diagnostics are useful in thinking about and planning against the full range of national security issues from insurgencies to invasions. It may be possible, with the refinement of this concept, to anticipate likely regions of conflict or even how to avert war. And if there is conflict, a knowledge of political performance could provide answers about how and where to fight, such as the critical swing regions in Afghanistan or, someday, Pakistan.

Political Performance represents a key ingredient in the integration process. It offers an explanation as to why the EU has advanced more than other such experiments and yet not as fast as many had anticipated. Once a policy of integration is chosen, the proposed new entity must implement goals. This requires an interaction between extraction and reach. Failure on either scale means failure for the integration effort.

We believe that political performance represents the first noneconomic statistical measure that has general and global applicability. It can be calculated horizontally and vertically. Consequently it gives promise of more accurately explaining critical changes to societies than economic factors alone. In a sense it has been the missing element in our calculations despite being part of our verbiage.

Models that account for systemic changes need to incorporate both economic and political factors to order to understand the complex interactions that maximize the performance of nations. This book attempts to show that an objective, empirical, and comprehensive measure of Political Performance is essential to this task. This is just a first step—but an essential first step—to provide researchers in political science, political economy, economics, and public administration with a new tool addressing key issues of the day.

Some nations grow; some stagnate. Some are enveloped in conflict; some bask in stability. Some meet their challenges head on; some are indecisive. This is the story of The Performance of Nations.

NOTES

1. GDP of course has a similar deficiency because it aggregates the input not the output value of the public sector.

2. The work by Kugler et al. (2011) on the consequences of war shows that advanced societies will recover largely from the ravages of war, while the least developed will descend into poverty and linger. We believe but have not yet shown that political performance in extraction, reach, and allocation can account for such differences. T. Kugler et al. 2013. "Demographic and Economic Consequences of Conflict." *International Studies Quarterly*, forthcoming.

Appendix

DATA ISSUES

Data Collection

Sources for RPC are chosen on the basis of consistent reliable data that is reported regularly and in comparable units. Sources share some standardization in reporting format and methods (e.g., the IMF, World Bank). The World Bank used to be the depository of all data collection; however, since 1972 the IMF has assumed responsibility for the collection. The IMF relies on national reporting—countries fill out forms required by the IMF and the IMF does not necessarily audit the data. Data can be reported and then updated by countries of origin, resulting in differences for IMF reporting for a country at different times. As is the case with any data reliant on national reporting, accuracy is not guaranteed; however, the data are consistent. Certainly more transparent countries and those with established internal checks and balances tend toward greater accuracy in reporting. Political objectives such as external debt may contribute to inaccuracy in reporting for some countries as well. Countries facing these problems may create ghost accounts in order to appear to be in better circumstances to external parties, resulting in inaccuracy in the most recent data. These reporting variances are typically adjusted with the passage of time. Updates in RPC require going back five years to assess and correct all of these reporting errors. National Central Bank reports and figures can also be used to fill holes in IMF reporting.

In some instances, different institutions stop reporting particular items or alter reporting mechanisms. Tax structures can dramatically change, as can currencies. When these changes occur, transition years can contain reporting under each structure or both currencies, making it difficult to consistently look at the measure.

Methodology for Overlapping Time Series

Comparisons of the rate of change are an initial starting point for making comparisons between series. Series often reflect different measurement units or methods. Consistency in the variance in observations contained in both series can be a basis for some confidence that the series are capturing the same variables. Applying the rate of change to existing measures prevents artificial introduction of variance created by differing measurement techniques or reporting agencies. Historical sources must be referenced in order to assure that steady change is occurring. The occurrence of dramatic or drastic change such as a coup, financial crisis, or natural disaster can massively affect the rate of revenue collection and national expenditure.

Quality Control

As in any other data collection situation we need to look at reliability and validity. The accuracy of the sources and the quality of the transcription of the data are of utmost importance. But there are also problems related to the level of change from year to year of the data that cannot be accounted for by a normal trend. For example, countries that suffer from high level of inflation might report data at different times of the year that are not comparable. Countries might change their currencies and the same problem presents: those two pieces of information are not comparable. These problems are usually highlighted when we work with ratios. Ratios that are very different raise a red flag to check for the reason for the outlier and permit us to "translate" all the information to common "currency." Another problem that often presents is the change of accounting systems.

So for quality control, working with absolute numbers in developing countries might lead us to ignore problems of the data itself. Of course, problems related to politics or natural disasters have their own explanations.

Tax revenues can suffer from poor reporting and variance in reporting, particularly in countries without strong financial institutions that collect information on a regular basis. Even in countries characterized by strong institutions and transparency, changes in accounting can contribute to the distortion of revenue figures. Inflation also contributes to the distortion of revenues and the allocation of expenditures and makes the reporting date an important issue, although monthly deflators correct these fluctuations.

Social security also suffers from inaccuracy in reporting, and the differences between and within countries (e.g., the elimination or implementation of a social security program, changes in the structure of collection and disbursement) compound the difficulty in accurate measurement across societies. At the same time, some countries have semiprivatized or privatized systems, making intercountry comparisons more challenging.

For the same reason, health expenditures also are difficult to measure comparatively across societies. Countries have different mixes of private and public health care systems that drastically alter the level of expenditures on health care by individual governments. These same countries change the degree of government involvement in health care provision over time, and different budget line items may be included under the umbrella of health care in some countries that may fall under other social services in others (e.g., hospice care and nursing homes in Scandinavian countries are included in health care expenditures—these are frequently private expenses in other countries). Although health expenditures have also been attached to developed countries' array of policy choices (private vs. public), more and more developing countries are making similar decisions both in social security and health.

Additional empirical challenges are presented at the subnational level. Data distortions caused by inflation, accounting changes, or even poor record-keeping practices are magnified at the subnational level. In some instances, different variables are reported in different currencies or measured differently (for example, GDP for the province in local market currency while the value added or revenue variables are reported in constant dollars or at constant levels). In addition, most data comes from national government sources, leaving far fewer sources to rely on for data on overlapping series when data points in the series are missing.

EMPIRICAL CHALLENGES

Demographic and economic data can suffer from poor reporting and variance in reporting, particularly in countries without strong institutions that collect information on a regular basis. Countries experiencing high levels of conflict may experience long periods of time without a complete or even partial census taking place. Even in countries characterized by strong institutions and transparency, changes in accounting can contribute to the distortion of revenue figures and economic data. Inflation also contributes to the distortion of revenues and the allocation of expenditures and makes the reporting date an important issue, although monthly deflators correct these fluctuations.

An additional problem evident with census data is that predictable but frequent intervals in census data require some filling of the data in order for a complete cross-sectional time series data set. Some secondary sources are available to fill in additional years; however, some variance is lost. In the current estimation, we used linear estimation techniques on a country by country basis.

Education data are often reported by national sources. Although we use a cross-national base for the data, we do rely on national sources for large amounts of the remaining required data. National governments can be politically motivated to inflate or address these education measures, a problem that occurs with the more historical data. Increased transparency and governance data collection efforts, in addition to more widespread survey research conducted cross-nationally, provide triangulation points for much of the current data. Fortunately, we are able to identify where historical numbers are grossly inflated by evaluating country by country trends over time. A final issue occurs with the definition of secondary education. While cross-national sources do contain consistent definitions for this measure, some national governments have different divisions for primary, secondary, and tertiary education levels.

Sample Size

In the current set of estimations, our sample includes eighty-five developed and developing countries.

There is a trade-off between expansion of the sample to include all countries and accuracy in the data (this is covered more extensively in the next section). For some countries, particularly extremely poor developing countries, accurate reporting of the components of RPC for the duration of the series is difficult to obtain. Inaccuracies in the data and gaps in reporting both influence whether data within a given country is reliable. Ex-Soviet republics and Eastern European countries reported net material product until the mideighties, and those series are difficult to convert back to the 1960s, when our data collection starts, to GNP or GDP. These countries will be added at the cost of having shorter time series.

At the same time, the model requires a large sample in order to be accurate. Without a sufficiently large sample, the establishment of a relative model does not yield results that reflect the capability of a country in comparison to others in the international system. A goal of data collection and extension of this data set should be to expand the sample to cover more countries in the world for the duration of the series. Improvements in transparency, reporting, and information access greatly facilitate this goal.

This relative model has relevance when tested within large samples. The smaller and the more homogeneous the sample, the less variance, resulting in predicted values that are not that different from actual values. This is a problem, especially when the availability of data for developed countries is greater than for underdeveloped countries. The need for data for developing countries should not be dismissed, and often it is better to make assumptions and accept lower quality data than to reject those series altogether.

MAJOR DATA SOURCES

Economically Active Population data comes primarily from Taylor and Jodice, with overlapping series from World Development Indicators, National Census, Banks Cross National Time Series Archive.

GDP per Capita is from the Penn World Tables (Summers and Heston). Overlapping series include data from the IMF, World Development Indicators, and National Sources.

Bureaucracy and Expenditure data come primarily from the Government Finance Statistics published by the World Bank. We also use data from the World Development Indicators, Europa Yearbooks, and National Sources.

Education data come primarily from Taylor and Jodice. We use data from the World Development Indicators and National Sources to supplement data where necessary.

Political Allocation (RPA): Data Collection

We collected every data from Government Finance Statistics (GFS) and International Finance Statistics (IFS) of IMF, UN National Accounts Main Aggregates Database, and World Development Indicators (WDI). For empirical assessment of the approach, we used balanced cross-section time series data for 152 countries from 1970 to 2007. We divided the whole dataset into four subsamples following World Bank's criterion of development levels: (1) Low income group when GNI per capita $975 or less, (2) Lower middle income when GNI $976–$3,855, (3) Upper middle income when GNI $3,856–11,905, (4) High income when GNI $11,905. Then we implemented four different regressions on each subsample categorized by specific income level to distinguish the specific optimal allocative portfolios and strategies at the different development stage.

Index

Afghanistan, 87–90, 192, 198; and Al-Qaeda, 89, 198; and Mujahidin guerillas, 88; and the Taliban, 89; and the US, 89–90; and USSR, 88–90; violence, 89

Africa, 145–160, 317; and accumulation of wealth, 146; and economic development, 145–151, 153, 155; and foreign aid, 150–151; and human development, 145–146, 153, 156–161, 170; and infant mortality rates, 157–159; and institutional development, 151–153; and oil resources, 166; and political capacity, 156

American Recovery and Reinvestment Act, 269, 287

Angola: and oil wealth, 147

Armed Conflict Database, 179

asymmetric power distribution: and regional integration, 104

birth rates, 245, 246; estimation of effects of political extraction on birth rates, 254, 255, 256, 257, 258; measurement of, 253; and per capita income, 245–247; and relative political extraction, 245–247, 251–259

black economy, 21, 24

Botswana, 23; and institutional development, 151–152; and political reach, 23

Britain: during WWII, 28–30, 81–82

Canada: and migration, 126

cash economy, 22

Chad: and oil wealth, 147

challenges to measurement of informal activity, 23

challenges to measurement of political capacity: cross-national measures, 19

challenges to political performance: in Afghanistan, 89

China: authoritarian regime, 8, 316; and the Cultural Revolution, 62, 214; and Foreign Direct Investment, 212, 215, 217–218, 222, 223; and growth rate, 64, 65; and migration, 125; and political allocation, 25; and political capacity, 41, 63; and political extraction, 38; and political violence, 173–177, 182–185; and provinces, 177; and relationship with US and India, 91–93; and relative political extraction (RPE), 181, 183; and relative political reach (RPR), 177–178, 180, 183–184; and social exclusion, 175, 183–184; and stability, 173–185, 252; and subnational analysis, 173, 184–185, 222–223; and urban population, 180, 183; and violence, 179, 183–185, 186

About the Contributors

Dr. Mark Abdollahian is Full Clinical Professor, School of Politics and Economics, Claremont Graduate University.

Constantine Boussalis is Empirical Research Fellow at Harvard Law School.

Travis G. Coan is Statistician and Lecturer on Law at Harvard Law School.

Yi Feng is the Luther Lee Professor of Government at the Claremont Graduate University.

Gaspare M. Genna is Associate Professor of political science at The University of Texas at El Paso and associate editor of the journal *Politics & Policy*.

Kristin Johnson is Assistant Professor of Political Science at the University of Rhode Island.

Matthew A. Jones is Assistant Professor in the Mark O. Hatfield School of Government at Portland State University.

Kyungkook Kang is Adjunct Professor in the School of Politics and Economics at Claremont Graduate University and Research Associate with the TransResearch Consortium.

Mariah A. Kraner is a Research Associate at Portland State University and the TransResearch Consortium.

Jacek Kugler is the Elizabeth Helms Rosecrans Professor of International Relations at the School of Politics and Economics, Claremont Graduate University.

Tadeusz Kugler is Assistant Professor in the Department of Politics and International Relations at Roger Williams University.

Hal T. Nelson is Research Assistant Professor at Claremont Graduate University.

Masami Nishishiba is Assistant Professor of Public Administration at the Mark O. Hatfield School of Government, Portland State University.

Peter Noordijk is an associated researcher with Portland State University's Center for Turkish Studies.

Saumik Paul is an Assistant Professor of Economics at the School of Economics, Nottingham University, Malaysia.

Marina Arbetman Rabinowitz is Research Professor with the TransResearch Consortium.

Siddharth Swaminathan is the Shri R.K. Hegde Chair and Professor of Decentralization and Governance at the Institute for Social and Economic Change in Bangalore, India.

Ronald L. Tammen is Professor of Political Science and Director of the Mark O. Hatfield School of Government at Portland State University.

John Thomas is Dean and Bashir Hasso Professor of Entrepreneurship at the Tom and Vi Zapara School of Business, La Sierra University.

Ayesha Umar Wahedi is Adjunct Professor, Mark O. Hatfield School of Government, Portland State University and Research Associate with the TransResearch Consortium.

Birol Yesilada is Professor of Political Science and International Studies, and Contemporary Turkish Studies Endowed Chair at Portland State University.